🌳 The Myth of Southern History

F. Garvin Davenport Jr.

THE MYTH
OF SOUTHERN
HISTORY

Historical Consciousness
in Twentieth-Century Southern
Literature

Vanderbilt University Press · Nashville

The author and publisher gratefully acknowledge permission to quote from the following works:
All the King's Men by Robert Penn Warren, copyright 1946 by Robert Penn Warren, 1953 by Random House, Inc.; *At Heaven's Gate* by Robert Penn Warren, copyright 1943 by Harcourt, Brace & Co.; *Brother to Dragons* by Robert Penn Warren, copyright 1953 by Robert Penn Warren; *The Legacy of the Civil War* by Robert Penn Warren, copyright © 1961 by Robert Penn Warren; *Night Rider* by Robert Penn Warren, copyright 1939 by Robert Penn Warren; *Segregation: The Inner Conflict in the South* by Robert Penn Warren, copyright 1956 by Robert Penn Warren; *Who Speaks for the Negro* by Robert Penn Warren, copyright © 1965 by Robert Penn Warren; *Absalom, Absalom!* by William Faulkner, copyright 1951 by Random House, Inc.; *Intruder in the Dust* by William Faulkner, copyright 1948 by Random House, Inc.; *The Sound and the Fury* by William Faulkner, copyright 1946 by Random House, Inc.; *The Mind of the South* by W. J. Cash, copyright 1941 by Alfred A. Knopf, Inc.; *Moral Man and Immoral Society* by Reinhold Niebuhr, copyright 1932 by Charles Scribner's Sons, renewed © 1960 by Reinhold Niebuhr; *The Children of Light and the Children of Darkness* by Reinhold Niebuhr, copyright 1944 by Charles Scribner's Sons; *Technics and Civilization* by Lewis Mumford, copyright 1934 by Harcourt, Brace & Co.; *On Native Grounds* by Alfred Kazin, copyright 1942 by Harcourt, Brace & World; *Stride Toward Freedom* by Martin Luther King Jr., copyright 1958 by Martin Luther King Jr.; *The Trumpet of Conscience* by Martin Luther King Jr., copyright © 1967 by Martin Luther King Jr.; *The Faulkner-Cowley File* by Malcolm Cowley, copyright © 1966 by the estate of William Faulkner, © 1966 by Malcolm Cowley; *I'll Take My Stand* by Twelve Southerners, copyright 1930 by Harper & Brothers, renewed 1958 by Donald Davidson (quotations from: "Reconstructed but Unregenerate" by John Crowe Ransom; "The Irrepressible Conflict" by Frank Lawrence Owsley; "A Mirror for Artists" by Donald Davidson; "Not in Memoriam, but in Defense" by Stark Young; "The Briar Patch" by Robert Penn Warren). Parts of Chapter I appear in "Thomas Dixon's Mythology of Southern History," *The Journal of Southern History,* XXXVI (August 1970). Copyright 1970 by the Southern Historical Association. Reprinted by permission of the Managing Editor.

Library of Congress Catalogue Card Number 76–112600
International Standard Book Number 0–8265–1151–1

Printed in the United States of America by
Kingsport Press, Inc., Kingsport, Tennessee

for Bern

✟ Preface

AMERICANS have never had much luck with history. In the 1960s the poles of racial and political confrontation have largely ignored the fact that history is ambiguous, complex change. For this student of American society, this characteristic was made strikingly evident at a meeting of the Southern Historical Association in New Orleans two years ago at which, on the day after the 1968 national elections, an overflow audience watched William Styron and several black members of the audience exchange rhetorical blows over the validity of the Nat Turner whom Styron had drawn in *The Confessions of Nat Turner*. On the same platform with Styron sat Robert Penn Warren, C. Vann Woodward, and Ralph Ellison, virtually ignored in the heat of the moment—that eternal American moment when the light of simple myth defies the shadows of complex reality.

This study does not include *The Confessions*. If it did, it would attempt to view the work neither as some kind of insult to so-called factual history nor as a conspiracy against some other cultural myth, but as a work well within the tradition of historically oriented Southern literature. Viewed from this perspective, Styron's book, along with many others not included, would lend support to the political purpose in writing this book, to whatever extent a motive beyond personal interest exists. This purpose is to suggest and to examine the existence of the idea of historical consciousness within American society and the importance of that idea to America in the 1970s. It is to suggest, as others have suggested, that history is not so much what happened as what people believe happened. History is a creative form of expression and is politically important to the extent that people use their imaginative understanding of the past to deal with the present. Americans as a rule have a very distorted or simplistic view of history. History is past and dead—never present and dynamic. What may be most dangerous about this view is that it tends to dismiss the past as irrelevant to the present and to that great American god, the future. In the short and violent decade which now draws to a close, Americans began to pay for that indifference and cultivated detachment. The South, it was argued by some, had been paying already for a century or more, while the rest of the nation sat back in self-righteous judgment. But now all the chickens had come home to roost, and they had come to Los Angeles and Detroit and Chicago as well as to the South.

The point is that there is evidence that the South, or at least some Southerners, have had more experience than the rest of America, or at least most Americans, in trying to figure out and create consciously a relevant approach to their history. The results of this historical creativity, which I have tried to record in this book, certainly offer no panacea for any of our collective or individual problems. I do believe that the results suggest some of the peculiar difficulties and paradoxes which face Americans who try to deal imaginatively and also morally with their past.

Anyone familiar with the works of Professor David W. Noble of the University of Minnesota will recognize my great indebtedness to him. As a teacher, adviser, and friend, Professor Noble has contributed countless insights and suggestions to this study. Professors Bernard Bowron, J. C. Levenson, and Mary C. Turpie also gave many useful suggestions and criticisms.

Many people read part or parts of the manuscript at various states of preparation and gave their time and ideas to many discussions of the various problems encountered. My parents, Professor and Mrs. F. Garvin Davenport Sr., read the manuscript and contributed many of their ideas about and knowledge of American history, and particularly Southern history. My former colleagues at the University of Minnesota, Professors Starling Price and William Marchand, were most helpful with their many questions and criticisms, especially in the early stages of the project. The enthusiasm, humor, and sage advice of my editor, Miss Mary Lee Tipton, have made the long process of revision and rewriting almost a pleasure. Miss Delphine Swanson typed the manuscript in its many and various stages, and no one could wish for a more considerate, perceptive, and patient typist. Financial assistance for the preparation of the manuscript was made available by Hamline University through the Faculty Enrichment Fund and the Shell Assists Program, and for this aid I am most grateful. My wife, Bernice, helped with the copyreading and proofreading and in addition lent her support and patience, as sometimes unwittingly did my children, Garvin and Paul.

FGD

Minneapolis
July 30, 1969

✤ Contents

If you could accept the past you might hope for the future, for only out of the past can you make the future.

Warren, *All the King's Men*

⚜ Introduction

AS long as Americans have been trying to define "the national character," they have also been concerned with the South's relationship to this "national" character. For the nineteenth and twentieth centuries this concern with the South has grown out of the seemingly obvious differences between the "Southern way of life" and the "American way of life." The overt focal points for this concern have always been conveniently provided by the economic and racial peculiarities of the South. Agrarianism and the Negro have been used as concrete symbols of a difference which one understands in different ways, depending on whether his sources are Thomas Nelson Page and Margaret Mitchell or Erskine Caldwell and William Faulkner. Nevertheless, the basic concept of distinction between the two regions has remained for many decades the same. The South is supposedly agrarian, aristocratic, patriarchal, fixed, closed. The North is supposedly industrial, democratic, egalitarian, mobile, open.

In recent years, the factual nature of these differences has been to some extent minimized by historical research which suggests that, throughout their history, the two regions have had generally parallel development insofar as economic, political, and social changes have been concerned. Nevertheless, there has remained a great deal of interest in the *concept* of regional difference itself for the light it throws on ways Americans think about themselves and their history. Beyond the purely scholarly interest in this problem lies the implication that America's own problems of race and region, as well as her response to, and place in, an increasingly non-white world, might be better understood if Americans could understand the peculiar nature of their own ironic affluence in a have-not world and the doubly ironic position of the South—a have-not region in the midst of this affluence—within this national history.

The difference between the North and the South is viewed, not as one of economics or climate, but as one of historical experience and consciousness. This viewpoint, best exemplified in recent years by the essays of C. Vann Woodward, shows the South as unique because it *has* experienced history: it has experienced defeat, humiliation, frustration, and poverty. It has experienced change, which is the essence of history; but unlike the national imagination, which sees change only as unending progress toward perfection, the Southern imagination has been forced to view history as turbulent and tragic. History can bring moments of victory, but its defeats and frustrations are usually better remembered. The South—unlike any other segment of the nation—has experienced social ostracism, military defeat and occupation, radical reconstruction, and institutional segregation in all of their fury and degradation.

One of the basic studies of this concept of a "divided culture" has been done by William R. Taylor in his book *Cavalier and Yankee: The Old South and American National Character*. Taylor traces the development of the idea of cultural division in the first half of the nineteenth century, primarily as it existed in the South. Because there *were* differences between the South and the North in terms of economic and political structure, and especially in racial attitudes, Southerners were forced into a rationalization of their racial institutions which would offset the increasing criticism coming not only from the northern United States but from the world. Thus, "Southerners carried on a peculiar kind of dialogue with the nation, sometimes constructive and harmonious, sometimes carping and critical. Through it all they persisted in seeing themselves as different and, increasingly, they tended to reshape this acknowledged difference into a claim of superiority."[1]

But at the same time the North also had its problems, in trying to cope with the new, increasingly materialistic civilization which had developed.

If swift change and social mobility of an unprecedented kind produced glowing optimism and expectation of a secular millennium, they also produced nostalgia and disquietude. Was all stability to give way to flux? Was an absorption in money-making and material things to replace the intellectual and spiritual heritage with which Americans had begun their national life?[2]

Such questions as these led many Americans from both regions to see in the culture of the South the security and stability, the sense of honor and "maintenance of domestic decorum" which they felt lacking in the national character. This concept called "national character" was being examined, not by Southerners alone, but by all Americans. This examination—with its assumptions of regional distinctions and uniqueness—has continued into this century with a tendency toward substituting for "Cavalier" the concept of historical burden and mission; and for "Yankee," the concept of historical innocence and cultural babbitry or anarchy.

Besides the historical basis provided by Taylor, my study also rests on Henry Nash Smith's definition of myth as stated nineteen years ago in *Virgin Land: The American West as Symbol and Myth*—"an intellectual construction that fuses concept and emotion into an image." While myths do not always reflect empirical fact, "they sometimes exert a decided influence on practical affairs," and on ways of thinking about one's self and about others. Myth is not synonymous with "fiction": it simply denotes one particular kind of perception. Myth has moved armies, nations, and civiliza-

1. *Cavalier and Yankee,* pp. 17–18.
2. *Ibid.,* p. 18.

tions and thus cannot be disregarded as a factor in the shaping of society. Besides the works of Taylor and Smith, Woodward's *The Burden of Southern History* was very helpful. Having read Dixon, Faulkner, and Warren, I discovered these essays, which enabled me to crystallize the type of comparative study I wished to do.

I have focused this study—which is basically critical and interpretative rather than biographical or bibliographical in nature—on both fictional and nonfictional works by white Southerners ranging roughly over the first half of this century, from 1903 into the 1960s. I have given special attention to five works which seemed to me of central importance in understanding the uses of Southern history. These include *The Leopard's Spots: A Romance of the White Man's Burden* (1903), a novel by Thomas Dixon; *I'll Take My Stand: The South and The Agrarian Tradition* (1930) by Twelve Southerners (John Crowe Ransom, Donald Davidson, Frank Lawrence Owsley, John Gould Fletcher, Lyle H. Lanier, Allen Tate, Herman Clarence Nixon, Andrew Nelson Lytle, Robert Penn Warren, John Donald Wade, Henry Blue Kline, and Stark Young); *Absalom, Absalom!* (1936) by William Faulkner; *All the King's Men* (1946) and *Brother to Dragons: A Tale in Verse and Voices* (1953) by Robert Penn Warren. Numerous other works of fiction, history, social essay, literary criticism, and sociology have been incorporated into the discussion as they shed light on my major concern, which is what Taylor calls the "dynamics rather than the origins or historical authenticity" of the myth, which I have named the myth of Southern history.

I realize that the South has many myths, but I hope that my avenue of concentration may lead to a sharper focus on at least part of the general problem. I am interested, first, in demonstrating that such a construct of ideas and images exists, sometimes overtly, sometimes covertly, in significant works by Southern artists and scholars during this period, and that this myth has embodied both a concept of Southern uniqueness and a concept of Southern mission to the rest of the nation. Second, I have tried to demonstrate that beyond the myth of Southern history and the older, more established myth of the Southern Cavalier there exists a tension brought about in large part by the fact, made clear by Taylor, that regional myths serve national needs. Thus, as the nature of national problems changes, the myths of the nation must also change. But while the older Cavalier myth reinforced the peculiar and democratically unacceptable pattern of race relations in the South, the needs of this century have made increasingly difficult the proposal or the acceptance of a South which condones racial inequality and injustice. Third, I have tried to see these Southerners and their ideas in a national context, wrestling with the problems of their United States, as well as in a regional context, struggling with the burden of their own historical consciousness. The South's task in this century has not been merely to rationalize its treatment of the Negro to an indignant nation but to explain in relevant terms to itself its own treatment at the hands of history. When success at this task is attained, the old defensiveness will no longer be necessary. Thomas Dixon and the Southern Agrarians attempted the explanation by taking a stand against pluralistic industrialism and the Negro. William Faulkner and, to a greater extent, Robert Penn Warren and C. Vann Woodward have moved beyond a defense of Jeffersonian America toward a new mythology more relevant to the problems of the United States as a great power in a world of have-not peoples. In addition, I have examined the suggestion that the culmination of the South's contribution to the development of historical consciousness in America may have come, not from the white community at all, but from the American Negro, whose sense of burden and mission is manifested generally by the whole Negro freedom movement of the post–World War II era and in particular by the beliefs and acts of Martin Luther King.

✤ I Early Conceptions of the Myth of Southern History

The Climate of Opinion

T H E imaginative history of the post-Reconstruction period of the South is directly related to the central body of myths by which the national community defined itself in the nineteenth century. Henry Nash Smith has noted that most Americans defined the distinctive national uniqueness which separated them from Europe in terms of a nature-*vs*.-civilization dichotomy. The United States represented a state of nature, while the Old World represented historical civilization. Thomas Jefferson believed that the majority of Americans, because they were yeoman farmers, could be free individuals—free from restraint by social institutions or traditions; free to live in harmony with nature's laws. This meant, for Jefferson, that Americans, unlike Europeans, could live in a state of innocence rather than corruption because power would be virtually absent from a community of free and equal men. In such a social and economic condition, there would be no rulers and no ruled.

The belief followed for most Americans throughout the nineteenth century that their democracy was the result of the unique gift of nature in the new world—a vast expanse of unsettled land.

From the historical and political apologist for Jacksonian democracy, George Bancroft, to Frederick Jackson Turner, who gave it explicit statement in 1893, the great number of Americans revealed their covert faith in the frontier as the origin of American democracy. They believed that their political life was not an expression of European traditions and institutions brought across the Atlantic but rather that their democratic practices were an organic growth from the social and economic conditions of freedom and equality that resulted from the virgin lands of the frontier.

The democratic yeoman farmer, therefore, became the symbol of the ideal American citizen. And it was against that ideal that the myth of the Southern Cavalier was contrasted. Yeoman *vs.* Cavalier represented democrat *vs.* aristocrat, nature *vs.* civilization, American culture *vs.* European, innocence *vs.* corruption. Ultimately these symbols seemed to find dramatic confirmation in the Civil War when the yeoman democracy of the North, according to national mythology, successfully defended national innocence against the conspiratorial effort of the undemocratic Cavaliers to impose the corruption of the institution of slavery on the entire nation. It was viewed as a righteous war led by the yeoman figure Abraham Lincoln against the sinister plans of the Cavalier, Jefferson Davis.

At first the national community defined Radical Reconstruction as a continuation of this just war, a continuation that was necessary to eradicate completely the Cavalier autocracy which had murdered Lincoln. Gradually, however, numbers of influential Yankees became aware that the Cavalier class was more a mythical than a real social entity. A wave of revulsion set in against the Radical Republicans, who had attempted to impose Negro equality on the South.

From Jefferson, through Jackson, to Lincoln, the yeoman had been defined as white; and white America had made it clear that it was unthinkable that the Negro could ever be integrated as an equal citizen. This national tradition of segregation now reasserted itself, and many in the North indulged in great sympathy for a white South that had faced the horror of racial equality imposed by a few New England fanatics. This sympathy was increased by the apparent commitments of Southern leadership in the 1870s and 1880s to the expansion of the industrial frontier that Yankees had been so busy creating during the previous quarter-century.

This "Road to Reunion" of regional reconciliation through a shared enthusiasm for industrial capitalism perhaps served to obscure an even greater national irony that had begun to develop as early as the 1790s. While most Americans had voted for the symbolic agrarianism of Jefferson, Jackson, and Lincoln, they had acted in the manner of that great enemy of agrarianism, Alexander Hamilton. Americans had poured more energy and ingenuity, more time and money, into building an urban-industrial nation than in preserving the spiritual heritage of virgin land.

Late nineteenth-century America was therefore desperately divided in spite of its public pose of optimism. On the one hand it was committed to preserving the landscape of Jefferson's yeoman farmer. On the other hand it was committed to building more and bigger factories and cities. Leo Marx has explored this cultural crisis in his book *The Machine in the Garden*. The national community seemingly could not surrender either of these two antithetical principles. And not only had the machine invaded the Jeffersonian garden, but the Negro remained an unwanted alien, as incapable as the machine, in the eyes of the white majority, of integration into a national community defined in terms of rural and small-town isolation.

This is the dramatic context of conflicting national mythology in which the mythology which is the subject of this study existed at the end of the nineteenth century. Still more rural in 1890 than the Northeast or Midwest, the South seemed to be the very citadel of Jefferson's vision of America as an agricultural garden peopled by innocent farmers freed from the corruption of institutional power. But Southerners also desired the fruits of economic progress. And, of course, they carried the major burden of the unassignable Negro population. The tensions between coveted affluence, mythical innocence, and racial burden could not easily be reconciled or even understood.

In contrast to these definitions of the South of 1890 which related it to the national mythology, there was, of course, the Southern experience of military defeat and occupation during the Civil War and Reconstruction. The South, unlike the rest of the American nation, had suffered disaster and humiliation. And, unlike the North, it had had Negro equality forced upon it. It was from these experiences, linked back to the pre–Civil War tradition of the aloof Cavalier, that, at the end of the nineteenth century, a new mythology of Southern history began to develop. But the myth of Southern history, while based on these facts of separateness, was also to be used by Southerners to seek resolution for the central contradictions of the national mythology—how Jefferson's white yeomen could retain their innocence in a society that was being invaded by the machine and the city and in which there was already present the alien figure of the Negro. This myth suggested that the South, because of its experience of defeat and humiliation, had developed a vision of history, a strength of character, and a sense of moral responsibility which made it alone of all the national regions strong enough to reconcile industrialism and the Negro with the Jeffersonian vision. Or, if reconciliation was impossible, the South would exile itself from the threatening forces and take its stand alone.

Thus, to the student of the twentieth-century South, it is significant that Paul Buck's study, *The Road to Reunion,* ends with the year 1900. For in this century, one of the dominant themes in Southern literature and letters has been the qualification of this theme of reconciliation and national patriotism which Buck traces through the closing decades of the nineteenth century. Like the earlier Cavalier mythology, this post-reconciliation theme has been built upon a belief in the uniqueness of the Southern identity, which has distinguished it from the dominant American or national identity. Furthermore, Southerners who have explored this theme have incorporated into it a suggestion that because of this peculiar uniqueness the South has a singular and vital contribution to make to the national life. The theme of Union, dominant in the era of reconciliation, becomes qualified by the concept of a special Southern mission to that Union. Both this mission and the conditions in the nation that make a mission seem necessary are eventually defined in terms of the Southerners' consciousness of their own past and their unique heritage. But unlike the Southern uniqueness which is associated with an "Old South" and which might be called sentimental comedy, the tendency evident in this century has been one toward ironic tragedy. The themes of righteousness and tranquility are crowded by the themes of guilt and violence. The tranquility of the plantation becomes first the burden of the subjugated Negro and eventually the "burden of Southern history."

This first chapter will examine selected writings of three Southerners from around the year 1902. The examination reveals the existence of all four concepts which contribute to the development of the "myth of Southern history." These four concepts are Union, Southern uniqueness, Southern mission, and Southern burden. Woodrow Wilson, who stands as a link between this century and the era of the New Patriotism studied by Buck, speaks of Union and reconciliation, assuming that disfranchisement has transcended once and for all the South's only problem, the Negro. William Garrott Brown expresses the paradoxical situation resulting from the juxtaposition of Southern uniqueness—the tranquil, leisurely, rural Southern "way of life"—with the dark weight of this same problem, the Negro. In Brown we see a consciousness of the pervasiveness of the past in the present, which anticipates, among others, William Faulkner. Perhaps because of this consciousness of the burden as well as of the uniqueness, Brown is unable to see any Southern mission to be undertaken for the benefit of the nation. It is for Thomas Dixon, racist and popular novelist, to bring together all four of the themes into something of a complete statement of the myth of Southern history.

As Woodrow Wilson, in his *History of the American People,* looked back upon Reconstruction and the years following, his major concern was reconciliation between the sections, which would allow the South to re-enter the national fold willing and able to go forward down the ever-widening road of national progress. Only the Negro, it seemed, created a barrier between the South and progress and prosperity. But immediately after the Civil War, unfortunately, the North had been unable to see the Negro in terms other than those of an "innocent . . . creature who needed only liberty to make him a man." Any attempt by Southerners to restrain the Negro could be seen by Northerners only as "vindictive defiance." Northerners "did not look into the facts; they let their sentiment and their sense of power dictate their thought and purpose."[1]

Had they looked to the facts, Wilson implies, they would have seen that the Negro was not a man and that political liberty could not make a man of him. They would have been concerned, not with the innocence of the Negro, but with the threat to American cultural innocence and racial purity that he posed. They would have seen that Negro liberty and equality threatened the hopes of Progress and Union. The political and social liberation of the Negro meant an attempt at "social revolution"[2] which would obviously undermine any hope of progress and national unity among white men. This danger of division and violence had been made clear during Reconstruction when this "veritable overthrow of civilization in the South" had provoked a white reaction of ugly terror and violence which was itself a threat to American democratic ideals and methods.[3]

But now, at the turn of the century, Wilson could write with some sense of relief that the threat of such undemocratic social revolution had been put down, simply by disfranchising the Negro. In finally disfranchising and segregating the Negro, Wilson writes, the South had rid itself of the only obstacle which had kept it from enjoying the fruits of this new spirit of nationalism and prosperity.

1. *A History of the American People*, V, 22.
2. *Ibid.*, p. 49.
3. *Ibid.*

For the North, this new spirit had meant nothing more than an "awakening," but for the South, the minority, it had been "practically the readjustment of conquest and fundamental revolution."[4] In *this* context of reconciliation and progress, revolution becomes for Wilson a virtue. He rejoices that the South had finally "been added as a modern economic force to the nation."

By 1882, according to Wilson, "The South, especially, was showing how it could respond to the economic stimulation of the time, to the general development of the resources of the country, *now that its corrupt governments, with their negro majorities, were lifted from its shoulders.*"[5] And finally, at the turn of the century, "The southern States were readjusting their elective suffrage so as to exclude the illiterate negroes and so in part undo the mischief of reconstruction; and yet the rest of the country withheld its hand from interference. Sections began to draw together with a new understanding of one another."[6] The new century was to see sectional understanding and national harmony, the perfection of industry, the reform of capitalism, the growth of manufacturing, and generally an undefined and presumedly unlimited progress. And for this new century, there was to be a New South. Wilson's version is similar to that envisioned earlier by such men as Henry Grady. The New South was to bury its isolation and its provincialism. Industry and progress would take precedence over agriculture and tradition in the minds of those New Southerners. The past and the Negro were to be buried and forgotten so that the South might move forward with the nation.

Wilson saw no further than reconciliation. He had no conception of the South's taking a self-conscious stand to lead the nation back from the abyss of racial, industrial, or moral corruption. Wilson saw no need of a special force of regeneration in American history; no need, in other words, for a Southern mission. The

4. *Ibid.,* p. 130.
5. *Ibid.,* p. 164, emphasis mine.
6. *Ibid.,* p. 300.

harmonious and simple destiny of the new nationalism was already shaped: Americans had only to live and guide it as it moved toward perfection. Black disfranchisement had been necessary in the South for reconciliation and reunion among whites. Beyond that it had no significance, and for Wilson the Negro had not tied the South to any kind of historical burden or responsibility. Several years earlier, in his biography of George Washington, Wilson had written that in the Congress of 1774, leadership had "naturally" fallen to the Southern delegates because of their personal dignity and broadness of mind—qualities lacking or less developed "at the front of trade or of legal practices" than in the operation of a plantation in an agricultural community.[7] But now, in 1902, there was no mention of sectional leadership. National co-operation was the new goal. The qualities developed at the front of trade were no longer to be sneered at, but coveted.

William Garrott Brown, like Wilson, was a Southerner and a historian. Wilson, the Virginian educated in the South and near-South, had believed in reconciliation and a promising future. He had assumed that any obstacle from the South's past had been eliminated with disfranchisement. Brown was an Alabamian, who had spent thirteen years of his life in the North, at Harvard, before he published in 1902 a small book of lectures and essays, *The Lower South in American History*. Unlike Wilson, Brown could not reconcile the South's past with the optimistic New Patriotism.

Brown would undoubtedly have liked to believe in the bright future of the Union. One of the final essays in *Lower South* deals with a Southern boy who becomes a hero in the Spanish-American War, thus proving the South's love of country. This theme is a common one for the period, as Paul H. Buck points out.[8] But significantly this essay is sandwiched between two longer, less

---

7. *George Washington*, p. 158.
8. *The Road to Reunion, 1865–1900*, pp. 305–307.

optimistic, less sentimental essays, one entitled "The Ku Klux Klan Movement," the other called "Shifting the White Man's Burden."

In "The Ku Klux Klan Movement" Brown suggests that "the end attained by the revolt against Reconstruction government was for the most part good. Southern society had been "righted" by it.

But the method of [this righting] survives in too many habits of the Southern mind, in too many shortcomings of Southern civilization, in too many characteristics of Southern life. . . . For thirty years they have continued to set one question above all others, and thus debarred themselves from full participation in the political life of the country. As they rule by fear, so by fear are they ruled. It is they themselves who are now befooled, and robbed of the nobler part of their own political birthright. They outdid their conquerors, yet they are not free.[9]

The South was not free from its own violence and disregard of law, justice, and liberty. Its own dark past had followed it into the new century. Disfranchisement, it is implied, would offer no permanent solution to the problem since it was itself merely a continuation of the old dilemma. The white man had not dealt justly or rationally with the Negro. He had only frustrated his own goals and desires for progress and democracy. He had made no step toward solving the race problem and until he did, if he ever was to, he had to "take up every new plan with the chastening knowledge that most of our devices have failed; that nothing which can be quickly accomplished will go deep enough to last; that no sudden illumination will ever come, nor any swift breaking of the clouds shed sunlight on our shadowed land."[10]

The image of darkness suggested by the "clouds" in the above passage is expanded:

Africa still mocks America from her jungles. "Still," she jeers, "with the dense darkness of my ignorance, I confound your enlightenment. Still, with my sloth, I weigh down the arms of your industry. Still, with

9. *The Lower South in American History*, pp. 224–225.
10. *Ibid.*, p. 271.

my supineness, I hang upon the wings of your aspiration. And in the very heart of your imperial young republic I have planted, sure and deep, the misery of this ancient curse I bear."[11]

As the rhetoric makes clear, Brown shared his generation's fears of racial corruption, symbolized by the "darkness" and "ignorance" of Africa. Only his extreme pessimism concerning any hope of escaping the "curse" and his open awareness of white guilt separates him from the ahistorical attitudes of most of his fellow Americans. For Brown the whole nation was bound to and cursed by the dark continent. But it was the South which had to bear the heaviest part of this burden. Already, in the first essay, Brown had shown his awareness of viewpoints which condemned the South as un-American and productive only of "tasks and perplexities."[12] And in writing of William L. Yancey, "The Orator of Secession," Brown pictured the grave of the dead agitator surrounded by so many other "graves of simple and honorable gentlemen who gave their lives and fortunes to the dreadful task he set them that one can fancy even his proud spirit crying out to be delivered from the body of that death."[13]

Throughout the book, mingled with a conventional, basically sentimental regional pride, is this theme of a dark and terrible burden which rested upon the South. And what was the South to do with such a past? Whatever it did, according to Brown, it could not forget it, could not disregard the sacrifice, the violence, the quandary of race. The bonds with the burdensome inheritance of racial injustice are everlasting.

Yet, the American experience, which another contemporary of Brown's, Frederick Jackson Turner, had earlier seen symbolized in the frontier, had *always* involved the breaking of the "bonds of custom" of the past. "Each frontier," wrote Turner, furnished "a gate of escape from the bondage of the past; and freshness, and confidence, and scorn of older society, impatience of its restraints

11. *Ibid.*
12. *Ibid.,* p. 3.
13. *Ibid.,* p. 152.

and its ideas, and indifference to its lessons."[14] On the other hand, it would be possible for the twentieth-century Southerner to recognize the falseness of this myth of spatial and temporal mobility and its accompanying ignorance of the mistakes and the moral debts of the past. The paradox, however, which we have seen in Brown, is that Southerners, as Americans, were also drawn toward an affirmation of this very innocence through spatial and temporal escape, which in light of their own experience seemed false and deceiving.

Both Brown and Wilson had sensed the attractions of the New Patriotism and the hopes of a new era of material progress for the reunited nation. But Brown, unlike Wilson, was held back by his consciousness of a cultural experience which suggested that Union and progressive harmony could not belong to a society which had undergone such violent change, conflict, and sacrifice, and which had hurriedly tried to bury the bloody issue of racial conflict, hoping against hope that it would not exhume itself. What Southerners like Brown needed was a way to reconcile violence with harmony, history with progress, and a sense of mission—a belief that the violence, the sacrifice, the conflict and injustice had served as means to a much greater, more significant *national* end. The merging of Jim Crow segregation with the new American Empire over the brown people in the Caribbean and Pacific was to provide the spark for the proclamation of this mission.

By 1900 it seemed evident to many Americans that their Anglo-Saxon heritage of progress and democracy was in danger of being submerged by an ever-rising tide of color. The "White Man's Burden" existed not only in South Carolina and in Mississippi but also in the islands of the Caribbean and the Pacific. America's foreign intervention had made wards of several million colored people, none of whom, it was assumed with but little argument,

14. "The Significance of the Frontier in America," *The Frontier in American History*, p. 38.

could be assimilated into the political or cultural life of the nation. This captive population was described by the *Nation* as a "varied assortment of inferior races which, of course, could not be allowed to vote."[15] At about the same time, the New York *Times,* commenting on domestic problems, observed that the "necessity of [Negro disfranchisement] under the supreme law of self-preservation is candidly recognized."[16] And as early as 1883, Richard Watson Gilder had written in the *Century* that "the negroes constitute a peasantry wholly untrained in, and ignorant of, those ideas of constitutional liberty and progress which are the birthright of every white voter." E. L. Godkin asserted, "I do not see, in short, how the negro is ever to be worked into a system of government for which you and I would have much respect."[17]

The lesson of Reconstruction had been well learned. The missionary spirit of abolitionism was long since dead. These "inferior" races, wherever they lived, must be denied participation in the cultural life of American society. For while they were inferior, they nevertheless threatened, with their ignorance and number as well as with their color, to undermine and destroy the whole structure of the white democratic civilization which had subdued them.

The inspiration for the South's new consciousness of its role in the national defense against these dark peoples took form, in part at least, in response to the growing belief by Americans that the South's resistance to Radical Reconstruction had not been treason but rather a recognition of the "facts" of racial inequality. In the national imagination the South's actions could now be equated with the defense of all of the values of white America—all the values of a great White Garden. The South received scholarly recognition for this role in 1896 when a New York historian, William Archibald Dunning, wrote that in disfranchising the Negro, the South had only recognized and upheld the truths known

15. Quoted in C. Vann Woodward, *The Strange Career of Jim Crow,* p. 54.
16. Quoted, *ibid.,* p. 55.
17. Quoted in Buck, *op. cit.,* p. 295.

by Jefferson, the father of the Declaration of Independence, and by Lincoln, who had saved the Union, not by freeing the Negro and certainly not by asserting the Negro's equality with the white man, but by freeing America, North and South alike, from the guilt of slavery. Dunning, who as a Northerner felt none of the sense of burden that Brown felt, pointed out that such men as Jefferson, Clay, and Lincoln had seen much more in the issue of slavery than the mere question of the "chattel relationship of man to man." But "in the frenzy of the war time public opinion fell into the train of the emotionalists and accepted the teaching of Garrison and Sumner and Phillips and Chase, that abolition and Negro suffrage would remove the last drag on our national progress."[18]

Fortunately, Dunning implies, this mission had failed. Gradually, the idea of the earlier statesmen—all Southerners by birth—came back into prominence. This idea was that

the ultimate root of the trouble in the South had been, not the institution of slavery, but the coexistence in one society of two races so distinct in characteristics as to render coalescence impossible; that slavery had been a *modus vivendi* through which social life was possible; and that after its disappearance, its place must be taken by some set of conditions which, if more humane and beneficent in accidents, must in essence express the same fact of racial inequality.[19]

Where Wilson had seen the Negro only as a sectional problem, Dunning says, in essence, that the South had come to the defense of the whole nation in its reassertion of the undefiled nature of the American Garden threatened by an inferior race. Wilson had understood the means but had not seen the larger end. For Dunning, on the other hand, the undoing of reconstruction had made explicit what Turner had earlier implied in his famous essay on the frontier —namely that in the Garden of Anglo-Saxon democracy "two races so distinct in characteristics as to render coalescence impossible" could not live together on equal terms.

18. "The Undoing of Reconstruction," *Essays on the Civil War and Reconstruction,* p. 384.
    19. *Ibid.*

For the Negro did not belong to the pre-1890 America of which Turner wrote. The Negro had not come willingly from Europe to escape old bonds but had been dragged from the dark continent in slavery. As far as white America was concerned, the Negro had not settled the frontier, nor had he carved a society out of the wilderness. In depicting the clearing of the forests in Mississippi, William Faulkner would later challenge the white exclusiveness of this frontier myth; for as the settlers sought to escape the bonds of the East, they became irreversibly entangled with the fates of both Indian aborigines and Negro slaves. But now, at the turn of the century, it would have seemed obvious to white Americans that the Negro did not share with his white superiors that "acuteness and inquisitiveness; that practical, inventive turn of mind . . . that masterful grasp of material things . . . that restless nervous energy" which had wrought the greatness of the American character.[20] In the Negro there was no individualistic antisocial antipathy to direct control which had from the beginning promoted democracy, according to Turnerian thinking.[21] In the Garden of America, the mythical force the frontier represented for Turner had not only promoted agrarian individualism and democracy against institutional cohesion and aristocracy; it had also served the purpose of assimilating the European white alien into the American mold. More significant for this study, it had excluded by definition the national black alien.

But what was to happen to the sanctity of the White Garden if this symbolic force of the frontier disappeared? The implications were that the outside forces of corruption and exploitation would then be unchecked. The alien from abroad would no longer be assimilated. Strange philosophies might now seep into the innocent New World. And finally, with no frontier continually regenerating American innocence by externalizing America's problems, the nation would have to admit that the problems—of which the Negro

20. Turner, *op. cit.,* p. 37.
21. *Ibid.,* p. 30.

problem was one of the most pressing—existed *within* the nation and therefore must be dealt with internally and, presumably, realistically.[22]

To all of these threats, beginning with and revolving about the threat posed by the Negro, Thomas Dixon had an answer embodied in the mission of a South conscious of, and inspired by, its past. The South would take a stand as a force of preservation and regeneration. Neither Dixon nor the Southerners who followed were offering the South as a frontier in exactly the same way in which Turner had thought of it—as a meeting point between civilization and savagery. But all of them struggled with a conception of the South as an intellectual and sometimes geographical force dedicated to a mission of national regeneration in the twentieth century in much the same way that Turner conceived of the frontier as a force of national regeneration in the nineteenth century. For these Southerners, the frontier was no longer a meeting and resolution between civilization and savagery. Rather it was a confrontation between tradition and progress. The forces and tendencies of industrial civilization were to be tempered and controlled by contact with the forces of tradition and history to create a harmonious, stable civilization. Later, with Robert Penn Warren and Martin Luther King, it would develop into a confrontation between historical responsibility and Christian forgiveness on the one hand and middle-class complacency and irresponsible repression on the other. In the moral and intellectual void left in the American imagination by the symbolic closing of the frontier and by the increasingly obvious fact that Jefferson's agrarian America had failed, all of these Southerners tried to build a conception of their history as a moral force capable of acting on the national character, and needed to guide the nation in a too-rapidly changing, urban-industrial world.

22. See William Appleman Williams, *The Tragedy of American Diplomacy* (New York: Dell Publishers, 1962), for a more complete development of this idea.

Thomas Dixon

The myth of Southern history approaches full devlopment in the early novels of Thomas Dixon. Dixon brought together the themes of reconciliation and union, Southern uniqueness, and Southern burden with the theme of Southern mission. The result was a conception of a new role for the South in the national life.

Dixon was a commanding spokesman for American racial separation. Colorful and indefatigable as an individual, he expresses racial views as detestable to a liberal modern reader as any of the verbiage of that particular heyday of American racism. But to pay heed only to Dixon's racial polemics—which are neither profound nor original—is to overlook the role he played as a participant in the development of the myth of Southern history. By examining in some detail his attitudes toward the South and the nation in the early years of the century as they are found in several of his novels, it is possible to establish a general outline of Southern concern and response. This will serve as a framework of reference as the major themes are repeated with significant variations in later years.

Thomas Dixon was born January 11, 1864, near Shelby, North Carolina, the son of a poor farmer. At 15, after a late start on his education, he entered Wake Forest College, and four years later he had earned both the B.A. and M.A. degrees. With the benefit of a scholarship, he entered Johns Hopkins University, where he became a "close friend of his classmate, Woodrow Wilson."[23]

After a year at Johns Hopkins, he went to New York to become an actor. Failing in this, he entered a law school in Greensboro, North Carolina, and received his law license in 1885. Before he had finished law school, he entered state politics and was elected to the state legislature; he was almost chosen Speaker of the House although he was not yet old enough to vote. Becoming discouraged, supposedly with corruption in politics,[24] he practiced law for

23. Raymond A. Cook, "The Man Behind the Birth of a Nation," *The North Carolina Historical Review*, XXXIX (1962), 521.
24. *Ibid.*, p. 522.

a short time. In 1887 he became a Baptist minister. Not satisfied with the huge audiences he was able to reach in such cities as Raleigh, Boston, and New York, he resigned from the ministry in 1899 to become a lecturer. Finally, at the age of 38, he began to write novels.[25]

Some years later, in 1915, millions of Americans learned from D. W. Griffith's motion picture *The Birth of a Nation,* which was based on Dixon's *The Clansman,* that the South's resistance to Radical Reconstruction and black supremacy in the South could only be considered heroic. When Oswald Garrison Villard and Moorfield Storey, who were active in the National Association for the Advancement of Colored People, tried to prevent the showing of the film, Dixon persuaded his old friend Woodrow Wilson, now President of the United States, and the members of the Supreme Court to view it. With such implicit approval of the picture, efforts to stop it were fruitless.[26] Wilson's comment on the film was: "It is like writing history with lightning. And my only regret is that it is all so terribly true."[27] While in fact it was not all true, Wilson's comment points to a dilemma in the minds of Southerners at the time. For what Southerners needed, and what such a motion picture as *The Birth of a Nation* could in part provide, was a way to reconcile regional knowledge and suffering with the concept of national innocence, violence with harmony, and an inescapable past with a faith in unhampered progress. Finally, it could provide a sense of mission—a belief that the violence, suffering, and injustice so much a part of Southern life before and after 1865 had been the means to a much greater, more significant national destiny. In other words, they needed a myth to replace the one shattered by the Civil War and Reconstruction.

Dixon's first novel was *The Leopard's Spots,* subtitled "A Ro-

25. *Ibid.,* p. 523.
26. *Ibid.,* pp. 530–533. See also Eric F. Goldman, *Rendezvous With Destiny: A History of American Reform,* rev. ed. (New York: Random House, Vintage Books, 1956), Chapter V.
27. Cook, *op. cit.,* p. 530.

mance of the White Man's Burden, 1865–1900." Its subtitle alone assured it of a national audience. This novel tells the story of Reconstruction, Redemption, and disfranchisement in North Carolina. Like Dunning and Wilson, Dixon saw Reconstruction as a greedy conspiracy against the people of the South, or, at best, a misled moral crusade. Like Dunning and Wilson, Dixon viewed disfranchisement as the only possible solution to the race problems created by the Civil War and its aftermath. Unlike either of these men, Dixon projected a new role for the South to play in the preservation and regeneration of national innocence. His synthesis of values represents a significant departure from that acquiescing and sentimental reconciliation reviewed by Paul H. Buck and suggested by Woodrow Wilson. Dixon's concern was a national crisis in which an older set of basically agrarian values was threatened by subversive alien forces represented specifically by the Negro threat and generally by a gamut-running, urban-industrial-scientific-capitalistic syndrome of materialism and racial degradation. His was a populist imagination,[28] basically antihistorical, and rooted in the mythical national covenant of racial innocence and harmony.

But if his concern was national, his response was profoundly regional. In his defense of Jim Crow, he was voicing the same basic concepts of a Southern mission that Woodward and Warren would later develop in their stand *against* Jim Crow. Yet the goals of this mission to regain the populist visions of innocence and harmony by doing battle with the forces of evil are sometimes darkened and made ambiguous by the sense of burden and tragedy which threads its way through Dixon's novels. The vision of innocence and harmony is always haunted by the specters of violence and frustration, which might occasionally threaten the Northerner but were always present for the Southerner.

The Leopard's Spots is the story of two men and their fight for

28. Richard Hofstadter, *The Age of Reform: From Bryan to F.D.R.,* Chapter I.

white supremacy. The elder of the two is the Reverend John Durham, Baptist minister of a small North Carolina town, Hambright. Durham stands throughout the novel as the philosophical spokesman for the American dogma on race. He also provides inspiration for the political hopes of the younger man, Charles Gaston. Gaston, whose own father had been killed in the closing days of the Civil War, grows from childhood during the dark days of Reconstruction when the evils of "Negro domination" are to be seen in every village street. Durham is his mentor, instructing him in the dangers which the Negro poses to the South and to the nation. At the end of the novel, Gaston finally becomes governor of the state on a disfranchisement ticket. Durham, himself sought after by a rich Boston church, rejects the offer and stays in Hambright, feeling it his duty to fight for Anglo-Saxon superiority in the South. As young Gaston grows to political maturity, he also falls in love with, and finally marries, beautiful Sally Worth, the only daughter of General Daniel Worth, a Civil War veteran and a "New South" industrialist who owns a complex of cotton mills near Hambright.

The novel also includes a cast of secondary characters who represent the various aspects of the Northern conspiracy against the South. Simon Legree is resurrected from *Uncle Tom's Cabin* to become a Reconstruction leader who succeeds in stealing enough money from the state government to set himself up on Wall Street as one of the most powerful industrialists in the country. George Harris Jr., "an educated Negro" and son of Miss Stowe's Eliza, reappears as the protégé of the Hon. Everett Lowell, a congressman from Boston and head of one of Boston's oldest and most distinguished families. Lowell has a daughter, Helen, with whom Harris falls in love. His suit, however, is rejected in the harshest terms by her father, even though he has championed Negro equality and Negro domination in the South. Because he is a Negro, George Harris is unable to find work in the North, even as a common laborer. Finally, at about the same time that Gaston's disfranchisement ticket triumphs in North Carolina, Harris gives up and becomes a distraught gambler traveling through the country on a macabre pilgrimage, laying wreaths at the sites of Negro lynchings.

In the beginning of the novel, as Dixon looks back to the close of the Civil War, he expresses the conventional sentiments of reconciliation and nationalism. Before the war, he notes, North Carolina had been the "typical American Democracy" (*LS*, p. 5), and this had not been changed by the war. The story opens with the return to Hambright of old Nelse, a loyal Negro slave, with the news of the death of his master, Colonel Charles Gaston. In final letters to his wife, the colonel had written that their son, Charles Jr., must be reared "to a glorious manhood in the new nation that will be born in this agony" (*LS*, p. 13). And to his son he had written: "You will live to see a reunited country. Hang this sword back beside the old flag of our fathers" (*LS*, p. 13).

We have already seen how Brown, in choosing an image to suggest this new union, pictured a young Southerner giving allegiance to the nation. Dixon also used this symbolic gesture in *The Leopard's Spots*, as well as later novels. The theme of reconciliation and union is seen in all of Dixon's early novels. Southerners are Americans, living and acting in such places as New York City, as well as in the South. Their hopes are the hopes of the nation—progress and national glory—and their concerns are the concerns of the nation, whether the focus is the Negro and other alien races or the trusts and socialism. In each case, Dixon's point was that Southerners could remain loyal to their regional heritage while at the same time helping to lead the nation into a more illustrious future.

The Burden

But reconciliation was not enough for Dixon. Wilson had made disfranchisement sound easy and had seemed to take it for granted, although he did show some concern that the methods by which it had been achieved threatened to bring social revolution and disunity. In several of his novels Dixon seems much closer to Brown in his consciousness of the immensity of a burden from the past—in this case the burden of blackness—which hung over the South.

Even as the defeated Southern soldiers limped back from Appomattox to take up their places in the new nation, a great dark shadow hung "in their hearts and over all the earth." The threat was the shadow of the freed Negro, "transformed by the exigency of war from a Chattel to be bought and sold into a possible Beast to be feared and guarded. Around this dusky figure every white man's soul was keeping its grim vigil" (*LS,* p. 5).

The significant words in this passage are "Chattel" and "Beast." The Negro has been changed from a legal abstraction into an organic threat. There is no sense of fear associated with the "Chattel." The fear comes from the "freed Negro," the "possible Beast." As a legal abstraction, the Negro had no place in a democratic society, no claim to the privileges of the White Garden. As a living freedman, a "Beast," he invades the sacred environment, bringing fear and danger with him. Most terrifying, he becomes a sexual creature, liberated from the restraints of the chattel. For Durham, the "towering figure of the freed Negro had been growing more and more ominous . . . throwing the blight of its shadow over future generations, a veritable Black Death for the land and its people" (*LS,* p. 33).

Again, as in the first passage, this passage suggests the white man's fear of the Negro's sexuality. The image of the towering Negro is phallic, throwing its blight over future generations. The bestial miscegenation which surely must come with Negro liberation and equality will corrupt the white race. This projected sexual threat to racial purity was Dixon's primary link with the national imagination. The Negro is viewed not only as a threat to the South but also to the nation. Turner and Dunning, among others, had conceived as Anglo-Saxon the American character which had led America to such greatness. Yet the Abolitionists were seen as having blindly tried to destroy this "racial integrity," not realizing, according to Dixon, that

one drop of Negro blood makes a negro. It kinks the hair, flattens the nose, thickens the lip, puts out the light of intellect, and lights the fires of brutal passions. The beginning of Negro equality as a vital fact is the beginning of the end of this nation's life. There is enough negro blood here to make mulatto the whole Republic. . . . *Can you build, in a Democracy, a nation inside a nation of two hostile races?* (*LS*, p. 242).

Dixon's answer to this question was "no." Yet he makes clear in the course of the novel that it was the South which had taken and would continue to take the stand against the subversion of racial purity.

If these passages and others like them anticipate Dixon's assertion of a Southern mission, they also reveal a thread of frustration and fatalism which sometimes threatens to show through the veneer of rhetorical swagger that Dixon puts forward as the battle cry of the Anglo-Saxon race. Early in the novel a company of drunken Negro soldiers break into the home of old Tom Camp, a virtuous Negro-hating Southern yeoman. The Negroes abduct Camp's oldest daughter from her own wedding ceremony. Without hesitation Camp commands his friends to fire upon the Negroes even though it is certain that they will hit the girl. "Shoot, men! My God, shoot! There are things worse than death!" Camp cries (*LS*, p. 125), and the others, led by the bridegroom himself, shoot and kill three of the Negroes. Unfortunately, they also hit the girl, who dies on the bed which had been prepared for her wedding night. Camp, in spite of his grief, then shakes hands with the men who have done the shooting, telling them that they have "saved my little gal" (*LS*, p. 126). The wedding of white innocents thus becomes a bloody funeral. White virtue has been saved, but at a cost so terrible as to make victory seem hollow to a contemporary reader. Camp's melodramatic response is so contrived as to be almost totally unconvincing. What the historian cannot overlook is the picture of American innocence being led to self-destruction by its own helplessness to deal concretely and rationally with a burden imposed upon it by the past.

Later in *The Leopard's Spots,* a Negro is burned alive for the rape and murder of Camp's other daughter. The purity of the white race again is avenged and asserted. Yet Dixon entitles the chapter "A Thousand-Legged Beast" and writes that the lynching crowd "seemed to melt into a great crawling swaying creature, half reptile half beast, half dragon half man, with a thousand legs, and a thousand eyes, and ten thousand gleaming teeth, and with no ear to hear and no heart to pity!" (*LS,* p. 380).

That the white race could be reduced to such levels of inhumanity is on one hand an implicit argument for complete segregation of the races in order to prevent such crimes in the future. On the other hand, Dixon's imagery reveals the despair of an individual caught in the contradiction of his own national culture. The desire to participate in the national life forces the Southerner to proclaim his region's cultural innocence and social harmony, fully conscious, however, of the guilt and tragedy which boil beneath the surface.

Both the tragedy and the absurdity of this position are demonstrated in Dixon's *The Sins of the Father* (1912). Soon after the Civil War, Tom Norton, a young white Southerner makes pregnant a mulatto servant girl, Cleo. Cleo goes away and gives birth to a girl who is but a few years younger than Tom Jr., Norton's legitimate son. Years later, Cleo, still a servant in the Norton home, brings a girl into the house and lets Tom Norton think that she is their daughter. Norton's son falls in love with the girl, Helen, and they are secretly married. The father reveals to the son that he has not only married his half-sister but a Negro. The father and son plan a joint suicide. Old Norton, who, in atonement for his earlier sins, has been conducting a vigorous campaign for Negro disfranchisement, tells young Tom:

There's no appeal, my boy! The sin of your father is full grown and has brought forth death. Yet I was not all to blame. We are caught tonight in the grip of the sins of centuries. I tried to give my life to the people to save the children of the future. My shame showed me the way as few men could have seen it, and I have set in motion forces that can never be stopped. Others will complete the work that I have begun. But our time has come—[29]

The "sin of centuries" will supposedly be stopped. But the forces that are to stop it are not explained. What is again clear is

29. *The Sins of the Father: A Romance of the South,* p. 452.

the image of the white Southerner driven to self-destruction by his entanglement in the paradoxical trap of white racial innocence. On one hand his own temptations and weaknesses force him to admit the imperfection of man and the complexity of human relationships. On the other hand, he is forced to deny this imperfection and these relationships for the sake of asserting his national innocence.

Old Norton wounds his son and kills himself. Tom Jr. recovers to learn that Cleo has executed a hoax: Helen is white. Tom takes up his father's disfranchisement work with "grim determination." The Negro must be shut out of white society. And after the death of his father, Tom "never again allowed a Negro to cross the threshold [of the Norton home] or enter its gates" (*SF,* p. 462).

This fact marks the Norton home with "peculiar distinction" for Dixon. The gesture, however, seems feeble, almost absurd, given the dimensions of the problem and the intensity of the emotions involved in the racial conflict. Rhetorical promises of great regenerative forces have been made, but only a single door has been slammed in bitterness and fear against a whole population. The image of Norton closing his house to Negroes is strangely anticipatory of an image of another closed house imagined some forty years later by Robert Penn Warren. Warren wrote of a strange old Southern white lady who, in her isolated, airless, old house, would sometimes telephone into town "that somebody was burning the Negroes out there on her place. She could hear their screams. Something was going on in her old head which in another place and time would not have been going on in her old head. She had never, I should think, seen an act of violence in her life. But something was going on in her head."[30]

The relationship between these two scenes is found in the sentence, "She had never . . . seen an act of violence in her life." "Indeed not," young Norton might have said, "for all of that has been eliminated by segregation, and its memory shut out by my closed door." And yet, it seems, it is a haunted innocence, vulnera-

30. *Segregation: The Inner Conflict in the South,* p. 112.

ble to sounds out of the past which the closed doors and airless rooms cannot keep back.

The Mission

If Dixon was aware of the burden of the past, he was also aware of the illumination and inspiration that the past offered. Out of the confrontation with the burden would come the moral strength to defend against its enemies an embattled tradition of Jeffersonian agrarian simplicity, once national in scope, now existing only in the South. It was the burden and the tradition together that for Dixon distinguished the South from the North. And for him it was this same pair of concepts which would secure the South's place in the national life.

The full dimensions of the national crisis against which the South must take its stand are suggested by an incident in *The Root of Evil* (1911), a muckraking novel about predatory capitalism and the social evils it breeds. In this novel, Dixon sends three Southerners to New York City. Jim Stuart and Nan Primrose are engaged to be married. Nan, however, is attracted by the wealth and position of John C. Calhoun Bivens, a Southern poor-white who has become a capitalistic master of trusts in the North. When Stuart, a lawyer, refuses to covet financial success in Dixon's version of the leisure class society, Nan breaks their engagement and eventually marries Bivens, surrendering her spiritual happiness and virtue for money. Although both Nan and her husband beg Jim to join the ranks of the wealthy as a Bivens lawyer, he resists the temptation and finally is able to say to Nan, "I've entered at last . . . into the Kingdom of Mind, that lies beyond the rule of greed, where beauty, heroism, and genius have built their altar fires and keep them burning."[31] His words anticipate the Southern Agrarians of *I'll Take My Stand* in choosing a "Southern" way of life as opposed to the "American" way of life represented by people like the Bivenses, who have been corrupted by the material-

31. *The Root of Evil*, p. 387.

istic greed of the "Industrial" or American way of life. Here, Dixon uses the South's Civil War–Reconstruction experience of privation and sacrifice to construct an ideal which will also reveal the South's moral superiority. Responding to the problems of an era which had suddenly become aware of the injustices and cruelties of industrial capitalism, Dixon looks, not to progressive politics and partial reform, but to national mythology, as interpreted through the South's experiences and goals, for total redemption.

Earlier in the novel, after the engagement has been broken, Stuart wanders through the sordid streets of the East Side. He walks into a filthy, smoke-filled basement saloon, observing the corrupted life around him. He is about to leave when suddenly

A fat beastly Negro swept by encircling the frail figure of a white girl. Her dress was ragged and filthy, but the delicate lines of her face, with its pure Grecian profile, and high forehead bore the stamp of breeding and distinction. . . . To the young Southerner the sight was one of incredible horror. . . . He looked about among all the men who filled the room, for a single face in which was left a trace of human pride. . . . He looked in vain (*RE,* pp. 99–100).

The imagery of black looming over white is again used as it is used in *The Leopard's Spots* in the suggestion of an association between the Negro and the corrupt urban-industrial environment. In a society in which this kind of degradation of the white race exists, there can no longer be a covenant of innocence with nature. The degradation is complete, for there is not one man in the room to share Stuart's outrage. This image suggests the basic and ulti-mate horror of the threat posed by what Dixon had earlier called the "metropolitan mob." For Dixon, this is the end result of the illusion of equality for the Negro, for it is only here in the depths of the urban hell which the capitalistic exploitation of such men as Bivens has created that the Negro is free to corrupt and prostitute the white female, symbol of Anglo-Saxon purity and regeneration. Stuart follows the Negro and risks his life for the privilege of "joyfully beating him into insensibility," an act of violence moti-vated more by frustration and horror than by pride. He rescues the girl and takes her to a home for wayward girls.

This single incident underlines Dixon's major thesis: just as Stuart attacks the Negro in order to rescue the white girl, so the South with its "clear" and unique perspective will willingly undertake the mission dictated by the crisis to eliminate the Negro from political and social participation in American life. The South will also take its stand against the materialism and spiritual degradation which make possible such violations of racial segregation. Such a mythological interpretation of racial injustice offered the security of a seemingly patriotic and Christian rationale as well as the illusion that the South could still act as a major influence in the life of the nation.

The antithesis to this picture of corruption and degradation in New York is suggested by the industrial world of General Daniel Worth in *The Leopard's Spots*. General Worth is Dixon's representative character of the New South, and it is in Dixon's description of Worth's home and mills that we see the ideal which the South represents.

First, Dixon describes Worth's home in the imagery of the myth of a Southern tradition which cannot be violated. Worth's home fits the stereotype of the plantation house as described by Francis Pendleton Gaines.[32] On a wooded hill overlooking the Catawba River, the ivory-painted brick structure rises with "big Greek columns" and wide verandas. "With its green background of magnolia trees, it seemed like a huge block of solid ivory flashing in splendour from its throne on the hill" (*LS,* pp. 214–215). The mansion is the traditional symbol of the South's uniqueness—the agrarian tradition of gentleman planters and happy slaves. The

---

32. *The Southern Plantation: A Study in the Development and the Accuracy of a Tradition,* p. 13. Gaines quotes a description of the mansion by Joel Chandler Harris as the "typical image of the mansion: 'a stately house on a wooded hill, the huge white pillars that supported the porch rising high enough to catch the reflection of a rosy sunset, the porch itself and the beautiful lawn in front filled with a happy crowd of lovely women and gallant men, young and old, the wide avenue lined with carriages, and the whole place lit up (as it were) and alive with the gay commotion of a festive occasion.' "

imagery suggests the Good Life supposedly enjoyed in such an environment of simplicity and harmony. It is the antithesis of the crowded, dirty city with its smoke and poverty that Jefferson imagined. But whereas the traditional image of the plantation represents racial harmony, Dixon's picture of the Worth estate—white and blending with nature—represents the ideal which the South must defend against both the Negro threat and against industrialism.[33] If industrialism is to come into the South, it must not violate this image.

The General's mills are also on the banks of the Catawba. That they are not the mills of Birmingham or of New England is made clear by the General's description of them. Their presence has disturbed none of the tranquillity or harmony of the Greek mansion on the hill. They are located in a pastoral setting of "wooded cliffs" and "moonlight." Their noise is like "ravishing music." They seem to the General to be a "living thing"—a living organism which suggests an actual vital attachment to, or relationship with, the community. The mills are operated by water, which is a natural, clean, nonpolluting source of power. Finally, even though they evidently operate rather long hours—while the General sits in the moonlight listening—they are capable only of good, for they not only provide work but weave fabrics which some day will "clothe the South in splendour" (*LS,* p. 380). The mills are in harmony with nature and at the same time serve a vital function to the

33. "Although in the realm of fact the difficulty of the study of race relations is commensurate with its importance, such is not the case with the tradition. Nothing could be simpler than the connection as ordinarily interpreted by the romancers. The chroniclers of the legendary plantation life, save a few abolitionists, focus attention on an idealized relation of feudalism, benign supervision and happy dependence. Even the anti-slavery writers, in deference to popular taste, include many episodes of idyllic nature. Abolition literature, it must be remembered, is not the norm of plantation narrative. From the rise of retrospective writings in the last third of the nineteenth century, a beautiful felicity of racial contact has been presented, not as occasional but as constant; an imperious kindness on the part of the whites, matched by obsequious devotion on the part of the blacks." Gaines, *op. cit.,* pp. 209–210.

community of man without violating the community's natural stability or the individual's dignity. They are subservient to the mansion. By defining the place of industry in terms which do not
violate the concepts associated with the mansion, the South is able
to master the new forces, reaping the benefits without giving up
any of its own agrarian innocence and freedom from industrial
complexity.

But General Worth's mills function harmoniously only because
he has gotten rid of the Negro. "We don't allow a Negro to come
inside the enclosure" (*LS,* p. 280), the General tells young Gaston. If he did hire Negroes, he says, labor trouble would end only
in anarchy or social revolution. The reader is also reminded of the
Reverend Durham's earlier concerns with the "towering figure of
the freed Negro" which had been "growing more and more ominous until its menace overshadowed the poverty, the hunger, the
sorrows and the devastation of the South, throwing the blight of its
shadow over future generations, a veritable Black Death for the
land and its people" (*LS,* p. 33). The image of black looming over
white—of the "fat" Negro over the "frail" white girl—can also
become the smokestacks hanging over the white mansion. Both the
Negro and the stacks threaten the simplicity of the South's mythical pastoral in white. The language suggests the blackness of soot
as well as the blackness of skin, the blight of poverty as well as
racial corruption, the mutilated land left by the mineral ravishers
as well as the black death of miscegenation.[34] Both concepts—the
Negro and industrialism—are linked in the imagery by their darkness and by their tendency to destroy the white harmony of the
White Garden symbolized by Worth's idyllic home and mills.

As long as the Negro and exploitative industrialism are excluded
from participation in the political and social life of the South, the

34. In the tradition, Gaines writes, miscegenation "is only a grey shadow,
not black. The net result is a mere sensationalism that gives piquancy to the
romance" (p. 210). Obviously, as this chapter suggests, Dixon—and Dixon's
generation—attaches far graver meaning to what Gaines calls "unchastity."
For Dixon, as the above quotations suggest, the shadow is definitely black.

"music of the mills" can continue. With its consciousness in the present of a more enriching, more natural life enjoyed in the simple agrarian past, the South will be able to take a stand against the so-called progress of the North, which is not really progress at all but a corrupting materialism which fragments man's relationship to nature by leading him into the tempting web of modern technology and finance.

Thus, Simon Legree, carpetbag thief, exploiter of Negro ignorance, manipulator of Negro domination in the South, can become a great and powerful capitalist in New York, taking by a kind of brute force whatever and whomever he wants much in the same way the Negro pimp in the East Side dive takes the white girl as his prostitute. Similarly, the scalawag Allen McLeod, who exploits the cause of Negro equality for his own political advancement, becomes the spokesman in the novel for the new scientific theory that ideal love and marriage blessed by God are myths and that physical passion is the only reality. McLeod's sexual "appetite" might even be compared to that of the Negro rapists in the novel. It is also "science" which takes part of the blame for the Negro threat itself. George Harris, who dares to ask permission to court his white patron's daughter, had been the subject of "an experiment of thrilling interest" in which he had been "collected" by a Bostonian matron as one of her most promising "specimens" of Negro boys to be sent North to be educated (*LS,* p. 49). The patron, Congressman Lowell, himself a man of "scientific mind" who has undertaken this "political study," draws the line at breaking the natural law of races. Lowell's rejection of Harris is one of the few instances in Dixon where the Negro is turned away from white society without violence being done by or upon the white person involved. The Northerner is threatened by the black burden of the South, but it is not the North's burden. There is no desperation in Lowell's actions. The reader feels that the dismissal is permanent, that Harris won't be back. It is Dixon, the Southerner, who, with at least some show of sympathy, records Harris's pathetic decay as a gambler.

Yet, for Dixon, it is this unique burden of the Negro which offers the South the chance to re-enter the national life more or less on its own terms. It must cast off this burden in order to preserve its own innocence. But if the South can succeed in getting rid of the weight of the Negro problem, it may then take its stand as a redeeming witness in the corrupted world seen by Jim Stuart in his descent into the hellish slums of New York. The ideal for which the South must take its stand and from which it must, in part, draw its strength is seen in the picture of General Worth's world. To these pastoral suggestions are added the Reverend Durham's rhetorical prophecies of doom and regeneration.

In rejecting the offer of the Boston church, Durham explains that it is his work to "maintain the racial absolutism of the Anglo-Saxon in the South, politically, socially, economically" (*LS,* p. 333). Here is the immediate mission. Second, Durham goes on to explain that the right to choose one's mate is the "foundation of racial life and civilization" and that the South must "guard with flaming sword" this "holy of holies." The purity of the race must thus be preserved. But now, third, the preacher goes on to speak of a more general mission for the South. He moves from the Negro to other forces which threaten the nation, and in doing so gives expression to one of the earliest twentieth-century conceptions of the myth of Southern history.

The South has been voiceless in these later years. . . . But when these children we are rearing down here grow, *rocked in their cradles of poverty, nurtured in the fierce struggle to save the life of a mighty race,* they will find speech, and their songs will fill the world with pathos and power (*LS,* p. 334, emphasis mine).

The "cradles of poverty" are the result of the war and Reconstruction—defeat and humiliation not in keeping with the nineteenth-century doctrine of American progress. Thus has the South been distinguished by history from the rest of the nation, for it has known the horrors of war and "foreign" occupation first hand. This experience has tempered the Southerner; and the confrontation with Negro domination has made the Southerner aware of dangers and tendencies which the North cannot see. Here, for a moment, Dixon seems vaguely to anticipate the responses of such Southerners as C. Vann Woodward and Robert Penn Warren toward the general nature of Southern experience. As we shall see later, of course, there are obvious and profound distinctions to be made between Dixon and the others. Yet what follows does not differ in its essential conception of a Southern mission in the national life from the "stand" of the Southern Agrarians nor even from Robert Penn Warren's later assertion that by dealing concretely with the moral problem raised by the Negro in the South, the South can offer some leadership in breaking out of the "national rhythm . . . between complacency and panic."[35] In this line, Durham continues:

> I've studied your great cities. Believe me the South is worth saving. Against the possible day when a flood of foreign anarchy threatens the foundations of the Republic and men shall laugh at the faiths of your fathers and undigested wealth beyond the dreams of avarice rots your society, until it mocks at honour, love and God—against that day we will preserve the South!
>
> .   .   .   .
>
> Believe me, deacon, the ark of the covenant of American ideals rests today on the Appalachian Mountain range of the South. When your metropolitan mobs shall knock at the doors of your life and demand the reason of your existence, from these poverty-stricken homes, with their old-fashioned, perhaps mediaeval ideas, will come forth the fierce athletic sons and sweet-voiced daughters in whom the nation will find a new birth! (*LS,* p. 334).

Atheism, socialism, capitalism, urban decay, materialism: all threaten the nation. The South holds the "covenant of American ideals" and in her struggle for racial purity will find the strength and courage to preserve this covenant until the nation can be brought back to the true and simple way. The South will act as a beacon on a hill, throwing the light to those in the outer darkness.

Thus, in *The One Woman: A Story of Modern Utopia* (1903) a Southern woman whose Midwestern husband has divorced her

---

35. Warren, *op. cit.,* p. 115.

saves him from execution when he becomes so depraved by socialism and free love that he commits murder as well as blasphemy against God and civilization. She forgives him and intervenes with the governor, also a Southerner by background and her former beau, to save her husband from execution. They are remarried by the governor himself, but it is not the conventional marriage of sectional reconciliation found so often in popular novels of the period. Rather it is a remarriage born of suffering and humiliation through which the South will rise to deliver the erring North from destruction. The Southerners' uniqueness lies in their strength of character, which allows them to rise out of the ashes of their own defeat and humiliation to restore some degree of virtue to those led astray by the false doctrines of a materialistic, immoral, urban society.

The Foolish Virgin (1915), which also illustrates Southern uniqueness, is the story of Mary Adams, a young schoolteacher in New York City who was originally from Kentucky. She marries Jim Anthony, a rootless and somewhat ruthless East Side inventor, who has been cheated by Wall Street lawyers out of the rights to an invention. Therefore, Anthony turns to crime. He uses his talents to perfect infallible safecracking tools with which he believes he can reclaim what is his in the dog-eat-dog society which industrial capitalism has spawned. Although a Southerner by parentage, he has grown up on the streets of the Northern city and is depicted as the victim of urban squalor and corruption. Only by being left for dead and then symbolically reborn in the mountains of North Carolina does he shed his sordid, Northern, urban past and eventually become worthy of his Southern wife and son. After his miraculous regeneration of "spirit" and "soul," he applies his inventive genius to the development of a new process for mining mica in the mountains.

Industrialism and capitalism had created the evils of the Northern city, but they pose no threat for Dixon in the Southern Garden, for here they exist in a unique framework of social harmony and simplicity shaped by the "ark of the covenant of American ideals."

Mica production can be doubled, but it will not conflict with the world symbolized by the idyllic log bungalow which Anthony builds "on the sunny slope of the mountain which overlooks the valley toward Asheville." At the end of the novel he and his estranged wife are reunited, to live lives of Southern simplicity in their mountainside home, far from the corruptions and complexities of the urban North.[36] That such regeneration can occur in the South is evidence for Dixon of the uniqueness of the region and its mission.

In *The Leopard's Spots,* the Reverend Durham had promised that the South would rise out of the ashes of its burden of defeat and poverty to save the nation from its enemies, both foreign and domestic. In *The Fall of a Nation* (1916), Dixon took the position that at least some of those foreigners were better Americans than complacent, politically duped natives. Written to support military preparedness, *The Fall of a Nation* again names "wealth beyond the dreams of avarice" and its corrupting influence as a major threat to the nation's moral fiber. But it is now the "might of kings"—European conquest—knocking at the door, demanding that Americans give a reason for their existence.[37] A fantasy of American paranoia regarding European conspiracy, the novel is not in a strict thematic sense a "Southern" story, although the novel's hero and chief spokesman for military preparedness, the young congressman John Vassar, is at one point likened to a Southerner for his "tall dark look of distinction" (*FN,* p. 70). Actually, Vassar is a Polish immigrant who holds Americanization classes in a neighborhood armory, where immigrants learn English and patriotism. These new Americans also support Vassar's fight for preparedness in the face of native indifference. He explains this support to Virginia Holland, a feminist and pacifist who has been duped by foreign espionage agents into opposing Vassar's armament bill: "You are American by the accident of birth. . . . We

36. *The Foolish Virgin,* pp. 230–234, 284–306, 326, 351–352.
37. *The Fall of a Nation: A Sequel to the Birth of a Nation,* p. 165.

are American because we willed to come. . . . We lifted up our eyes from a far country—amid tears and ashes and ruins—and saw the light of liberty shining here across the seas. . . . It is *our* country . . . as it can't be yours who do not realize its full meaning" (*FN*, pp. 66–67).

For Dixon, the immigrant, like the Southerner and unlike the Northerner, knows the realities of the burden of history and is thus in a better position to appreciate the meaning of American freedom. The immigrant, again like the Southerner, is also much more aware of threats to this freedom and to the American way of life. Later in the novel, after the United States is invaded and temporarily conquered by the European powers, these same immigrants play key roles in the resistance movement which eventually defeats the invading armies with the aid of a secret organization of white-robed, horse-riding, female guerrillas whose dress is reminiscent of the Ku Klux Klan. Dixon concludes: "Taught wisdom at last in the school of defeat, a mighty nation lifted her head and girded her loins for a glorious future" (*FN*, p. 362). Once again, through the devices of melodrama and plot-contrivance, Dixon resolves a national crisis—thus furthering the cause of Union—by using the experience of the South and of those societies like the South which had experienced history as defeat and tragedy to suggest that righteousness and virtue were ultimately strengthened by the perspectives and insights gained through the burdens of frustration and defeat. Four decades later C. Vann Woodward noted parallels between the South's burdensome heritage of "frustration, failure, and defeat" and the "common lot of mankind," especially in the underdeveloped nations of the world. From this point of view, the national myths of "opulence and success and innocence" are put on the defensive.[38] The South is able to stand with the world, or with at least a good part of the world, in judgment on the North's illusions about the value and the just and wise use of affluence and

38. "The Search for Southern Identity," *The Burden of Southern History*, pp. 19, 25.

power. While taking full account of the vast differences between the specific uses of Southern history implied by each man, it may be suggested that at a general level, the uses of the past concerned Dixon at the beginning of the century as much as they would concern Woodward nearly fifty years later.

Paradoxically, the light of the redeeming Southern beacon is born in darkness. For Gaston, innocence and harmony are recovered, not by escaping history, but by drawing moral fortitude out of the knowledge and conflict and suffering which have been experienced in the South's peculiar and tension-filled relationship with the nation. Worth's isolated little world is the ideal, but it can be preserved only by knowledge, and by sacrifice and labor in history. Worth wants to ignore history, to "leave the Negro and politics alone" (*LS,* pp. 280–281). Young Gaston, reared in the postwar, "poverty-stricken" South sees that this is not enough. If the Negro threatens the ideal, then the Negro must be dealt with concretely, politically, in history; and this Gaston sets out to do, through political, institutionalized segregation. Worth's concept of the past is static and sentimental. Gaston's is dangerously more dynamic, for he admits change and sees the necessity of political action if the racist structure of American society is to be preserved. Such characters as young Tom Norton in *The Sins of the Father,* and Jim Stuart in *The Root of Evil* share this view. Nevertheless, one must ultimately conclude that Dixon sought to use history only to escape from history. This is the contradiction that is never resolved. He seems to be conscious of history only insofar as it can be used to escape back to the illusionary innocence of an all-white America. Southern history is then only a means, similar to the concept of the mythical frontier, toward the preservation of Anglo-Saxon supremacy.

✢ II   The Southern Agrarians

The Symposium

THREE decades passed between the publication of *The Leopard's Spots* in 1902 and *I'll Take My Stand* in 1930.[1] The focus of national attention had shifted. In 1900, Dixon had written of the Negro as the primary threat to both Anglo-Saxon supremacy and Anglo-Saxon democracy. He had in addition vaguely sketched the coming day when industrialism and capitalism would corrupt the simple fabric of American life. By 1930, however, there was already some evidence of shifting national attitudes toward the Negro. But industrialism and capitalism loomed larger than ever as major concerns in American society. The prosperity of the pre-

---

1. Two recent studies of the Southern Agrarians, both of which go far beyond the scope of this study, are Alexander Karanikas's *Tillers of a Myth: Southern Agrarians as Social and Literary Critics* and John L. Stewart's *The Burden of Time: The Fugitives and Agrarians.* Virginia Rock's "The Making and Meaning of *I'll Take My Stand:* A Study in Utopian-Conservatism, 1925–1939" is an extensive study of the development of that book. I am indebted to all three studies for the facts and insights they offered.

vious decade had not resolved the old conflict in the American mind between rural simplicity and urban-industrial complexity. Material acquisition was nice, but so was the uncomplicated simplicity associated with the rural past. The popular literature of the 1920s abounded in tales of escape into the wholesome primitiveness of unspoiled nature, while Americans believed to the very end and beyond that the simple economic structure extolled by President Hoover would bless the nation forever. The First World War was forgotten and capitalism was sacrosanct, yet the conflict remained. George Babbitt worked to boost the glory of Zenith in the day but dreamed of his fairy child at night. Jake Barnes fished the trout streams of provincial Spain but could not forget the war which had left him a cripple in mind, body, and spirit. The furious pace of the Roaring Twenties hid the conflict from easy view, but, as almost every serious artist of the decade made clear, it *was* there.

The twelve Southerners who contributed to *I'll Take My Stand* tried to utilize the South's mythical past to meet the threats which industrialism posed to a humanistic society. But in attempting this, they failed to adapt the Southern racial issue to changing national patterns of thought. Without this adaptation, their attempt to relate Southern history to national needs was to prove futile.

Thirty-four years earlier, the election of 1896 had marked the final defeat of agrarian forces in American politics. From that point, urban industrialism would become an increasingly significant factor in shaping the politics as well as the cultural imagination of the nation. But in the South such men as Dixon and Thomas Watson continued to warn against the evils of Yankee capitalism and did what they could to protect the agrarianism of the rural South against what they saw as Northern, urban, or industrial ideas. The chief manifestation of this turning in upon itself, which coincided with the defeat of the old agrarian values at the national polls, was the South's attack upon the Negro. The South believed it could preserve its agrarian economy and social structure—the Garden—only if it was defined as a White Garden, a garden from which the Negro would be excluded at all cost. And while the South turned against the Negro in regional reaction to national urban industrialism, it also opposed urban industrialism out of fear of Negro advancement. The framework of Southern thought remained basically rural, not only because there was little actual industrial development in the South as a whole during these years, but because only a rural, agrarian orientation guaranteed the racial stability necessary to Southern peace of mind. Nevertheless, by 1930 the Southern status quo was threatened more than ever. Earlier Southern victories over the Negro had done nothing to halt or even to brake the advances of industrialism but had only obscured, temporarily, the totality of the industrial-pluralistic victory over agrarian individualism. In fact, advocates of the "New South" paradoxically sought to encourage the development of industry in the South without encouraging even moderate change in the region's caste structure. Yet an industrial society, unlike an agricultural society, was bound to make racial discrimination quite obvious and therefore less tolerable, even though at the same time it might intensify class division. Such Southerners as Donald Davidson recognized the danger that the mixture of industrialism with democracy posed to the status quo. In fact, all of the men who contributed essays to *I'll Take My Stand* proclaimed the importance of a Southern tradition that had supposedly allowed the South to resist much of the social disruption of industrial capitalism and thereby to have escaped the fate of most of twentieth-century America.

As Dixon's chief concern had been the Negro, so the Agrarians spoke of "Industrialism" as the immediate crisis. Like the Agrarians, Dixon had proclaimed the myth of plantation simplicity and had associated it with Jeffersonian agrarianism. But for Dixon, the South's mission to the nation had been the political and social disfranchisement of the Negro which was to be achieved through the manipulation of institutional politics. The Agrarians, on the other hand, professed the same plantation mythology, the same Southern "innocence," but were unable to put their "stand" into a context which would appeal to the population at large or which was capable of being instituted in the social structure. The Agrarians' approach to the problem of industrialism was in large part defined by their intellectual heritage from the generation of Dixon and Watson—the politics and sociology of Jim Crow—and for this reason, given the shifting attitudes of the times, the Agrarians were not able to relate the myth of Southern history to the current problems of the nation successfully.

The symposium's contributors were writers, critics, and social scientists, all Southerners by birth and, with a single exception, by early education.[2] Their identification with the South went deep. In speaking of the "unanimities in attitude" of the group, Virginia Rock writes of "an identification often closely enmeshed with a sense of belonging not only to a certain locale but to a particular kind of locale—a rural, agrarian environment characterized by open fields and woods and by growing crops on small farms, where the 'hastening ills' of a mechanizing civilization had not yet destroyed the 'natural beauty.' "[3] "To the Agrarians," according to Miss Rock, "the traumatic experience of the Civil War, the humiliations of Reconstruction, and the effects on Southern economy were not mere abstractions in history textbooks; they were part of the lives of their own people—of their ancestors and their ancestors' neighbors."[4] The significance of such a consciousness of the past is suggested in a passage from Stark Young's *The Torches Flare,* published in 1928 and quoted by Miss Rock. The central character of that book observes, "It's only natural, of course, that a people who had lost their cause and had a hard time afterward and were so poor and had their pride hurt so, and saw a thing they had been born to dying away from them in a new age, should have created a defense in some sort of beautiful tradition."[5] This "beau-

2. Rock, *op. cit.,* pp. 10–11. Henry Blue Kline attended Case Institute of Technology for two years before entering Vanderbilt.

3. *Ibid.,* p. 13.

4. *Ibid.,* p. 20.

5. *Ibid.,* p. 22.

tiful" and defensively created tradition of Southern history as it stood in 1930 is the subject of this chapter.

The dozen essays in *I'll Take My Stand* cover varied themes: the philosophy of agrarianism; the role of economics, history, religion, and education in an agrarian society; a criticism of the philosophy of progress itself; and a discussion of the Southern race problem. Each essay was written by an individual member of the group to contribute to a fuller understanding of the book's general thesis. This general thesis, agreed upon by all of the contributors, was "to support a Southern way of life against what may be called the American or prevailing way; and all as much as agree that the best terms in which to represent the distinction are contained in the phrase, Agrarian *versus* Industrial."[6]

Even the South, however, because it was isolated as one of a few such agrarian sections in the nation, was seen by the Agrarians as itself in danger of capitulating to the industrial ideal or the "decision of society to invest its economic resources in the applied sciences" (*ITMS,* p. xi) with continually increased production and consumption of manufactured goods as the only end or goal. But according to the Agrarians, echoing heirs to a long line of European and American anti-industrial sentiment, this materialism has played havoc with man and with civilization. Man himself suffers because of the increased and "fierce" tempo and consequent strain in an industrial society. The worker's sense of security is decreased because of the constant danger of unemployment. Labor is made to seem degrading and undesirable, while the new leisure gained through the machine is empty and without meaning. In such a society neither the arts nor religion nor the "amenities of life," such as the "social exchanges which reveal and develop sensibility in human affairs," are able to survive (*ITMS,* p. xv). Melville and Thoreau, James, Twain, Howells, and Dreiser, not to mention

6. Twelve Southerners, *I'll Take My Stand: The South and the Agrarian Tradition,* p. iv.

Fitzgerald and Dos Passos and Lewis, had all made the charges and had in fact portrayed and documented their views much better than the Agrarians ever would. But now in 1930, after liberal dissent had been centered for a century or more in New England and, to a lesser extent, the Middle West, it was the South's turn to call the nation to account for its wandering away from the simple truths of the Jeffersonian dream of an agrarian, decentralized republic; for only the South, so ran the theme, still contained more than a shred or two of that virtuousness. Opposed to the industrial society, the Agrarians claimed, was the agricultural society which was able to assimilate limited industrialism and urban development without destroying the basic fabric of a leisurely, humane existence. Agriculture, which was seen as the best and "most sensitive" of vocations, had economic preference and employed the maximum number of workers. For the Agrarians, this fact made possible the leisure and sense of human fulfillment found in an agrarian society.

The Static Frontier

In June of 1920, John Gould Fletcher, poet and critic, returned to the United States from Europe. In a letter, he expressed the disillusionment of an entire generation of American intellectuals at what America had seemingly become. He wrote:

When I arrived at New York, I suffered so badly from disillusionment that I was tempted to return by the next boat . . . New York is simply one vast orgy of spending. . . . The war has not made the remotest effect—it has only increased the amount of money people have to spend, speeded up machinery everywhere, made everyone a cog in the vast money-making, soul-destroying grind. . . . Outwardly this country is prosperous to a degree never imagined before.
But inwardly this prosperity masks a profound and hopeless failure to get the most out of life. . . . American people are simply struggling on the edge of a vast abyss. I do not exaggerate. As the machine gets more and more perfect, life becomes more and more impossible. The machine must either be destroyed or life will cease to exist on this [planet?].[7]

7. Quoted in Rock, *op. cit.,* p. 71.

This is a succinct statement of the temperament of the "Lost Generation" of American intellectuals which, it should be remembered, included Southerners as well as others. The war to end wars had failed. The dollar and the machine reigned supreme. The ideals of simplicity, basic to the concept of the national covenant, had been put aside. American society teetered on the edge of an abyss of materialism dug by its own technology.

For the Agrarians, Thomas Dixon's prewar prophecies of the corruption and defilement of American ideals and institutions had become the realities of postwar America. For Dixon had seen the day when "a flood of foreign anarchy" would threaten the "foundations of the Republic"; a day when men would "laugh at the faith of your fathers" and when "undigested wealth beyond the dreams of avarice" would rot American society "until it mocks at honour, love and God" (*LS,* p. 334). The specters of 1900 seemed to have become the realities of the 1920s. Anarchism, materialism, conformity, complacency, crumbling morals, and new levels of wealth and high living "beyond the dreams of avarice" were to be found. Those who found themselves revolting against this society were confronted by the same industrial, capitalistic society—the same quest for the Big Money—that Dixon's Jim Stuart had fought against in *The Root of Evil*. They "feared the effect upon themselves and upon American culture of mass production and the machine, and saw themselves as fighting at the last ditch for the right to be themselves in a civilization which was being leveled into monotony by Fordismus and the chain-store mind."[8]

Throughout the 1920s and even before, "in scores of letters, critical articles, and poems . . . attacks and oblique criticisms were directed against industrialism, specialization, urbanization, mechanization, and finance capitalism" by various members of the group who at the end of the decade were to unite under the

---

8. Frederick Lewis Allen, *Only Yesterday: An Informal History of the Nineteen-Twenties,* pp. 236–237.

Agrarian banner.[9] Like other intellectuals of the period, one of their basic concerns in this dissent from American society was the fate of the arts and of the artist in a materialistic society. There was also a concern with morality in the age of the machine. Like Walter Lippmann, writing at the same time, they spoke of the need of a religion of the "spirit." With Lewis Mumford they saw the necessity of subduing the machine to human ends. And like Charles Beard, they called for a subduing of "physical things to the empire of the spirit." But unlike any of these Northern intellectuals, all groping at the same time for a regeneration of idealism in the face of overwhelming materialism, the Southern Agrarians discovered the source of such regeneration in a concept of regional history and the mission which that history dictated.

Their development of this mythological construct and its implications for their lives and for a Southern mission crystallized slowly throughout the 1920s. The turning point, however, was most certainly an incident which took place in 1925 and more than any other single event turned the attention of such men as John Crowe Ransom, Donald Davidson, and Allen Tate to a deliberately self-conscious examination of the relationship between the South and the rest of the nation. The Tennessee legislature had passed and signed into law in March an antievolution bill which prohibited the teaching of Darwin's ideas in state-supported schools. To test the law, John T. Scopes, a young high school science teacher, agreed to teach Darwin's theory in order to precipitate a trial. The trial took place during the summer of 1925 and might have passed unnoticed by the future Agrarians as well as by everybody else, had it not been for the coverage of the trial by the Northern press. The sensational and often vicious "boob-baiting," in which H. L. Mencken and a host of lesser talents indulged, pictured the South as a land of yokels and reactionaries where ignorance was a virtue and where the virtues of civilization were unknown and, strangest of all, unwanted. It was "Tennessee *vs.*

9. Rock, *op. cit.,* p. 65.

Truth," and "Tennessee *vs.* Civilization," and "Tennessee: Where Cowards Rule"; it was too much for the sensitive Southerners.

Before the Scopes trial, the legend of the Old South had not particularly appealed to the young Fugitives. Ransom, for instance, was more interested in medieval Europe as a standard against which to measure the present. Nor had Davidson used the Old South in his poems of escape from a crude and common world. In the same year Tate wrote that "The modern Southerner does not inherit, nor is he likely to have, a native culture compounded of the strength and subtlety of his New England contemporary's."[10] And Robert Penn Warren, preparing to leave for the University of California, was not at all interested in the Dayton affair or its implications. But the attacks on the South by Mencken and others stirred the future Agrarians into a new mood of defensive anger, followed by concentrated study of their region. Their declaration which followed, not only defended what they understood by "Fundamentalism," but offered this same fundamentalism as an answer to the corruption of morality observable on all sides. Two years before *I'll Take My Stand* was published, Davidson wrote that fundamentalism, rather than being apologized for, should be seen as a positive value system since "it offers a sincere, though a narrow solution to a major problem of our age: namely, how far science, which is determining our physical ways of life, shall be permitted also to determine our philosophy of life."[11] Davidson argued that in going along with "progress," the South should pick and choose, for with its traditional conservatism, it had kept intact "old ways of life" which gave it "definite character. In this time of change it can and ought to be deliberate. Whatever the South may find to emulate in the example of other sections of the United States, it may also find mistakes to avoid."[12]

Davidson's article was indicative of the direction in which at

10. Quoted in Stewart, *op. cit.,* p. 113.
11. Donald Davidson, "First Fruits of Dayton: The Intellectual Evolution in Dixie," *The Forum,* LXXIX (1928), 898.
12. *Ibid.,* p. 901.

least four members of the future symposium—Ransom (who specifically defended fundamentalism in *God Without Thunder*), Tate, Davidson, and Frank Lawrence Owsley—were by then moving. The Northern and city journalists, like the abolitionists before them, had taken much pleasure in debunking the sentimental legends of an Old South which was leisurely and genteel, exposing the South as a land of barbarity and sloth. And like pre–Civil War Southerners, the Agrarians came to the defense of what was attacked, not because they were already its sworn advocates, which was hardly the case, but because outsiders had attacked something Southern. William Jennings Bryan, however, was not a Southerner, and the conflict in which the Southerners found themselves was not merely a sectional quarrel but a national dilemma, the old conflict between agrarian innocence and urban-industrial complexity. It was 1896 all over again, and the points of view from which Bryan, and later the Agrarians, argued were as antiquated in 1925 as cries for free silver would have been. It was not that capitalism and industrialism were above criticism in 1925 or 1930. The influence of science on morality was certainly a legitimate question, if not a solvable problem, but what the Dayton incident did in the long run was to encourage the Agrarians into criticizing these systems and institutions, using as their base an illusionary fiction rather than viable myth. They defended and asserted the Old South and the Southern way of life. But this was not the South and the tradition they would have discovered had they been more directed toward finding a really usable Southern past and less involved in answering an insult and in defending the innocence of the American Anglo-Saxon Garden. Scientific materialism with its new environmental tendencies endangered not only Protestant fundamentalism but white supremacy in the South and in the rest of the nation. Warren, least involved of the group in their response to the Scopes trial, soon began working his way back to a more profound investigation of Southern history, and he was undoubtedly aided indirectly by another Southerner not overly concerned with Dayton, William Faulkner. In any case, the symposium which resulted, in part, from the Dayton trial not only links the Agrarians solidly to the continuing national quest for a regeneration of "the spirit" but also stands as a testament of their peculiar involvement with the myth of Southern history that would fulfill the South's continuing quest for an honorable reconciliation with the Union on terms which would allow dignity rather than humiliation, and which would call for a national recognition and utilization of the South's own peculiar past.

The nationalistic context of their stand is suggested in the Introduction:

The communities and private persons sharing the agrarian tastes are to be found widely within the Union. Proper living is a matter of the intelligence and the will, does not depend on the local climate or geography, and is capable of a definition which is general and not Southern at all (*ITMS*, p. xi).

The values they defend are seen as more than regional, and several of the reviewers of the book for Northern publications found the Agrarians' thesis attractive and sound even if hopeless. Therefore, the Agrarians ask:

Should the agrarian forces [of the South and West especially] try to capture the Democratic party, which historically is so closely affiliated with the defense of individualism, the small community, the state, the South? (*ITMS*, p. xix).

But the basis for the incorporation of ideal into political action is power, and the Agrarians had neither the means nor the imagination to translate their beliefs into action by manipulating, or by motivating others to manipulate, political power. Unlike Dixon, who knew about political power firsthand and who was able because of the climate of opinion in which he operated to motivate the manipulation of white power against the black man, the Agrarians were isolated in political innocence—a virtue among the Lost Generation—and no speculation could have been more ill-fated than that which looked to the Democratic party on the eve of the New Deal, World War II, and the welfare state for a standard-bearer in the fight to redeem the lost agrarian innocence of America's Jeffersonian dream.

Yet these themes of agrarian individualism and self-reliance were as American as Walden Pond. Indeed Thoreau would have found much to agree with in their advocacy of a society in which men and nature "live on terms of mutual respect and amity." And one could think of Melville's "Tartarus of Maids" when Lyle Lanier spoke of a spirit of individualism which was "natural in an agrarian society where there was considerable isolation and personal autonomy" but which "had no place in a machine age where the conditions make for an aggregate mental and emotional life." And even when John Crowe Ransom made his often-quoted assertion that "The South is unique on this continent for having founded and defended a culture which was according to the *European* principles of culture" (Ransom, *ITMS,* p. 3, emphasis mine) he was merely using a "European" setting to reinforce the old myth of *American* simplicity and harmony with nature. Ransom's "Europe" was only a somewhat older and more pastoral version of the North Carolina estate portrayed in *The Leopard's Spots.* In such a setting man "concludes a truce with nature and he and nature seem to live on terms of mutual respect and amity, and his loving arts, religions, and philosophies come spontaneously into being" (Ransom, *ITMS,* p. 7).

In this setting man was able to build his institutions as long as they were "comfortable" and to pursue prosperity as long as it was "modest." The significance of such qualifications as these is that they allowed a relationship in which man might enjoy the fruits of his collective civilization without losing the leisurely innocence of a "provincial" and individualistic relationship with nature.

One does not have to go back, however, to the beginnings of English civilization to find the virtues of this compromise extolled. It is perhaps just as fruitful to note how similar to the historical theory of Frederick Jackson Turner are Ransom's views of the proper relationship between man and nature. Like Turner, Ransom wrote of the modification of the social institutions of civilization by direct and continual contact with nature. The advantage that Ransom's resolution of civilization and nature has over Turner's—and the purpose served by placing it in ancient England—is that it provides for moral regeneration in a static, past-oriented society rather than in a mobile, future-oriented society. Thus an actual physical frontier is no longer needed. Regeneration occurs by the powers of the spirit and of the mind through consciousness of tradition and stability rather than through the Turnerian escape from "Old World" values. It was this tradition-consciousness which would help preserve the Jeffersonian equality and social simplicity which the Agrarians associated with eighteenth-century America. Ideally, it was to provide, not escape, but inspiration and strength to act in the present. Thus it was quite natural that Ransom deplored the forces which had brought the South's "institutions into disrespect [and which had sapped] continually at her courage"; as well as the "false pride to inspire a distaste for the thought of fresh pioneering projects" (Ransom, *ITMS,* p. 15).

Such conditions are to be deplored, suggested Ransom, because the South *could* take a role in the national life by championing the "English" compromise between man and nature; by proclaiming and insisting upon the application of tradition-oriented consciousness in working toward a resolution of the ideals of simplicity and the forces of complexity in which the former would subjugate the latter, and in which man would voluntarily return to his rightful place in nature. Unfortunately, Ransom admitted, the "contemporary form of pioneering" is industrialism, "a pioneering on principle, and with accelerating speed . . . a program under which men . . . sacrifice comfort, leisure and the enjoyment of life to win Pyrrhic victories from nature at points of no strategic importance" (Ransom, *ITMS,* p. 15).

This helps to explain why mobility—so important in Turner's thesis—could no longer be part of the regenerative force for the Agrarians. Mobility is associated with industrial progress with its sacrifice of a comfortable, human-centered society. Mobility allows only for exploitation and meaningless conquest. Progressive mobility will ultimately destroy nature and with it man's chances to live harmoniously in nature. Industrial progress is war with nature as Ransom's phrase "Pyrrhic victories . . . of no strategic importance" suggests. War, itself a force intimately linked with industrial society, is another symbol for the harsh regimentation, inhumanity, and exploitation which destroy art, religion, social simplicity, and individualism. Tradition, on the other hand, is believed to promote a gradual and lasting development of these coveted values and modes of expression.

In spite of industrialism's steady advance, there was still hope for the preservation of such values in America:

there is something heroic, and there may prove to be yet something very valuable to the Union, in [the South's] attachment to a certain theory of life [Agrarianism]. They have kept up a faith which was on the point of perishing from this continent (Ransom, *ITMS,* p. 16).

There could still be a regeneration of American innocence and simplicity. There could be a new frontier to redefine the necessary compromise between nature and civilization, between the primitive and the complex. Mobility and the ideology of progress had failed. Stability and the consciousness of tradition must succeed. But to find these qualities, the nation had to look to the South.

For while the Agrarians were participating in the continuing national quest for a rehabilitation of agrarian innocence and simplicity, they professed a regional uniqueness which we have already seen suggested in Ransom. The South was the America of Jeffersonian ideals and eighteenth-century agrarianism. According to Davidson, there was, in the pre–Civil War South,

a fair balance of aristocratic and democratic elements. Plantation affected frontier; frontier affected plantation. The balance might be illustrated by pairings; it was no purely aristocratic or purely democratic South that produced Thomas Jefferson and Andrew Jackson, Robert E. Lee and Stonewall Jackson (Davidson, *ITMS,* p. 53).

This Old South, of which the twentieth-century South is the only remaining manifestation, was seen as a land of small farmers and planters, each group serving as a force of moderation on the other. The aristocratic element kept the democratic element from becoming too acquisitive, either politically or economically. The democratic element returned this same favor and, presumably, also helped to keep the aristocrats from becoming too removed from the virtue-giving soil. Civilization modified the materialism of the frontier; the frontier in turn shed its democratic spirit on civilization. The result was a stable society, a balanced "diversity within unity" rather than the mobile, progressive democracy suggested by Turner. For the Agrarians, the tendency of this latter kind of democracy was toward an open industrial society: "Only as democracy becomes allied with industrialism can it be considered really dangerous. . . . Democracy if not made too acquisitive by industrialism, does not appear as an enemy to the arts" (Davidson, *ITMS,* p. 49).

If democracy was not the enemy of the arts, neither, as we shall see later, was it the enemy of an organic, individualistic society.

The blending of these elements of social structure—democracy and aristocracy—with the concepts of nature and civilization is suggested even more vividly by Owsley's portrait of George Washington:

Washington . . . inhaled the smell of ripe corn after a rain, nursed his bluegrass sod and shade trees with his own hands, and . . . kept vigil with his sick horses and dogs, not as a capitalist who guards his investments, but as one who watches over his friends (Owsley, *ITMS,* p. 71).

It was a simple life based on a harmonious, organic relationship with nature. Such an existence was "a way of life" and not merely a means to material acquisition. Washington was not a capitalist or merely an aristocrat but a gentleman planter endowed with the yeoman's love of and respect for nature; ready on the other hand to serve as first President of his country. Owsley's Washington is involved in the same kind of "comfortable" and "modest" life as Ransom's prototypal English pioneer.

But while the good life lived in such surroundings was in part

due to the influence of the democratic yeoman virtues, the aristocratic element was revealed in the agrarian Southerner's unique
concern for others. Stark Young found a self-restraint and a sense
of responsibility to community and to other individuals the mark of
the true Southerner (Young, *ITMS,* p. 350). This Southerner is
always aware of a responsibility to others—black slaves, white
tenants, or peers. This restraint of individualism prevents the social
anarchy of industrial democracy where only the "strongest" can
hope to survive. At the same time, this concern for others makes
unnecessary and unjustifiable the concept of the welfare state. For
both societies—the laissez faire jungle and the welfare commune
—stifle the creative potential of their individual citizens. The
Agrarian compromise allows for both the freedom of the one and
the unity and wholeness of the other.

This involvement in society—a much sought-after concept at the
end of the 1920s—was not seen as an attitude to be self-consciously cultivated by isolated individuals within the society.
Rather, it was seen as part of an inherited regional consciousness
of tradition which pervaded all segments of the society. And while
debt to the Cavalier literary tradition is obvious, we must observe
that the myth was not put forward as a nostalgic escape. Rather it
was promoted as a theory of community which must be preserved,
not for the sake of its memory, but for the contribution it could
make to the national life by resolving the conflict between the
individual life centered in freedom and the industrial life centered
in regimentation.

Similarly, Lewis Mumford, at almost the same time, wrote in
Technics and Civilization that the goal of modern America and of
the modern world

is not *increased* consumption but a vital standard: less in the prepara-
tory means, more in the ends, less in the mechanical apparatus, more
in the organic fulfillment. When we have such a norm, our success in
life will not be judged by the size of the rubbish heaps we have
produced: it will be judged by the immaterial and nonconsumable
goods we have learned to enjoy, and by our biological fulfillment as
lovers, mates, parents and by our personal fulfillment as thinking,

feeling men and women. Distinction and individuality will reside in the personality, where it belongs, not in the size of the house we live in, in the expense of our trappings, or in the amount of labor we can arbitrarily command. *Handsome bodies, fine minds, plain living, high thinking, keen perception, sensitive emotional responses, and a group life keyed to make these things possible and to enhance them*—these are some of the objectives of a normalized standard.[13]

How like the Agrarian's conception of life in the Old South— the essential South—is Mumford's hope for American life. And how like the old Progressive hopes, voiced by such intellectual heirs of Emerson and Whitman as Louis Sullivan and Van Wyck Brooks, do both Mumford and the Agrarians sound in their preference for an "organic" society.[14] And even a Southerner like Thomas Wolfe, who could ridicule "the young Gentlemen of the New Confederacy" who, catching the "last cobwebs of illusion," retire "haughtily into the South . . . at one of the universities," from which they can "issue in quarterly installments very small and very precious magazines" which celebrate "the advantages of an agrarian society"—even this young Southerner could go on to remind Northerners that to their cold land of "sky-aspiring brick . . . cold salmon-colored panes . . . weary grey of . . . stony-hearted pavement," Southerners had brought "a warmth of earth, an exultant joy of youth, a burst of living laughter, a full-bodied warmth and living energy of humor, shot through with sunlight and with Africa, and a fiery strength of living and faith and hope."[15] To the tarnished nation, the South could give back some of that innocence, some of that organic wholeness now subjugated to technics.

In the traditions of their region the Agrarians also found an atmosphere congenial to the arts. "Art depends, in general, like religion, on a right attitude to nature; and in particular on a free

13. *Technics and Civilization*, p. 399, emphasis mine.
14. E.g., Louis Sullivan, *Autobiography of An Idea* (New York: Dover, 1924), pp. 285–329.
15. *The Web and the Rock*, pp. 242, 247–248.

and disinterested observation of nature that occurs only in leisure" (*ITMS*, p. xv).

Davidson says in "A Mirror for Artists," that

So far as the arts have flourished in the South, they have been, up to a very recent period, in excellent harmony with their milieu. The South has always had a native architecture. . . . The South has been rich in the folk arts and is still rich in them. . . . As for the more sophisticated arts, the South has always practiced them as a matter of course (Davidson, *ITMS*, p. 55).

Such Midwesterners as Ernest Hemingway and F. Scott Fitzgerald had fled Babbitt's Zenith for New York and Paris and the provincial streams of Spain. Several members of the Agrarian group too had been abroad and the spirit of expatriation from America was certainly present among them. But here, in their symposium of 1930, they found in a concept of regional history what others had migrated to Europe to find—a provincial freedom not crushed by industry and finance, a society in which art was still a vital part of the "milieu."

The harmony of the Southern arts with their environment is vividly suggested in Davidson's brief description of the South's "native" architecture.

nothing more clearly and satisfactorily belongs where it is, or better expresses the beauty and stability of an ordered life, than [the South's] old country homes, with their pillared porches, their simplicity of design, their sheltering groves, their walks bordered with boxwood shrubs (Davidson, *ITMS*, p. 55).

This is the familiar image of the plantation house which stands for the ordered Southern life. The great houses suggest simplicity, order, and unity as opposed to complexity, disorder, and fragmentation. These houses, which at the same time represent civilization and intellectual sophistication, blend in very well with the sheltering groves and boxwood shrubs of nature. The "walks" stretch out like arms from the world of man through the world of a benign nature, whose harmony and simplicity are reflected in the harmony and simplicity of the buildings. All together the estate becomes a symbol not only of the covenant with the "sheltering groves" of nature but of a pervading consciousness of tradition. This eighteenth-century world of order is threatened by the industrial anarchy of the nineteenth and twentieth centuries which cuts down the "groves" and fragments life into a disconnected series of conditioned responses for the sake of momentary physical survival and unnatural gains in wealth and power for a few. For Dixon, it had been the threatening shadow of the Negro which loomed over this pastoral image. For the Agrarians, the shadow of the smokestack fell across the pillared porches. For both Dixon and the Agrarians, the eighteenth-century pastoral order symbolized by the mansion insured caste stability, while the industrial democracy of the nineteenth and twentieth centuries endangered the sanctity of the Anglo-Saxon Garden.

That this image of the pillared, pastoral South had a national as well as a regional significance is suggested by two illustrations by Wilfred Jones which appear in the one-volume edition of Charles Beard's *The Rise of American Civilization* (1930). In the first illustration, heading a chapter entitled "The Politics of Economic Drift," a large, pillared, Greek-revival Southern mansion is shown close to the foreground, dominating the picture. Its great door and front facade are illuminated by natural light. Hanging moss creates a frame of repose if not of nostalgia. The several human figures include two young women dressed in great billowing skirts, one of whom is talking to a young gentlemen mounted on a horse which is attended by a docile Negro. In the background and far in the distance there is one smokestack and part of a building, perhaps a factory, showing. In the second illustration, in a chapter entitled "The Approach of the Irrepressible Conflict," a similar house is seen from a greater distance, its door and facade now in dark shadow. The moss is gone and no human figures appear on the quiet lawn. On the hill rising slowly in the background are now seven or eight tall smokestacks. The threat of Northern industrialism has driven the leisurely residents away. The doom of a civilization looms overhead. The "progress" of industrial democracy is about to destroy the simple pastoral life. Thus the plantation doomed by the factory, as well as the plantation in its pristine splendor, is part of the national mythology. This insoluble paradox is both the dynamics and the dilemma of cultural myth in America. For none of the psychological and social rewards which myth promises by definition are available in any context other than tenuous moments of seeming resolution. Mythology which does not solve the problems it is created to solve results in cultural frustration and increasingly shrill or superficial attempts to make it work somehow. Nevertheless, as Taylor notes in *Cavalier and Yankee,* nineteenth-century Americans disturbed by the rapid change and flux of their "progressing" society did sometimes find in the South a soothing image of security and stability. The function continued into the twentieth century, as indicated not only by such minor pieces of evidence as the Jones drawings but by the many favorable and nostalgic remarks which reviewers used to describe *I'll Take My Stand* and the public response, first to the novel and then to the motion picture *Gone With The Wind.* In the anxious and troubled 1950s and 1960s, *Gone With The Wind* has remained a box office favorite, not only in the United States, but in such countries as England as well.

Describing his travels through Alabama in the same period, another Northerner, Carl Carmer, tells of a large house built on a summit overlooking Birmingham. The structure is a replica of the temple of Vesta in Italy, but this "classic glory with a garage in its base" is also, for Carmer, "a symbol of the big town's [Birmingham] quality." Birmingham, according to Carmer, has no traditions. She is the New South:

On one side of her rises a mountain of iron. On another a mountain of coal. She lies in the valley between, breathing flame. *The dark shafts of her smokestacks mock the beauty of the temple columns in the sky above her.*[16]

The symbolic smokestacks, the fire and smoke of this industrial hell, threaten the tranquillity and order of the temple on the hill,

16. *Stars Fell on Alabama,* p. 80, emphasis mine.

even if the temple does have a garage in its basement. Carmer continues:

> The valley of the furnaces is an inferno. Molten steel, pouring from seething vats, lights the night skies with a spreading red flare. Negroes, sweating, bared to the waist, are moving silhouettes. On the top of a big mold they tamp the sand in rhythmic unison—a shambling frieze. Steel cranes, cars of the juggernaut, screech above the simmering red pools of spitting, rippling metal. . . . [Birmingham is] . . . an industrial monster sprung up in the midst of a slow-moving pastoral.[17]

How different, then, is his industrial hell—this inferno of seething vats, red pools of spitting metal, and half-naked, abstracted, almost dehumanized Negroes—from General Worth's simple Anglo-Saxon industrial valley in *The Leopard's Spots*. Dixon's visions have failed to materialize. Industrialism as defined by the North rather than by the South has invaded, and even the Northerner senses the threatened destruction of the "temple on the hill." But for Carmer, as for the Agrarians, there was still hope. Nature, in Mumford's words, had not yet been wholly "dismembered" and "resynthesized," for far above the valley of the industrial inferno, "in the gardens that circle the temple on the quiet mountain the irises stand straight and cool in the moon-shadows."[18]

And it is the attempted moral, and perhaps even political, application of this image of classic simplicity and order, of the "slow-moving pastoral" which defined, for the Agrarians, the myth of Southern history. "If a community, or a section, or a race, or an age, is groaning under industrialism, and well aware that it is an evil dispensation, it must find the way to throw it off" (*ITMS*, p. xx).

Somehow, the Agrarians insisted, the South must find this way and must act as a bulwark, must "determine" itself, preserving the older American values at least upon its own soil as an example to, and refuge for, the rest of the nation. If the simplicity of the American garden could be preserved in the South, it could perhaps

17. *Ibid.*, p. 81.
18. *Ibid.*

be preserved for, if not in, the entire nation. But the Agrarians had no concrete proposals as to how to do this. Ironically, they were hampered by Southern history.

"The Briar Patch"

Though the Agrarians wrote of taking a "stand," they were unable to utilize that which *really* distinguished the South's history from that of the rest of the nation. The existence of the Negro and the Civil War defeat—the two factors which even Dixon recognized as the South's actual mark of uniqueness—are the social realities which offer the foundations for a dynamic mythology of Southern history. Yet of the Civil War the Agrarians said nothing except to blame it for the initial destruction of the plantation. And in what they wrote about the Negro, they were involved either in apologetics for the slavery of the eighteenth and nineteenth centuries or in acquiescence in the Jim Crow discrimination of the twentieth. The Agrarians' whole conception of Southern society was built on what was even then, in 1930, the increasingly tenuous assumption that the racial situation created in Dixon's day and still upheld in their own day by an increasingly fanatical minority would, and in fact must, remain unchanged. By 1930, however, Jim Crow was no longer in the mainstream of the national imagination.

In 1900, racism had been a concept of nationalism. By 1930, the situation was changing and showed signs of changing even more. On the one hand, the record of racial violence during the 1920s and 1930s is well known. Jim Crow legislation was actually "elaborated and further expanded" during these years.[19] Yet a decade later, in 1941, W. J. Cash was to write of the South during the 1920s that perhaps "the very Klan and Fundamentalism themselves testify in the end to the beginning of the subtle decay of the old rigid standards and values, the ancient pattern."[20] Cash's

19. C. Vann Woodward, *The Strange Career of Jim Crow,* p. 102.
20. *The Mind of the South,* p. 350.

suggestion calls attention to the fact, often overlooked, that the 1920s were not given over entirely to the Klan and American racism. The resurgence of racism was itself a response and at the same time a stimulus to trends which had been developing from the end of the World War in which race relations in America were beginning that long period of development, the climax of which we may have yet to witness. Once again, in the 1920s—and increasingly thereafter—the South felt the pressure of growing national censure because of its "peculiar" institutions.

Already in the 1920s American scholars and journalists were taking a new look at the American Negro. "A spate of articles and books published in the 1920s seriously analyzed and attempted to understand the Negro's place in the nation. The dozens of volumes about Negroes written by pseudo-scientists and racists at the turn of the century were now replaced by works which attempted to cut through racial stereotypes . . . and tried to find some viable program for 'interracial cooperation.' "[21]

Along with the academic interest in race relations came more visible signs of change from American Negroes themselves, including protest from an increasing number of Negro organizations, many of which were founded in the 1920s. There was also evidence from the Negro community of new efforts in the arts, education, and politics.

"In the years that immediately followed the first World War," according to John Hope Franklin, "no meeting of a national Negro organization neglected to register its protest against the failure of the United States to grant first-class citizenship to the Negro."[22] These organizations included the National Association for the Advancement of Colored People (NAACP), the National Race Congress, and the National Baptist Convention. In 1919 the NAACP held a national conference on lynching with Charles

21. Gilbert Osofsky, "Symbols of the Jazz Age; the New Negro and Harlem Discovered," *American Quarterly*, XVII (1965), 233.
22. *From Slavery to Freedom: A History of American Negroes*, p. 478.

Evans Hughes as chief speaker, and in 1921 the first anti-lynching bill was introduced in Congress by Representative L. C. Dyer of Missouri. In addition, throughout the 1920s the NAACP "undertook to secure in the courts the rights which Negroes could not otherwise obtain" and met with varying degrees of success, one of the more heartening victories coming in *Nixon v. Herdon* (1924) in which the Supreme Court found the Texas statute denying Negroes the right to vote in Democratic primaries to deny the Negroes rights under the Fourteenth Amendment.

Other signs of change were to be seen in the numerous organizations founded in the 1920s which in one way or another reflected the new concern of Americans—black and white—with the plight of the Negro. In 1919 the Commission on Interracial Co-operation was founded and, confining its activities primarily to the South, established educational programs in race relations at the state and local level. Three years earlier, in 1916, Marcus Garvey had established the first American chapter of the Universal Negro Improvement Association in New York City. Garvey's organization, unlike other Negro organizations, appealed chiefly to the lower socio-economic groups of the Negro population.[23] In 1920, the Friends of Negro Freedom was established to fight discrimination in Negro employment,[24] and in 1925 the American Negro Labor Congress met for the first time. Although the Labor Congress eventually failed, it was a significant, interracial effort toward justice and equality of opportunity for the Negro. "The most significant step toward the unionization of Negroes"[25] also came in 1925 when the Brotherhood of Sleeping Car Porters and Maids was organized. Even George Baker, "Father Divine," had his beginnings in 1919, and his "Peace Missions" were interracial as early as 1926.

To further the advance in Negro education, philanthropic aid

23. *Ibid.*, p. 481.
24. *Ibid.*, p. 485.
25. *Ibid.*, p. 486.

from the North continued to flow into the South after the Civil War. Between 1913 and 1932 the Julius Rosenwald Fund, for instance, aided in the construction of over 5,000 Negro school buildings in fifteen Southern states. Of the funds going into these buildings, 17 percent of the contributions came from " 'a flood of small contributions of Negroes themselves—striking evidence of the desire of members of this race for schooling for their children.' "[26] Enrollment of Negroes in colleges continued to increase after World War I, with more than 38,000 Negroes enrolled by 1933. Of these, 97 percent were attending colleges in Southern states.[27]

In the arts, the Negro found a new mode of protest and also another important avenue into membership in American society. Franklin writes that "the literature of the Harlem Renaissance was, for the most part, the work of a race-conscious group. Through poetry, prose and song the writers cried out against social and economic wrongs."[28] The Harlem Renaissance was "essentially a part of the growing interest of American literary circles in the immediate and pressing social and economic problems." Thus the new inclusion of the Negro in American literature was not confined to literature *by* Negroes alone. Such efforts in drama as Eugene O'Neill's *The Emperor Jones* (1920) and *All God's Chillun Got Wings* (1924) and Paul Green's *In Abraham's Bosom* (1926) suggest the new place of the Negro in American literature. It was not that the Negro had never been used for literary purposes before, but now "the Negro was studied, not merely talked about or discussed. Instead of being caricatured or typed, he was seriously portrayed as a person."[29]

Politically, the Negro was also beginning to exert his influence. As early as 1923 Negroes had started to oppose the senators who

26. *Ibid.*, p. 535.
27. *Ibid.*, p. 539.
28. *Ibid.*, p. 491.
29. Margaret Just Butcher, *The Negro in American Culture*, p. 250.

had been responsible for the death of the Dyer anti-lynching bill.[30] By 1928 when the Republican party made a strong bid for the white leadership in the South, the "disaffection of Negroes in the party of Lincoln" was a political fact.[31] In 1930, the year *I'll Take My Stand* was published, Negro opposition helped cancel John J. Parker's confirmation to the Supreme Court because of his outspoken objections to Negro participation in politics. Later, this same Negro participation in politics which Parker had denounced helped to defeat three other senators who had voted for Parker's confirmation.[32]

In January of 1929, the director of publicity for the NAACP looked back on "Twenty Years of Negro Progress," noting the various instances where a new concern and a new frankness in discussing the race problem in America had "let in the light up[on] a realm where light more than anything else was sorely needed."[33] Perhaps most influential in allowing this "light" to enter were new, increasingly scientific approaches to the role of environment in defining the relationships which exist between the individual and society. For if an individual's social potential and contribution were believed to be determined in large part at least by his social, cultural, and economic environment rather than by his race, a change in public attitudes toward the Negro was already a fact and the reconstruction of the Negro's place in American society already under way.

This new interest in the total environment had had its beginnings several decades earlier, but now in the closing year of the 1920s evidence of the changes it had brought about as well as the change such a trend might bring about in the future could easily be found. Thus, in discussing the National Interracial Conference of 1928, Walter White wrote in *The Nation* that the conference,

30. Franklin, *op. cit.,* p. 515.
31. *Ibid.,* p. 513.
32. *Ibid.,* p. 515.
33. Herbert J. Seligmann, "Twenty Years of Negro Progress," *Current History,* LXXX (1929), 620.

representing all sides of the issue, was a step "in taking discussion of this most difficult of American problems out of the realm of hysteria and conjecture into the clear light of *scientific and factual approach.*"[34]

In the same year, the provost of George Peabody College for Teachers in Nashville wrote that a new Department of Educational Sociology, made possible, incidentally, by a Julius Rosenwald grant, would allow students to "continuously be making surveys of conditions in negro schools, negro homes, negroes in the courts, negroes in labor, and negroes everywhere." Eventually these students would be able to "deal with fact with a freedom from prejudice and bias that was impossible to [their] fathers."[35]

And finally, in an article published by the National Conference of Social Work in 1928 entitled "The Effect of Changed Economic Conditions Upon the Living Standards of Negroes," Forrester B. Washington, director of the Atlanta School of Social Work, discussed, among other problems, increasing Negro crime and insisted that

this situation is certainly not due to the old myth that Negroes are inherently criminal. . . . It can be due to nothing else but changed economic conditions . . . for it is commonly known that when men and women, irrespective of race, are hungry and cold they will steal and commit other atypical acts to provide food and shelter for themselves and their families.[36]

Here, we are struck not only by the rejection of old racial explanations in favor of environmental explanations—a procedure which is repeated continually in the article—but by the humanity and sentiment allowed to the Negro as a human who commits "atypical acts," not because of racial qualities, but because of a sense of family responsibility.

34. "Solving America's Race Problem," *The Nation,* CXXVIII (1929), 43, emphasis mine.
35. R. B. Binnon, "Solving the Negro Problem Through Education," *Current History,* XXX (1929), 236.
36. *Proceedings of the National Conference of Social Work—55th Annual Session, Memphis, Tennessee, 1928,* p. 470.

Granted that trends toward a new emphasis on environmentalism did not constitute a major or total shift in the climate of opinion, they do suggest the clouding of the relatively simple picture of race which had predominated earlier in the century. In such an atmosphere the attempt by the Agrarians to use the Southern past without somehow adapting the Southern racial issue to this new tendency in the national imagination could not succeed. Yet, on the other hand, the Agrarians as Southerners could not tamper with the racial status quo.

First, and most obviously, their own regional identity made such a move philosophically impossible. If the Agrarian resistance to industrialism was to have any effect, it must have the support of the Southern whites. Even to suggest a liberalized approach toward the Negro would be to alienate and fragment this needed support. This concern is clearly seen in the intragroup controversy which arose over Robert Penn Warren's essay on race relations in the South before the book was published. To several of the Agrarians, especially to Donald Davidson, Warren's essay seemed too liberal and too glib in its discussion of the Negro in the South. Expressing doubts that Warren could even write such an essay, Davidson asked in a letter to Allen Tate,

Would [Warren] say "Mrs. Robeson" in referring to a negro woman—especially in a book expected to go to a Southern audience? Would [he] talk of "negro society" and of "equality" with such glibness as he here exhibits?[37]

And Lanier focused on the real issue by noting that race "is the only real issue on which Southerners can be differentiated from people in other sections [as well as the only question] on which any real unanimity of thought and action can be secured from Southern people at present."[38]

Both of these remarks are revealing in their concern. Lanier rightly saw the race question as the only real uniqueness that the

37. Quoted in Rock, *op. cit.*, p. 264.
38. Quoted, *ibid.*, p. 266.

South possessed. But "unanimity" was possible only by saying something less than Warren had said, possibly by saying nothing at all. At no point in their symposium were the Agrarians so pragmatic—so aware of the reality of the political environment—as they were on this issue of race in the South. For if such phrases as "Mrs.," applied to a Negro, and "Negro society" and Negro [economic] "equality" could provoke such a response from men of such broad experience as the Agrarians, one could well imagine the sensitivity of the average Southerner on the issue. The fact that they could do no more than respond in a regionally conditioned manner to the clichés of racial caste and to its threatened violation demonstrates the futility of any attempt they might have made to utilize the Southern past in a more dynamic way.

Second, this concern for the racial status quo points up another paradox in the Agrarians' resistance to industrialism. Industrialism was to be opposed because it stifled and eventually destroyed the individual. And yet to resist industrialism, a great mass of individuals, the Negroes, were to be stifled and suppressed. To advocate any actual change in the status quo would not only give aid and comfort to industrialism, since it would provide a new labor market to exploit, but it would also mean increasing competition between the races in the labor market and eventual political and social equality for the Negro. Industrialism, symbol of exploitation of the individual, would rudely threaten the peculiar exploitation of the individual so central to Southern society. One reviewer of *I'll Take My Stand* noted that "The Neo-Confederates have seen the shadows of the smoke stacks and have become as alarmed as ever did a Kluxer at the sight of a healthy bodied Negro."[39]

And no wonder, for they represent the same thing—the challenge of urban-industrial, multi-racial democracy to the race caste system of the South and, as we have since learned, of white America. Davidson's concern about "democracy made too acquisitive by industrialism" takes on larger overtones in this light which

39. Quoted, *ibid.,* p. 335.

shows industrial democracy equated with racial equality. Warren himself writes in his essay "The Briar Patch," the one essay in the Symposium that defined a "stand" on the Negro question, that

It has been the custom to some degree in the South, and probably to a greater degree elsewhere, to look forward to industrial progress as the factor which would make the Southern negro's economic independence possible. This industrial progress, which one sees heralded in the census reports, in announcements of chambers of commerce, and in the gaudy full-page advertisements of national magazines, is to strike off the shackles and lift the negro from his state of serfdom, ignorance and degradation (Warren, *ITMS*, p. 255).

The Negro's economic independence would lead to greater social independence: to be rid of the shackles of serfdom, ignorance, and degradation was to be rid of social as well as of economic barriers. But to Warren there was something ludicrous and at the same time frightening in this: "Such an expectation involves an exorbitant act of faith—an act of faith, not in the negro's capacity, but in the idea of industrialism" (Warren, *ITMS*, p. 255).

The expectations were somewhat ludicrous because of the irony of humane values being "heralded" in the statistics and "gaudy" advertisements of an impersonalized, commercial society dedicated to the false ideal of material progress. They were frightening to Warren because of their threat to the racial status quo. Industrialism could help the South and the Negro "only if it grows under discipline and is absorbed into the terms of the life it meets. It must enter in the rôle of the citizen and not of the conqueror—not even in the rôle of the beneficent conqueror" (Warren, *ITMS*, p. 256).

The analogy suggested by Warren's rhetoric of "shackles" and "conqueror" is that of a second Reconstruction of the South by the self-righteous North. And it is the fear of such reconstruction with its racial and social implications which implicitly lies beneath the abstract rhetoric of Warren's statement that if industrialism was to come into the South it must "grow under discipline" and must be "absorbed into the terms of the life it meets." That is, industrialism must accept the framework of Jim Crow; must operate within it and must contribute to its preservation by agreeing not to exploit the Negro labor market beyond the limits set by the white community. Industrialism must be controlled to preserve the White Garden. One must note in passing that as white control of American industry has been very slowly undermined by the ever-expanding demand for equal rights and opportunities, the retreating frontier of white America has been expanded slightly from the industrial front to include also the neighborhood and household fronts, which today, along with the sacrosanct "neighborhood" school, form the last lines of defense for the White Garden. Middle-class and lower middle-class areas where "the best" of nature and civilization supposedly meet are white America's last chance at that regeneration and purification envisioned by Frederick Jackson Turner. The closed doors of neatly trimmed rambler America rather than the closed shop will be the last stand for American racism.

For the Agrarians in 1930, however, the boundaries of the Negro's ventures into society would be set by the social pattern of Jim Crow separation. Thus, in admitting a strong "theoretical" argument in favor of higher education for the Negro, Warren suggests that such arguments would be "badly damaged if at the same time a *separate* negro community or group is not built up which is capable of absorbing and profiting from those members who have received this higher education" (Warren, *ITMS*, p. 251, emphasis mine). Does the Negro, Warren asked, "simply want to spend the night in a hotel as comfortable as the one from which he is turned away, or does he want to spend the night in that same hotel?" (Warren, *ITMS*, pp. 253–254). If the former, its fulfillment depends upon the extent to which the Negro is able to gain his own economic independence. But the Negro radical, Warren knew, would not accept this, would not accept Booker T. Washington's Atlanta Compromise, and would hold out for that "millennium" when the two races "regularly sat down at the same table" and in which "the white woman filed her divorce action through a negro attorney with no thought in the mind of any part to these various transactions that the business was, to say the least, a little eccentric" (Warren, *ITMS,* p. 254).

Obviously, Warren implies, the Negro must accept the "separate but equal" status assigned him by Washington and *Plessy v. Ferguson* three decades earlier and which had since been translated— and Warren would agree, somewhat perverted, since conditions were *not* equal in the two castes—into the system of Jim Crow segregation.

But "even if the policy of the factory was to employ white labor only" there was danger of racial conflict, for the Negro's

mere presence is a tacit threat against the demands which white labor may later make of the factory owner. This fact and the related fact of the negro's lower standard of living have been largely responsible for the race riots which have occurred in the North since the days of the war, when *pillars of smoke from Northern factory chimneys first summoned the Southern negro out of the land of Egypt* (Warren, *ITMS,* pp. 256–257, emphasis mine).

If a similar situation were allowed to develop in the South, if "the manager of a factory in the South can look out of his office window on a race of potential scabs," then *"it will be a new era of the carpet bag"* and of exploitation and "reconstruction" from the North. Once again, the image of the smokestacks rose up and was associated with the racial trouble which had arisen in the North and which might arise, with even more disastrous results, in the South if industrialism were allowed to come in, uncontrolled by the community. A new era of the industrial carpetbag with its implications of Negro rule and social equality between the races loomed over the relative tranquillity of the South, which, with perhaps only partial dissidence, Warren called the "land of Egypt."

How then was the South to meet the paradoxical threat of industrial dehumanization and racial egalitarianism implicit in an urban-industrial society? We have already suggested that, unlike Dixon, Warren in 1930 could not meet the problem by calling for the exclusion of the Negro from American society and culture. Yet the only other alternative—and the third obstacle to their moving away from the assumption of racial stability—was to assume, as Southerners and as Americans, responsibility for the plight of the Negro in the South and in the nation and thereby to admit that the old White Garden was unfeasible in the world taking shape in 1930. To take this position would be to deny the Southern uniqueness which the Agrarians professed. It would mean that the South, too, had been defiled by the greed and indifference of an industrial, capitalistic society and must now not only accept existence in such a society but must also participate in an attempt to reconcile America's exploitative treatment of the Negro with the American ideals of political democracy and social equality.

Such an admission in its full implications would be a painful refocus on the agrarian defeat of 1896, not only as the symbolic defeat of agrarianism, but as the turning point in America's attitudes toward its own environment. As we saw in our discussion of Dixon, Turner's synthesis, in essence an environmentalistic approach to American values, was also an Anglo-Saxon *racial* agrarianism, a racial relationship with redemptive nature which excludes alien peoples from what becomes an exclusively Anglo-Saxon garden. The new America of the twentieth century was to be urban and industrial, bringing with it a new kind of environment and the pressing need of social re-evaluation and reform. "Inevitably," writes Ralph Henry Gabriel of the late nineteenth century, "a changed social scene led to changed social thinking. The social sciences, developing swiftly in the invigorating atmosphere of the Great Liberation speeded the evolution of social theory appropriate to the new day." Gabriel notes that "in the 1920's and 1930's as the idea of cultural relativism emerged, the anthropologists discovered that culture conditions, perhaps determines, the behavior of the individual." Social scientists investigated the group as "mediator between the individual and society" and found that through this group the individual received particular "intimations of the outlook and values of society. . . . By the end of the 1920's, the evolution of social theory had left behind the simple doctrine of the free individual of the eighteenth and nineteenth centuries. The study of the social process through which the infant and child is taught the ways of his culture marked out boundaries to individual freedom."[40] Complex social structure, not quasi-mystical virgin land, shaped the individual, and both the processes and the boundaries were most evident in the least pastoral, least Turnerian parts of the new urban-industrial environment, the parts most often inhabited by nonwhite Americans. With these people the "processes" were usually better described as severe cultural and economic deprivation and the "boundaries" as gross exclusion from participation in white society.

Thus with this new, more scientific approach to, and study of, the American environment came a new exploration of interracial problems and solutions, some of which I have already briefly discussed in looking at the record of racial progress in the 1920s. But the Agrarians, heirs both of Turner and of Jim Crow, were bound to a racial environmentalism inseparable from Southern suppression of the Negro.[41] The Agrarians were thus caught in the proverbial vicious circle. To deal with "industrialism" they must also deal with the Negro. To offer leadership in combatting the evils of industrialism would have necessitated offering leadership in solving the problem of race in the South and in the nation. Yet to suggest, as had Dixon, that the South, because of its experience with the Negro question, should take a position of leadership in solving this problem would have meant in 1930 to adopt the methods and attitudes of the new social sciences. This in turn would have only encouraged the development of that urban industrialism in the South which the Agrarians feared would corrupt the Southern tradition. It would have also encouraged further Negro liberation, which would have led again to a repetition of the cycle, a cycle bound to destroy Southern unity and the white man's illusionary sense of security. The task for the Agrarians was to

40. *The Course of American Democratic Thought*, 2d ed., pp. 425–427.
41. For an examination of the Agrarians' hostility to science generally and the social sciences particularly, see Karanikas, *op. cit.*, pp. 123–143. Also Rock, *op. cit.*, pp. 37–81 *passim*.

appeal to the nation without threatening the racial status quo in the South—and in most of the North. They asked for followers when they could offer no leadership and no convincing example. The clock was stopped, in effect, at 1896, or at the moment of Charles Gaston's triumphant anti-Negro speech in *The Leopard's Spots;* stopped at that moment when racial agrarianism was frozen into the Southern imagination while the rest of the nation was moving on in new directions, albeit laboriously and with much hesitation.

In struggling with this dilemma, Warren finally chose an expedient compromise between total exclusion and inclusion, calling for a strict interpretation of the "equal" in the old "separate but equal" doctrine. Warren wrote that the Negro must be given a separate but truly equal economic stake in the future of an agrarian, rural South. Only in this way could the Negro be kept from the clutches of industrialism. The acquiescence to segregation in Warren's essay is reinforced by the almost total absence of discussion of contemporary race problems in the other essays and by the fact that of all the major areas of discussion, Warren's is the only one which is neither outlined nor even referred to in the introductory "Statement of Principles."

That in the minds of the Agrarians the cause of Southern self-determination and preservation of values had nothing to do with a changing status for the Negro is the conclusion that must be drawn, not only from Warren's essay, but from the general tone of indifference and omission in the rest of the book. Frank Lawrence Owsley suggested the Agrarian point of view in writing of the Negro in the Old South. The Negroes came in such numbers that "people feared for the integrity of the white race. For the negroes were cannibals and barbarians, and therefore dangerous. . . . Slaves were a peril, at least a risk, but free blacks were considered a menace too great to be hazarded. Even if no race wars occurred, there was dread of being submerged and absorbed by the black race" (Owsley, *ITMS,* p. 77). Four years later, Allen Tate wrote in the *American Review:*

I argue it this way: the white race seems determined to rule the Negro race in its midst; I belong to the white race; therefore I intend to support white rule. Lynching is a symptom of weak, inefficient rule; but you can't destroy lynching by *fiat* or social legislation; lynching will disappear when the white race is satisfied that its supremacy will not be questioned in social crises.[42]

That the Negro was a threat to the American virtues that the Agrarians associated with the life of the soil was also suggested by Tate's remark that in the Old South the Negro slave "was a barrier between the ruling class and the soil."[43]

But if, as we have seen, Warren's essay was basically only a restatement of Washington's conservative compromise position, why was it so controversial among members of the group? Although the reference to "Mrs. Robeson" which bothered Davidson was excluded, the references to "Negro society" and Negro "equality" remained.[44] And to suggest Negro "equality," even if it was only economic equality, was in itself a step away from the plight of the American Negro in 1930. The system of Jim Crow, it must be remembered, was less than "separate but equal" in its restrictions and discriminations. It was "separate and unequal" as the Supreme Court was later to conclude in 1954. Thus when Warren suggested that "If the Southern white man feels that the agrarian life has a certain irreplaceable value in his society, and if he hopes to maintain its integrity in the face of industrialism or its dignity in the face of agricultural depression, he must find a place for the negro in his scheme" (Warren, *ITMS,* p. 263), he was, from a Southern viewpoint in 1930, suggesting much more than a citizen of the 1960s may be capable of giving him credit for. "One must be careful," notes John L. Stewart, "to avoid underestimating just how far Warren *had* gone when he insisted on respect for the rights and dignity of the Negro as an individual, and one must recognize

42. Quoted in Karanikas, *op. cit.,* p. 90.
43. Quoted, *ibid.,* p. 89.
44. Rock, *op. cit.,* p. 267.

that the essay is everywhere suffused with a quiet humanity and decency."[45] In its economic aspects Warren's essay echoes the pre-1896 Populist proposal of a union between blacks and whites pulling together to resist the antiagrarian forces of the Northeast. That Warren even suggested such a union of separate races joined in a common cause would make him suspect to the sensitive Southerner of 1930. True, as Stewart also points out, one feels in Warren's essay "too little realization of what humiliation of the individual even such kindly proposals as [Warren's] might involve." Yet there is also the suggestion in Warren's essay that the whole South *should* take responsibility for the plight of the Negro and that to begin with, the white South might work to provide the Negro, as well as the poor white, with a better education. Warren was suggesting, perhaps unconsciously at this point, that the South had been touched by the corruption of history and that if it was going to express its potential for uniqueness and leadership, if it was to remain untouched by the corruption of a dehumanized faith in progress already knocking at the plantation door, it must take responsibility for that portion of history with which it was so irrevocably involved. To whatever extent such suggestions were present, they were anticipations of later developments of Warren's thinking. At this point, however, one could have indeed wondered with Davidson what was going on in the mind of this young man from Kentucky studying abroad at Oxford. This question and the later involvement of Warren with the myth of Southern history will be examined more closely in later chapters.

What finally emerges, however, from our inquiry into the ideas of Dixon in 1903 and the problems of the Agrarians in 1930, are two pictures of the myth of Southern history according to Jim Crow. In Dixon's case, a successful synthesis was possible because Southern attitudes on race matched national attitudes. In the Agrarians' case, this was no longer true. Warren's attempt to find a resolution led only to a reaffirmation of the older racial guidelines

45. Stewart, *op. cit.,* p. 165.

set down by the Supreme Court of a fading era. Ultimately, the Agrarians' attempt to reconcile the South with the nation by means of the uniqueness of its own pastoral mythology of the "beautiful tradition" which was depicted as a virtue lost to the rest of the nation—this attempt failed. Not only did their ideal fade in the years of depression, world war, and a new technology, but many of these same men have lived to see the essential symbolic meaning of their innocent South vulgarized into the politics of "white backlash." Their witness has been one of frustration, resentment, and often, outrage. To the image of the plantation, which itself has been taken over by the chambers of commerce and the tourist bureaus, has been added the dime-store Confederate flag, symbol of police brutality, schizophrenic defiance of national efforts toward racial justice, and a paranoiac retreat into an illusionary world of simple, violent answers to complex problems. It is this debased use of the Southern past and of Southern uniqueness which all Americans have had set before them in the headlines of the last fifteen years, and which many have unwittingly embraced.

✤ III   William Faulkner

The Essential Biography

WILLIAM FAULKNER was born in 1897 at New Albany, Mississippi, and died in 1962 at nearby Oxford, Mississippi. Most of his life was spent in and around Oxford, in a land spotted by weather-grayed cabins and roadside monuments commemorating this or that battle or rendezvous of the Civil War. Although Faulkner earned no academic degrees in his lifetime, he read and knew the classics of Western literature, understood man's dilemma as universal, and found his response to the history of his region intensified by this understanding. One might have expected such knowledge to have set him off from the South, to have made of him an expatriate-in-residence, or at worst a self-conscious professional Southerner claiming that his knowledge of the classics was somehow native to that region and only to that region, since, so the story goes, learning is dependent on leisure and leisure is impossible in a highly industrialized society such as the North.

Instead, Faulkner's intellectual experiences seem to have contributed to an insight into the nature of the South's past which raised his art above exposé, above provincial chauvinism, and most certainly above the limitations and abstractions of political rhetoric, into the realm of creative cultural myth. Faulkner's rendering of the myth of Southern history suggests a South tempered by defeat and frustration into the recognition that man's history is tragic and ambiguous rather than progressive and harmonious. While the particular failures of history must be accounted for and eventually atoned, they can be resolved, if at all, only by forgiveness, humility, and love. Faulkner believed that the crime against the American Negro must be righted. But a second Reconstruction imposed by federal law would ignore the complexity and entrenchment of Southern institutions and traditions and the involvement of Southern individuals in these institutions and traditions. It would ignore the bitterness and resentment left by the earlier attempt at Reconstruction and would deny the necessity for forgiveness. On the other hand, as the destruction of the Sutpen family in *Absalom, Absalom!* suggests, the South could not ignore its own guilt and the necessity to assume its own historical burden, for this would be acting with the same absolutism and righteousness that had marked the Northern abolitionists of every generation. It would deny the responsibilities inherent in the tragic experience of man's history.

Rather than lagging behind the main stream of national movements as did the Agrarians, or riding a momentary crest of popular racism as did Dixon, Faulkner seems actually to have anticipated a consciousness of history which still, thirty years after *Absalom, Absalom!,* has made only small headway among American intellectuals—liberal or conservative—Reinhold Niebuhr being a notable exception. Faulkner's wide reading was blended with an inherited consciousness of the South's past, which in turn was reinforced by his living among the farmers and storekeepers of Oxford. But it is impossible in this short book to ascertain just how these influences worked together to produce such a synthesis. The biographical uniqueness of Faulkner's life seems to lie first in his lack of formal education and second in his relative isolation from influential literary and political groups of his day. Alone in the Mississippi countryside, with Shakespeare and the Old Testament, Faulkner seems to have come around to a basically tragic conception of history and man's position in nature. According to the American cult of nature, isolation from institutional complexity is supposed to preserve simplicity and innocence rather than to lead to a vision of the complexity and tragic ambiguity of human experience; yet Faulkner was alienated from the national myth of cultural innocence rather than from a sense of the tragedy of historical burden and complexity in nature. His work renders the dilemma of the South caught between the assertion of new-world innocence and the obviously contradictory lesson of the Southern disaster, defeat, and humiliation.

Five aspects of Faulkner's work can be isolated to show how he related the dilemma of the South to national ideals and to universal history. These are the imagery of the plantation house, the concept of national innocence, the concept of regional burden, the literary form of imaginative historiography, and the proposal and execution of a specific Southern mission to the nation. With the exception of the last theme, all are best illustrated in *Absalom, Absalom!,* published in 1936. Since the concept of mission can be fully discussed only with reference to *Intruder in the Dust,* published a decade later, I have centered the last short section of the chapter around this book.

The year 1936 also saw, besides *Absalom, Absalom!,* the publication of Margaret Mitchell's *Gone With the Wind,* and a few months later, in 1937, John Dollard's *Caste and Class in a Southern Town.* In 1941 W. J. Cash's *The Mind of the South* was published. In addition, the 1930s was an important decade in Southern historiography. The "revisionist" movement again suggested that novelists and historians were moving on parallel courses in their interpretations of the South. Because all of these books and developments seem to add to an understanding of Faulkner and the South, they too have been incorporated into the discussion. They offer a perspective on my thesis that during the 1930s the myth of Southern history underwent a transition in Faulkner's novels which prepared the way for later explorations of the myth by Robert Penn Warren and C. Vann Woodward, who adapted it not only to the domestic Civil Rights crisis of the 1950s and 1960s but to America's postwar involvement with a defeated, discouraged, and "underdeveloped" world at large.

The Plantation

Both Dixon and the Agrarians, as well as many other American authors writing about the South, had found in the great houses of the plantations a symbol of Southern uniqueness. The image of the house and its surrounding grounds symbolizes among other things order, innocence, and white supremacy as well as the important concept of stability and permanence unaffected by history. Such associations have the same appeal to the national imagination as they do for Southerners, evoking that nostalgic sense of Southern uniqueness and a vanished simple and good life which Taylor so accurately described in *Cavalier and Yankee*. Two generations of Americans remember "Tara" and "Twelve Oaks" in Margaret Mitchell's *Gone With the Wind*. Of "Tara," which was not, strictly speaking, a Greek-revival structure, Mitchell wrote, "From the avenue of cedars to the row of white cabins in the slave quarters, there was an air of solidness, of stability and permanence."[1] "Twelve Oaks," the home of Ashley Wilkes, is more in the tradition: "the white house reared its perfect symmetry before her, tall of columns, wide of verandas . . . a stately beauty, a mellowing dignity" (*GWW,* p. 94).

As in the rhetoric of Dixon and the Agrarians, the mansions stand for a society in which order, permanence, and leisure are still possible. The destruction of many of these large houses by the Northern armies during the Civil War does not negate their symbolic usefulness but only adds a peculiar fierceness to memories of their destruction. What they stood for lingers after them in their ruins. Though she despairs as she views the ruins of "Twelve Oaks," Scarlett vows to rebuild the splendor of "Tara," and at the end of the novel, when everything else is lost, she clings to the

1. *Gone With the Wind,* p. 48.

image of "Tara," "and it was as if a gentle cool hand were stealing over her heart. She could see the white house gleaming welcome to her through the reddening autumn leaves, feel the quiet hush of the country twilight coming down over her like a benediction" (*GWW*, p. 1036).

An equally romantic vision of the ruins of the South is provided in Thomas Dixon's *The Traitor* (1907) which is "A Story of the Fall of the Invisible Empire." John Graham, state chief of the Ku Klux Klan, takes his love, Stella Butler, daughter of a Northern judge, to the ruins of a great plantation, "Inwood," where "towering in solemn, serried line on a gentle eminence still stood the six great white Corinthian pillars of the front facade of the house."[2] The classical ruins in the afternoon sun and the solemn shade of stately old firs suggest all of the pastoral tranquillity of an eighteenth-century landscape painting. Later John Graham restores the mansion "on its original foundations, rebuilding it of native marble behind the stately old Corinthian pillars around one of which the ivy is yet allowed to hang in graceful festoons."[3]

"Inwood," like General Worth's plantation in *The Leopard's Spots,* also becomes the site of a complex of mills owned by the Graham Brothers. On the very site of the older ruins, an order rises which can incorporate the new technology without losing any of its older qualities of classic, agrarian simplicity. The Klan may be dead, but white supremacy prevails. But this vision of a South which is both pastoral and industrial is violently desecrated in the early novels of William Faulkner.

In the tone of that naturalism and realism which were his literary heritage, Faulkner drastically rejects this sentimental and contradictory stereotype of the South. In *The Sound and the Fury,* for example, on the morning after Jason's niece, Quentin, has robbed his money box and run away with a circus worker, Dilsey, the old Negro servant, returning from the Easter service at the

2. *The Traitor*, p. 227.
3. *Ibid.*, p. 331.

Negro church, cries out the tragedy of the Compson family and of the whole South: "I've seed de first en de last. . . . I seed de beginnin, en now I sees de endin." In the passage immediately following these often-quoted words, we see the full, tragic meaning of her statement for that South represented by the great shining plantation houses.

Ben shambled along beside Dilsey, watching Luster who anticked along ahead, the umbrella in his hand and his new straw hat slanted viciously in the sunlight, like a big foolish dog watching a small clever one. They reached the gate and entered. Immediately Ben began to whimper again and for a while all of them looked up the drive at the square, paintless house with its rotting portico.[4]

Quietly and unpretentiously, Faulkner turns upside down the stereotype of the Old South: the idiot white man follows like a "big foolish dog" behind his black keeper, a "small clever dog." In the robbery, the house before them has just witnessed another disgrace, another step in its own ultimate destruction. Now, Dilsey alone offers the stability of an earlier era. Father is dead of drink; Jason is a petty, frustrated merchant whose inability to cope with life is suggested by his violent allergy to the smell of gasoline, the basic fuel of the new century; and Mother reveals symptoms of paranoia. Thus, the image of "the square, paintless house with its rotting portico" does indeed underline Dilsey's tragic words, "I seed de beginnin, en now I sees de endin."

Two years later, in 1931, the controversial novel *Sanctuary* was published; and again a ruined plantation set a scene entirely lacking in romance and nostalgia. The Frenchman place is a gutted ruin—gaunt, stark, set in a jungle, desecrated by poor white farmers in search of easy firewood and by gullible local adventurers in search of imaginary Cavalier gold. It is also the hideout of Popeye—"psychopath, sadist, and murderer." In the later Compson *Appendix,* written for Malcolm Cowley's *Portable Faulkner* in 1946, Faulkner completed the narrative of the destruction of the

---

4. *The Sound and the Fury,* p. 313.

symbolic plantation house in a world now dominated by Snopeses. After the final disintegration of the Compson family, the house had become a boarding house and after that had been torn down for a golf course. Finally the land, still called the "old Compson place," had become the site of a colorless, crowded, low-income housing development (*SAF*, p. 9). The tradition for which the houses stood—the tradition of a Cavalier South built on leisure and dignity—no longer has relevance.

In *The Mansion* (1959), Flem Snopes "imports" Wat Snopes to rebuild his house, complete with tall white columns. The architectural form is not actually destroyed but consciously exploited as a petty status symbol, a symbol of wealth and respectability, virtues which in the world of the Snopeses need no further qualification or definition than that afforded by an ostentatious house with a false facade.[5] Snopes senses the value of the stereotype to his own ambitions but is ignorant of its more complex symbolism.

Absalom, Absalom! (1936) gives Faulkner's most complete and most significant treatment of the plantation image. Like the other plantation houses which we have discussed, Thomas Sutpen's house, built at "Sutpen's Hundred," reflects both a specific relationship with nature and a particular way of life. But as in *The Mansion,* relationships are inverted so that the house, instead of being a symbol of the Old South's harmony and leisure, becomes the symbol, finally, of an American attitude toward nature and toward man, an attitude which holds the seeds of its own destruction.

Absalom, Absalom! begins in the summer of 1910, just before Quentin Compson leaves Jefferson to attend Harvard. Quentin hears from Miss Rosa Coldfield the story of Thomas Sutpen, who had come to Jefferson in 1833; carved out a great plantation, "Sutpen's Hundred," from the virgin land; married Rosa's sister, Ellen; fathered two children by her; and settled down as a well-established, if not fully respected, planter. As Rosa Coldfield nar-

5. *The Mansion*, pp. 153–154.

rates her version of Sutpen's life—a version to be modified and clarified by later narrators—Quentin imagines Sutpen's entry into the little isolated frontier village eighty years before. Smelling of hell and demonism, Sutpen "abrupts" upon the pastoral virginity of the land. He is followed by a gang of slaves, "half tamed," and a captive French architect, "grim, haggard, and tatter ran" (*AA,* p. 8).

Then in the long unamaze Quentin seemed to watch them overrun suddenly the hundred square miles of tranquil and astonished earth and drag house and formal gardens violently out of the soundless Nothing and clap them down like cards upon a table beneath the up-palm immobile and pontific, creating the Sutpen's Hundred (*AA,* pp. 8–9).

As a picture of the American's relationship with nature, this passage contradicts the Jeffersonian dream of the simple agrarian, living in harmony with a fruitfully submissive virgin land, which somehow retains its qualities of innocence even after it has been cleared and planted and settled. The description of Sutpen's entrance with such words as "overrun" and "drag" house and fields "violently" from a "tranquil and astonished earth" suggest a rape more than the establishment of any kind of harmonious relationship such as Ransom had suggested in *I'll Take My Stand.* Sutpen's venture brings to mind, not the scholar-planter sipping mint juleps on the veranda while he reads the poets, but, as Cleanth Brooks has noted, the cold, satiric rhetoric of Thorstein Veblen discussing "methods of demonstrating the possession of wealth" and status, among which are "conspicuous leisure" and "conspicuous consumption." The great house which Sutpen builds is only part of his materialistic design, a scheme to move up from the lower moneyless class into a kind of "barbarian leisure class," through emulation and invidious competition with older, more established leisure classes. Sutpen is no Virginia Cavalier come west, but a propertyless Jacksonian common man on the make who moves west into the great valley of the Mississippi looking for social and economic opportunity. The design which Sutpen dreams is as contrived as

Flem Snopes's rebuilding of the De Spain house a hundred years later. For after Sutpen is humiliated by the Negro butler of a Tidewater planter who tells the boy "never to come to that front door again" (*AA,* p. 237), Sutpen's purpose becomes revenge by emulation.

The house that he builds as the chief symbol of this design is even larger and whiter than the one from which he had been turned away as a boy by a Negro slave. In revealing the motives of achievement and emulation behind the building of Sutpen's house, Faulkner takes exception both to the myth of the Cavalier and to the myth of the yeoman, as these figures supposedly shaped the two sections during the nineteenth century. There was no break with the East, just as there had been no break with Europe in the seventeenth century. The institutions and motivations of an exploitative society moved west with the pioneers. On each successive frontier, nature was violated and subdued, having little if any purifying and simplifying effect upon those who violated it. The savagery of the frontier had no influence on spreading civilization. Civilization came with its own built-in form of savagery in the guise of invidious emulation and conspicuous leisure and the greed necessary to support these forms of behavior.

As Sutpen's mansion is built in violence, so is it destroyed. The beginning contains the seeds of the end. The destruction comes from neither an invading army nor from the ravages of time, but from a moral tragedy within the house of Sutpen. The decay and final destruction of the Sutpen mansion testifies to the demise of a false concept of civilization and history, which is no more Southern than it is American or Western. When Quentin visits the old Sutpen house with Miss Coldfield, this unreal quality is made evident.

It loomed, bulked, square and enormous, with jagged half-toppled chimneys, its roofline sagging a little; . . . Quentin saw completely through it a ragged segment of sky with three hot stars in it as if the house were of one dimension, painted on a canvas curtain in which there was a tear; now, almost beneath it, the dead furnace-breath of air in which they moved seemed to reek in slow and protracted violence with a smell of desolation and decay as if the wood of which it was built were flesh (*AA,* p. 366).

The house appears as the backdrop to an illusion-based drama. The design of which the house is the chief symbol has been perpetuated at the cost of at least a dozen lives, and the house seems built of rotting flesh. The mansion is finally destroyed by fire while a Negro idiot, Jim Bond, bellows out one final, nonhuman protest against the injustice done against man and family in the name of the Sutpen design.

What Faulkner does to the myth of Southern history may be seen by contrasting Dixon's triumphant picture of Tom Norton, closing the door of the Norton home to Negroes, with the closing of the great white door of the Sutpen mansion in the face of Charles Bon, Sutpen's mulatto son by his first marriage. Dixon, writing *The Sins of the Father* in 1912, saw the slamming of the door, a contemporary event for him, as the final exclusion of the Negro from American society. Faulkner, twenty-four years later, found in the closing of the white man's door to the Negro, not the final solution to the race problem, but a judgment against such Americans as Sutpen who are caught up in the myths of achievement and moral innocence—myths which perpetuate great evil. The burning of the Sutpen house occurs in 1910, about the time Dixon was writing *The Sins of the Father*. Faulkner found in this decade, which saw the formation and triumph of most of the South's Jim Crow legislation, the final destruction of the plantation myth, and the beginning of great social affliction and frustration for the South. Only the retarded mulatto, Jim Bond, the hopelessly entangled and doomed Quentin Compson, and Gavin Stevens, a contemporary of Quentin's, are left to poke among the ashes for meaning and new direction.

Faulkner's rendering of the symbol's corruption and devaluation finds its analogies in the political and social context of the times. If *Gone With the Wind* appealed to a popular yearning for more simple times and for escape from Depression economics, *Absalom, Absalom!* more closely paralleled a re-evaluation of the South taking place at other levels of American society at the same time. A clue to this political and social context is provided by President Roosevelt's view of the South's relationship to the nation in 1938. For Roosevelt, the South was "the nation's No. 1 economic problem—the nation's problem, not merely the South's."[6] Roosevelt pointed to the economic unbalance in the nation as a whole as stemming from the conditions in the South. The task to end this unbalance "for the sake of the South and of the nation" was one which embraced neglected natural resources, absentee-ownership, industrialism, child labor, farm tenancy, housing, education, taxation, and health. This situation, expressed in the rhetoric of practical politics, parallels the demise of the plantation stereotype which we have already traced through Faulkner's major works. Yet only a few Americans read *Absalom, Absalom!* in the 1930s, while millions read and viewed the story of Scarlett O'Hara; and the sensational exposés of poor-white degradation which brought Erskine Caldwell's *Tobacco Road* (1932) and *God's Little Acre* (1933) into popular fame, while seemingly closer to the South depicted by Faulkner and by Roosevelt, were perhaps no less escapist and stereotyped in the end than Miss Mitchell's long novel. Thus when W. J. Cash wrote that *Gone With the Wind* "ended by becoming a sort of new confession of the Southern faith," he suggested only part of the truth, for in fact it had become a confession of the American faith or at least of the remnants of that faith. It was the same faith which had inspired the Agrarians. Henry Steele Commager, in a review for the New York *Herald Tribune* lamented that what was gone with the wind was "a way of life and of living, something deeply rooted, genuine and good, something . . . 'with a glamour to it, a perfection, a symmetry like Grecian art.'" Commager, like the other historians discussed so far in this study, obviously shared with contemporary novelists the imagination of his times.

6. Quoted by Frank Freidel, *F.D.R. and the South,* pp. 94–100.

The escape novels told their truths only unintentionally. And even if frustrated readers of Faulkner complained that *anything* Faulkner might reveal was strictly unintentional, the fact remains that *Absalom, Absalom!* is an artistically conceived revelation of a cultural symbol's devaluation at the hands of its own culture. What appears to be Gothic and romantic in *Absalom, Absalom!* is not the rhetoric of sentimental escape but rather the inescapable burden of an imperfect and guilt-ridden past.

Articles and reports in journals and popular magazines reinforced Roosevelt's less-than-tranquil picture of the South. In *Scribner's Magazine* for May 1936, John Crowe Ransom and V. F. Calverton presented two conflicting views of Southern culture. Ransom called the South a "bulwark against marxism and monopoly," and Calverton, a Marxist critic, proclaimed "The Bankruptcy of Southern Culture," charging that the South lacked responsible and realistic intellectual leadership and that it was mired down in shallow romanticisms about itself. Ransom's article is illustrated with a drawing of a yeoman farmer against a background of fields and small farm buildings, the image of the small American agrarian living in harmony with a bounteous nature. Calverton's article is illustrated by a single Greek column, without capital or entablature and entwined by a dead, straggling, nondescript vine. John Dollard's *Caste and Class in a Southern Town* offered more cold facts weighted against the myth of the Old South. The book, published in 1937 from field research done in 1935 and 1936, is a study of the community structure of a small Southern town and more specifically of the relationships between the two races in this town. Dollard's central thesis is built upon the observation that the community is organized first, and basically, by caste. There is a white caste and a black caste, and the boundary is, with notable exceptions, tightly drawn. Second, each caste tends to be stratified into the usual socio-economic classes: upper, middle, and lower. But social mobility is primarily determined by caste rather than by class. A middle-class Negro, for instance, is considered inferior to a lower-class white person. The white caste dominates, regulates, and exploits the black caste; and Dollard specifically reviews the economic, sexual, and prestige gains made by members of the white caste at the expense of the Negroes.[7]

Dollard's observations, while provocative and scholarly, are less than profound in their exposure of race relations in the South. Most of the same conditions had already been exposed in some form or other by generations of abolitionists and other "outside" observers. Yet in the very words "provocative" and "scholarly" lies the key to the book's far-reaching implications as one pioneer document in the modern chapter of relations between the South and the rest of the nation. Reviews of Dollard's book suggest quite clearly the impact which this study and others preceding and following it were to have in the future. One reviewer wrote in the *American Political Science Review* that "As one follows his fascinating portrayal . . . of the sham and hypocrisy which characterize a society tortured by a consciousness of guilt, the impression grows that here is a portrait not alone of a Southern town but of the South."[8] Others viewed Dollard, not as a muckraker or do-gooder, but as a scientist who had written a "scientific appraisal." Thus, another reviewer wrote, "no Southerner with any pretense to intellectual honesty can raise the cry . . . about the inability of outsiders to understand the South's peculiar problems. . . . [Dollard has shown] an understanding of the agrarian South's 'problems' which few in the region, and probably none in Southern-town, can approach."[9] Dixon's contempt for the new scientific approach to race problems seems to have been fully warranted by 1937, at least from the conservative's point of view. The implication was that the Southerner would now have to admit, if he was intellectually honest, that he had been wrong, and worse, unscientific, in his supposed "understanding" of the Negro problem.

But instead of confessing, the South, in the person of Donald

7. *Caste and Class in a Southern Town,* p. 99.

8. Peter H. Odegard, "A Review of Caste and Class in a Southern Town," *American Political Science Review,* XXXI (1937), 982.

9. John D. Allen, "Southerntown," *The Saturday Review of Literature,* XVI (1937), 167, emphasis mine.

Davidson, responded to these charges and implications with a bitter attack upon Dollard and his book. The simple agrarian South was once again being invaded by "metropolis," and the black knight this time was the devilish Dr. Dollard with his "obscene and defamatory caricature" of the South. The misdirected science of the North was once again leading an invasion in an attempt at self-righteous reconstruction of the simple Agrarian South. "If we may judge by the past," Davidson wrote, "its findings are likely to be put to use in the next wave of social reform directed at the South. Are the great research funds that once were devoted to such understandable and worthy projects as the attack on yellow fever and hookworm now to be extended to the eradication of the so-called 'psychoses' of the Southern mind?" The link between the conspiracy of science and the conspiracy of "metropolis" abolitionism comes a few lines later when Davidson declares that "The Southerner who reads Dr. Dollard's book is compelled to feel that he has not much more chance for a fair hearing before this particular variety of social scientist *than he had before the old-time abolitionist.*"[10]

What Dollard found in Southerntown was true in large part, and Faulkner's major novels are further documentation for much of Dollard's thesis. But Faulkner's novels also suggest what Davidson's rhetorical polemics only suggest—that the danger in a purely scientific approach to the South is that the complex *historical* context of the problem will be overlooked. For instance, in speaking of the upper class in Southerntown, Dollard writes, "In its day this was a functioning class leading in statecraft and agriculture, and disciplining its individuals for leadership. Nowadays it seems to be based largely on memories. . . . There are echoes of old transactions, such as whose relative sold what house and piece of land to whose grandfather. . . . The ancestors are potentially present every time an upper-class group gathers; even though in

10. Donald Davidson, "Gulliver With Hay Fever," *American Review,* IX (1937), 167, emphasis mine.

the case of the younger members of this class there is less frequent trading of memories and old associations."[11]

In fact, Dollard is describing a situation applicable to some families such as Faulkner's Compsons, and his observations are enlightening in studying Faulkner's characters. But the sociological observation remains flat and without historical meaning. Warren, according to Alexander Karanikas, touched on this problem in discussing liberal propaganda novels where the author is so "haunted" by the sociological facts and factual "truths" of his abstractions that he misses the complexity of the event itself. "Characters and events interested the liberal novelist only as illustrations of his preconceived notions. Hence the novel created by him could be nothing more than a political pamphlet in disguise."[12] It is Faulkner's portrayal of such a fictional character as Quentin Compson—which we shall examine shortly—that adds the dimension of human complexity and the depth of historical construct to the sociological fact.

While incorporating elements of both, Faulkner stands farther removed from the vision of the Old South put forward in *Gone With the Wind* than he does from that of the New South suggested by *Caste and Class*. Dollard's observations lack a sense of historical perspective. But Miss Mitchell's romantic epic of the past lacks, from Faulkner's point of view, historical sophistication. Both Dollard and Miss Mitchell seem to see their particular South in juxtaposition to, but not as part of, the national imagination: Dollard because the South is basically immoral and unprogressive; Miss Mitchell because the Old South alone is moral. Faulkner's uniqueness lies, not only in his insight into the complexity and tragedy of Southern history itself, but in his rendering out of this regional epic a meaning which is national in implication. Sociology cannot record the burden of history. Regional romance cannot comprehend its own history in terms of national experience. In the

11. Dollard, *op. cit.*, pp. 80–81.
12. Quoted in *Tillers of a Myth*, pp. 136–137.

self-centered innocence of Thomas Sutpen, Faulkner portrayed the Southerner as American. In Quentin Compson, we are to see the burden of historical consciousness which the American as Southerner must bear.

Innocence

The first chapter of *Absalom, Absalom!* is narrated by Rosa Coldfield, sworn enemy of Thomas Sutpen, now forty years dead. She calls Sutpen a demon for whom no crime, no outrage, no perversity is impossible. Gradually, this diabolical picture of Sutpen is modified. The reader is never given one authoritative judgment of Sutpen's character, but the picture that emerges associates Sutpen's sin not with demonism but with innocence. This aspect of Sutpen's character illuminates Faulkner's response to certain cultural prototypes of the national imagination as well as his involvement with the myth of Southern history. Thomas Sutpen was born in 1807 in the mountains of what is now West Virginia, "one of several children of poor whites, Scotch-English stock" (*AA*, "Genealogy," fol. p. 378). Faulkner describes him coming out of an almost purely Lockean state of nature, where the sanctity of the individual was absolute, where nature was held in common by all men, where there was no invidious comparison and emulation nor any individual responsibility to the other inhabitants, where "men and grown boys . . . hunted or lay before the fire on the floor while the women and older girls stepped back and forth across them to reach the fire to cook" (*AA*, p. 221).

One day Sutpen's father, who is employed in a menial capacity by one of the wealthy gentleman planters, sends young Sutpen to the planter's mansion with a message. The boy walks up to the front door of the house, past the lawns and gardens, "never for one moment thinking but what the man would be as pleased to show him the balance of his things as the mountain man would have been to show the powder horn and bullet mold that went with the rifle" (*AA*, p. 229).

But the child's curiosity is rudely shocked. Instead of the planter, a Negro butler meets him at the door, bars it to him, and tells him "never to come to that front door again but to go around to the back" (*AA,* p. 232).

The boy's sense of natural equality is humiliated by the slave of a man who would not have spoken to him, Sutpen suddenly realizes, even if the Negro had not come to the door first. The state of nature has been corrupted. He has suddenly been exposed to that usurpation of the common earth which for Rousseau had marked the beginning of "wars, crimes, misery and horrors." The barbarian standard of comparison and emulation is born in the young boy's mind. The moment is portentous. "When the boy . . . ragged and barefoot, comes to the door of the plantation house, he is punished for the unforgivable American crime, the crime of poverty. This crime is unforgivable because poverty is the result of shiftlessness and well-known remedies exist for it."[13] As all of this gradually becomes clear to young Sutpen, he vows to make up for it. Certainly for the sake of revenge, and supposedly in order to be able himself to meet the poor white boy next time and to admit him into the great house, he sets out to create his design. His escape to the West Indies is the beginning of Sutpen's escape to the West, the traditional American escape from complexity to the simplicity of nature. Sutpen, like Huck Finn and, later, Jack Burden, "lights out for the territory": "What I learned was that there was a place called the West Indies to which poor men went in ships and became rich, it didn't matter how, so long as that man was clever and courageous" (*AA,* p. 242).

The islands are a microcosm of the New World itself, a world in which the "incredible paradox of peaceful greenery and crimson flowers" provides a backdrop for "all the satanic lusts of human greed and cruelty." This greed exploits not only the land but human flesh as well. The New World, then, had never been, and could never be, a garden of undefiled harmony and simplicity. Europeans had not escaped the burdens of history or the evils of

13. John Lewis Longley, *The Tragic Mask: A Study of Faulkner's Heroes,* p. 217.

civilization by coming to the New World any more than Sutpen had escaped the system which had brought about his humiliation. Sutpen is influenced, however, by a cultural innocence which motivates the individual toward, and rewards him for, the exploitation of his environment and his fellow human beings for his own pecuniary gratification while teaching no principles of individual responsibility toward the environment and the people. The self-made man, even the self-made Cavalier, is not his brother's keeper in nineteenth-century America, the myth of the Old South notwithstanding. The image of the Tidewater Cavalier becomes for Sutpen a model for imitation, as contrasted with the innocent comparison of possessions in which the boy had hoped to participate when he went to the planter's house. The symbol of this goal is the big house itself. The Cavalier myth contributes to and encourages the very exploitation and crass worship of material goods which other Southern traditionalists claim that it opposes. Sutpen's design is the American Dream of success, but in Faulkner's novel it also becomes a cultural tragedy because of this paradoxical innocence which makes Sutpen insensitive to the evil done to men and nature in pursuit of this success. Thus Sutpen repudiates his first wife, the daughter of the West Indies planter for whom he works, and their son when he learns that his wife has Negro blood: "I found that she was not and could never be, through no fault of her own, adjunctive or incremental to the design which I had in mind, so I provided for her and put her aside" (*AA,* p. 240).

This desertion of his wife and child is only the first in a series of fateful decisions in the execution of the design. Yet Sutpen is, as Longley correctly states, "only one more example of the kind of heroes America had before it created Horatio Algers, Jr. As everybody knows, in America the path to success is clear and simple, and any poor boy may follow it: marry advantageously, get a big house, and found a dynasty. The unspoken corollary is: get it at all costs, no matter how."[14] Sutpen's innocence is the self-sufficiency of the rationalist and positivist. Later in his life, he is not

14. *Ibid.*

concerned with "whether or not it was a good design" (*AA,* p. 263) but with "where he had made the mistake which kept his actions from being, as modern scienteers would say, 'effective!' "[15] There is no element of conspiracy nor any sense on Sutpen's part of guilt or of wrongdoings. His is an innocence "which believed that the ingredients of morality were like the ingredients of pie or cake and once you had measured them and balanced them and mixed them and put them into the oven it was all finished and nothing but pie or cake could come out" (*AA,* p. 263). By providing financially for the repudiated wife and child, Sutpen assumes not only that he has met his responsibility to them, but that he has actually done more than might be expected of him since he had been deceived about his wife's Negro background. That a man owes nothing else, not even recognition, to children who do not fit his own purposes is the fateful assumption which ultimately leads to Sutpen's failure. That the white South—as well as white America—can reject the legitimate demands of its minority population for recognition and inclusion in society without reaping a terrible humiliation and defeat seems just as explicit, albeit with the hindsight afforded by the 1960s. In history, man is responsible for man. In the 1930s, the Marxists claimed to be concerned with the working man. Such conservatives as the Agrarians spoke in the interest of the human element in life. The New Deal took the economic burden of men and women upon its shoulders. The immediate needs of man in this present moment were discussed everywhere—our term would be "dialogue"—and relief and reform provided the backbone of political response. Yet the plight of man in history was still incomprehensible. The popular response to *Absalom, Absalom!,* as reflected in popular reviews, centered around the difficulty of Faulkner's style, with little if any interest in the themes of race and history. Yet Faulkner's book was about history—specifically, about American history and the Amer-

15. Hyatt Waggoner, *William Faulkner: From Jefferson to the World,* p. 166.

ican burden of innocence. The story could generally be best expressed within the framework of classical myth and symbol (that
is, the title, itself a reference to the biblical story of David and his
sons, and the analogies to Greek families and characters), and
specifically could best be illustrated by the South's entanglement
with history through the burden of the Negro and the burden of
defeat.

From the West Indies, Sutpen travels west and north, eventually
wandering into the virgin Mississippi valley in 1833, settling upon
Jefferson, Mississippi, as the scene for the second attempt at the
design. Here, with his gang of wild slaves from the West Indies and
his captured French architect, he builds the great house and fur-
nishes it with imported furnishings and ornaments. A daughter,
Clytemnestra, who is destined to destroy the Sutpen house eventually, is born to a Negro slave the following year. In 1838, Sutpen
marries Ellen Coldfield, Rosa's older sister, who bears two children, Henry (1839) and Judith (1841). In 1859 Henry goes to
the new University of Mississippi at Oxford where he meets
Charles Bon, Sutpen's repudiated son by his West Indian wife.
Guessing who Bon really is, Sutpen refuses to let him marry
Judith; and when he persists—as Shreve and Quentin piece the
story together, using their imaginations and conjecture to supplement what few facts they have—Sutpen tells Henry that Bon is not
only a half-brother to Judith but that he is part Negro. Henry
himself forbids Bon to see Judith again, and, when Bon persists,
Henry, who loves Bon as much as he loves his own sister, kills him
at the gates of the Sutpen mansion and is forced to flee. It is now
1865, and Sutpen is not only destitute because of the war but is
also once again without a male heir to his design. He makes the
proposition to Rosa Coldfield that if she will bear him a son he will
marry her. Rosa is outraged and leaves the plantation, not to
return for almost forty years. Finally, in a last desperate attempt to
get a male heir, he "takes up" with Milly Jones, the illegitimate

granddaughter of a poor white man, Wash Jones. Milly gives birth to a girl, and Sutpen rejects her. Wash Jones, who had thought of Sutpen as a grand and brave hero and gentleman, murders Sutpen with a rusty scythe for the betrayal of his granddaughter. In 1881, Charles Bon's son and his "full blooded negress" wife come to "Sutpen's Hundred," and Jim Bond, their idiot son, is born in 1882. In September of 1910, "Rosa Coldfield and Quentin find Henry Sutpen hidden in the house," and in December Rosa returns to take Henry to town. Clytemnestra, now a dried-up old crone, sets fire to the house, destroying herself and Henry, thinking that she is saving him from arrest for the murder of Bon half a century earlier. Only Jim Bond is left, to howl around the house and finally disappear.

Sutpen's flaw is his inability to live in history as represented by the acts and relationships for which he is responsible but for which he will take no responsibility. His flaw is pride in his self-sufficiency. Earlier in the story, it is suggested that if Sutpen would only recognize Charles Bon as his son, by a word or a look or even a transmitted emotion, he, Bon, would not persist in his engagement to Judith but would leave, gladly, never to return. But Sutpen will not give this recognition. The great white door under the portico is slammed in Bon's face, not by a slave, but by the white master himself; and Bon is not even given the chance to go around to the back door, not given even the token recognition that he asks for. Here one might make an analogy with the statement by some contemporary Negro leaders that what the Negro wants is not the white man's daughter, but his good will, or at least his recognition of the Negro as a human being. But again, it must be stressed that the central concept of the novel is the necessity of moral responsibility in history: the idea that in history, personal and social relationships and responsibilities must be assumed; that emulative "designs" toward "progress" must be defined by these obligations; and that the man or the society which tries to escape these obligations, these complex relationships—the man or society that denies the necessity of love and forgiveness in the name of some material design or some illusionary concept of progress—will live in vain and perish in defeat. Like the Agrarians, Faulkner criticized predatory capitalism and the radical individualism which personified this capitalism. Unlike the Agrarians, he criticized it because it ignores the complexity of history and the claims of common humanity rather than because it violates a mythical tradition of harmony and stability based on a doomed white supremacy. The scythe, symbol of time, wielded by a poor white against a once-respected leader who had failed to assume his responsibilities, captures the essential meaning of the novel. Innocence, or this irresponsible self-sufficiency, if not cast off voluntarily, will be violently destroyed. If a society does not assume its responsibilities when it has the chance, it may never get the chance. History is not of itself moral. But if the Wash Joneses and the Flem Snopeses and the Jim Bonds are not to be the inheritors of the earth, man must by his own will introduce morality, and must, as Jack Burden in *All the King's Men* later discovers, learn to live in the "agony of the will." *Absalom, Absalom!* suggests that the nature of history makes impossible the American dream of economic plenty and simple harmony with a docile nature. It also poses the question: Does the American Dream make responsibility in history equally impossible?

One reads in *Absalom, Absalom!* the sealing of the South's fate —and the nation's—in this century, sealed and determined, not in 1833 or 1865, but in 1910; for it is in 1910 that Quentin Compson fails to resolve the paradox of his culture as a Southerner and as an American. Because Quentin is unable to comprehend the national *or* regional implications of Sutpen's prideful innocence and the South's burden, he is unable to resolve the problems of his own time in history. Until the ideals of the plantation myth and the myth of achievement can be resolved with the realities of racial injustice and the economic exploitation of the land, the South cannot hope to reconcile itself either with the nation or with itself.

Even the violent destruction of the plantation house itself in 1910 is not enough to show Quentin the futility of his illusions about the South. Because Quentin is obsessed with the ideas of Southern honor and Southern innocence, he tries, in *The Sound and the Fury,* to destroy time, thereby escaping history. He succeeds only by destroying himself. *Absalom, Absalom!* is the prelude to this final act of violence of the South upon itself. In Ilse Dusoir Lind's words, the "desolation of the mansion is the key to Quentin's own, and in the story of a design that failed we may read the meaning of the decline of the South,"[16] which, it should be added, may have national as well as regional implications.

Like Quentin, Joe Christmas in *Light in August* tries desperately and continually, although with a terrible resignation to ultimate defeat, to escape history, to escape his own past in which black and white are inseparably fused, yet, paradoxically, always isolated from one another, each hating the other. In the same novel, the Reverend Gail Hightower lives only for a frozen moment in the imagined past, a scene from the Civil War in which his grandfather led a raid in Jefferson against Northern supplies: *"time had stopped there and then for the seed and nothing had happened in time since, not even him."*[17]

Hightower's schizophrenia helps us to distinguish clearly between the burden of the past, under which all of these characters labor, and the burden of history. The image of arrested time haunting the present represents the burden of the past. For the Southerner, time has stopped, and the point of this stoppage is always the Civil War. In *Intruder in the Dust,* Faulkner writes:

For every Southern boy fourteen years old, not once but whenever he wants it, there is the instant when it's still not yet two oclock on that July afternoon in 1863 . . . and Pickett himself . . . waiting for Longstreet to give the word and its all in the balance[18]

16. "The Design and Meaning of *Absalom, Absalom!*," in *William Faulkner: Three Decades of Criticism,* ed. Frederick J. Hoffman and Olga W. Vickery, p. 304.
17. William Faulkner, *Light in August,* p. 55, emphasis mine.
18. *Intruder in the Dust,* p. 194.

This is the moment of smashed progress—the moment of the Lost Cause. Something happened to the South during such moments, something catastrophic, for it froze the imagination of the South against a shallow, progressive view of history while failing to reveal exactly what might take the place of this view. It is the burden of the past which too often appears in *I'll Take My Stand.* We see a calculated distrust of the doctrine of progress and a seemingly sterile self-consciousness concerning the past, because there is no acceptable explanation as to why any of this has happened to the South or what it means, if anything, for the present.

In other words, the burden of history, to distinguish it from the burden of the past, suggests that the defeat, the humiliation, and the social catastrophe give fruitful knowledge of the human condition rather than the impotent, self-destructive idea of self-sufficient innocence; responsibility rather than irresponsibility; motion and action to replace political immobility and moral stagnation. Quentin's problem is that he is caught between the two. He cannot escape the past, nor can he accept the implications of Sutpen's suicidal quest for innocence as he and Shreve piece the story together in their room at Harvard in 1910.

Shreve understands the moral issue well enough to construct an acceptable imaginative account of the events which demonstrate Sutpen's selfish innocence. Quentin knows, if he does not understand, the burden that this past has placed upon him. He, too, like Henry, has already made in *The Sound and the Fury* a vain attempt to defend, or at least to avenge, some already crumbled concept of Southern honor and principle which he sees in his sister Caddy's lost virginity.[19] But Shreve cannot feel the burden. "We don't live among defeated grandfathers . . . and bullets in the dining room table," he says (*AA,* p. 361). Quentin, on the other hand, has only the reality of the burden, without the strength necessary to act. Quentin is like the South, already immobilized by the past, unable either to escape this past or to relate it to the present. Nor does he understand the national implications of Sut-

19. *The Sound and the Fury,* pp. 95–197 *passim.*

pen's story. There is no explicit statement in *Absalom, Absalom!* to the effect that the South might use its burdensome past and its own peculiar involvement with the tragedies of history to make a contribution to the life of a nation which, because of its own uninterrupted affluence and progress, has never been forced to face the tragedy of history. But Faulkner did show the dilemma of the modern South caught between a belief in the national faith of moral salvation through economic progress and a sense of moral burden which contradicts such easy faith in progress. The irony of Southern history is further underlined in *Absalom, Absalom!* by the "skepticism and detachment" of the outlander, Shreve, which allows him to play the game of Sutpen as one might play the game of "Clue," but which also allows him to dismiss the "tragic problem" of history and the "irrational claims from which Quentin cannot free himself and which he honors to his own cost."[20] Quentin, the Southerner, literally stakes his life on the solution to the problem and loses. Shreve stakes nothing and loses nothing because the story has no meaning for him. By his own confession, he is ahistorical. That both Quentin's dilemma and Faulkner's unwillingness to accept more traditional explanations of Southern culture were parts of a broader re-evaluation of the South taking place in the 1930s is revealed by the efforts of selected historians and social scientists during the decade in which "revisionism" became a major trend in Southern historiography.

The Content of History

An increasing interest in the complexity of Southern history was evident in all of the major areas of Southern historiography during the 1930s. It has been suggested that even the Agrarians themselves, in their quest for illusionary order and leisure, made a major contribution in the area of historiography by suggesting that historians might profitably explore "the patterns of conflict and

20. Cleanth Brooks, *William Faulkner: The Yoknapatawpha Country,* pp. 317–318.

antagonism in modern southern history."[21] The interpretations of
the past which an earlier and basically more optimistic generation
had created seemed less adequate to a generation increasingly
aware of both the region's unique historical burdens and of the
factual inadequacies of accepted explanations of the South's role in
the national life. Not only were new facts discovered, but, in
addition, point of view and tone shifted through the process of
"revisionism" from the self-assured, apologetic rhetoric of much
New South history and New South fiction toward an ironic, almost
hesitant awareness of more basic motivations, of contradictory acts
and words, and of paradoxical entanglements in the ambiguities of
culture. "The grave emergency precipitated by the depression,"
wrote Virginius Dabney, "has served to emphasize the fact that
there is a serious lack of clarity and coherence in our political and
social concepts, and has brought into prominent relief the need for
a reexamination of many hypotheses which we had previously
regarded as axiomatic."[22] Dabney saw in this situation a mission in
which Southern liberalism could "reassert itself as a vital force in
our national life. By furnishing an adequate answer to some of the
principal questions raised by the existing economic distress, Southern statesmanship could establish itself once more as a controlling
factor in the national councils. At the same time it should thereby
be able to give to the dignity and worth of human beings everywhere a greater measure of reality."[23] W. T. Couch, in the Preface
to *Culture in the South* dissented from the Agrarians' naive insistence that the agrarian way of life in the South was better than
industrial life. Pointing to the South as the home of close to two
million tenant farmers and as the last stronghold of child labor and
overworked females, Couch wrote, "The system is so thoroughly
bad that no laws can be devised which, so long as the system lasts,

21. Paul M. Gaston, "The 'New South,'" in *Writing Southern History:
Essays in Historiography,* ed. Arthur S. Link and Rembert W. Patrick, p.
327.
22. *Liberalism in the South,* p. 424.
23. *Ibid.,* pp. 424–425.

can protect the women and children who are a part of it."[24] In what was to become a standard textbook of Southern history, William B. Hesseltine debunked the plantation image of "goateed squires of undreamed virtues who sipped mint juleps in an aura of lavender and old lace," as a coverup for the less romantic task of keeping " 'the niggers in their place.' "[25] The New South, Hesseltine wrote, had had its beginnings with the distinguished figure of Robert E. Lee giving "his efforts to building a new society."[26] But he went on to note without added comment that the tradition as it developed under men like Lee—and Grady—had "been responsible for the industrial system of the South—for its textile factories, its mill villages, its railroads, its tourist camps and resorts, its public utilities, and its wage scales."[27] At best, the blessings seemed mixed.

Other scholars chose prose more metaphorical if no less informative in which to express their revisionist attitudes toward the Old and New Souths. Benjamin Kendrick and Alex Arnett viewed the Old South in terms of the ancient Greek belief "that the spirit of a man wandered disconsolately until his body received the religious ceremony of burial."[28] For decades the ghost of the Old South "has stalked abroad to bedevil in some sort the placidity of Southern and, to a lesser extent, of American life."[29] Neither Reconstruction nor the New South had given proper honor and interment to the body—the one had mutilated the remains while the other had been too willing to bury the body quickly in a shallow, unhallowed grave. In trying to reassess the meaning of the South's past, Kendrick and Arnett wrote, "We neither praise nor blame [the Old South] or its enemies but insist that it did not deserve the hard fate of being cut off in the flower of its age. From the way of life which

24. *Culture in the South,* p. viii.
25. *A History of the South,* p. 647.
26. *Ibid.,* p. 646.
27. *Ibid.,* p. 648.
28. *The South Looks at Its Past,* p. 103.
29. *Ibid.*

history and tradition ascribe to it, we may glean much for the creation of a better and a newer South."[30] Thus would the Old South be given decent burial and at the same time be evoked as a guide and standard in the twentieth century. The choice of metaphor and language in such a view of the idea of the Old South left the problem more open-ended than Hesseltine's ironic debunking of the "goateed squires." Like the Southern Agrarians, Kendrick and Arnett tried to emphasize what was valuable in the Old South but concluded their book on the hope that what was of value in the Old South would not blind the present generation to regional detriments including the "blight of slavery; the tragedy of the 'poor whites'; and the curse of ignorance, prejudice and superstition."[31]

Many scholars stressed the dangers in oversimplification of the South's past and its meaning for the present. "The most dramatic and tragic group of crises," Howard W. Odum wrote in 1936, "is that centering around secession and war."[32] Any evaluation of the South, or any utilization of its various qualities would have to take this complexity into account. "It is not possible," Odum wrote, "to dismiss with a mere verdict the backgrounds of a dynamic folk whose changing cultures have provided the most dramatic episodes in American history and whose experiences have comprehended all the basic elements in the architecture of modern civilization."[33] In his biography of Tom Watson, C. Vann Woodward made a point of rejecting "political epithets" and easy, stereotyped explanations as means by which to understand the life of a complex individual living in an equally complex society. To make Watson responsible for "the sinister forces of intolerance, superstition, prejudice, religious jingoism, and mobbism," as one liberal journal had done, Woodward wrote, "would be to assign him far too important a role, a role that belongs to the vastly more impersonal forces of economics and race and historical heritage." Rather, Watson was a

30. *Ibid.*, pp. 103–104.
31. *Ibid.*, p. 7.
32. *Southern Regions of the United States*, p. 11.
33. *Ibid.*, p. 23.

product of such forces, and for Woodward, this was what had made Watson's life not only a "personal tragedy," but "also in many ways the tragedy of a class, and more especially the tragedy of a section."[34] In *An American Epoch: Southern Portraiture in the National Picture,* Odum, an eminent sociologist by training and reputation, felt compelled to explain the book's unorthodox narrative style:

If the present narrative reflects emotional episodes alongside the quantitative statements of facts, even so any adequate picture of the South must combine the poetic with the scientific. It is as if a new romantic realism were needed to portray the old backgrounds and the new trends and processes.[35]

Such a "romantic realism" was one way of describing what Faulkner (and later Warren) offered to the historian and social scientist—a realism which did not end with the rather severe limitations of quantitative facts. The form and general approach of *An American Epoch* may also have influenced another Southerner, Wilbur J. Cash, who, compelled to narrate the ambiguities of his culture at the end of the decade (1941), published his somewhat romantic yet insightful *The Mind of the South.* Cash, like Faulkner and like other artists and scholars of the decade, made a major contribution to the intellectual and cultural re-evaluation of the South. And Cash, like Faulkner, did a great deal to move the issues and problems beyond the dead end which had been the fate of *I'll Take My Stand.*

The Mind of the South parallels the struggle in which Faulkner and Quentin were already engaged. Cash wrote his book to facilitate an understanding of just what the nature of the South's uniqueness was and was not, and to preface that understanding he insisted that we "disabuse our minds of two correlated legends— those of the Old and the New Souths." The legend of the Old South, "in its classical form," is the plantation South, "a sort of stage piece out of the eighteenth century, wherein gesturing gentle-

34. *Tom Watson: Agrarian Rebel,* p. xii.
35. *An American Epoch,* p. x.

men moved soft-spokenly against a background of rose gardens and dueling grounds. . . . They dwelt in large and stately mansions, preferably white and with columns and Grecian entablature."[36] Like Faulkner, Cash begins by attacking the central image of this mythical South, the plantation and the "big house." He is just as critical of the "legend" of the New South in which "the Old South is supposed to have been destroyed by the Civil War and the thirty years that followed it, to have been swept both socially and mentally into the limbo of things that were and are not, to give place to a society which has been rapidly and increasingly industrialized and modernized both in body and in mind" (*MOS,* pp. ix–x).

The fact that both images of the South exist together is for Cash proof that paradox is the essence of popular thinking, and here we can agree with him since both images, the simple order of an agrarian life and the progress of industrialism, are essential elements of the American Dream. The true picture, for Cash, is that there was an Old South, though very different from the one he debunks, and that this Old South has determined the newer South to a far greater extent than it itself has been changed.

The mind of the section, that is, is continuous with the past. And its primary form is determined not nearly so much by industry as by the purely agricultural conditions of that past. So far from being modernized, in many ways it has actually always marched away, as to this day it continues to do, from the present toward the past (*MOS,* p. x).

This passage demonstrates the paradox in Cash's mind which we have already seen in Quentin Compson. There is a continuity with the burden of the past which pervades and obstructs the Southerner's cultural response to the present: thus the bullet holes in the dining room table which Shreve doesn't understand. Like Quentin, Cash did not understand that what prevents resolution of the paradox is no peculiarly Southern quality—vice or virtue—but a national quality, the belief in innocence through the self-sufficiency

36. *The Mind of the South,* p. ix.

and self-reliance of the individual and the desire for harmony and simplicity in nature which must always deny the claim of history. It is this paradoxical position in which the South finds itself which Robert Penn Warren and C. Vann Woodward do eventually resolve, at least within their own works, if not for their society.

Cash's dilemma is clearly seen in that to the very end of his book he describes as uniquely Southern qualities of personality and culture which are parts of a national mythology. In his uneasy flirtation with the South of the Agrarians and Dixon, he first destroys and then recreates a myth of Southern uniqueness which ironically denies the uniqueness which the South actually possesses: "Proud, brave, honorable by its lights, courteous, personally generous, loyal, swift to act, often too swift, but signally effective, sometimes terrible, in its action—such was the South at its best. And such at its best it remains today" (*MOS,* p. 439).

These are the agrarian virtues professed in *I'll Take My Stand,* but what is all of this but the myth of American democracy with its individualized, spontaneous, simple way of life? And as for the "South's" vices—"Violence, intolerance, aversion and suspicion toward new ideas, an incapacity for analysis, an inclination to act from feeling . . . an exaggerated individualism and a too narrow concept of social responsibility, attachment to fictions and false values, above all too great attachment to racial values and a tendency to justify cruelty and injustice in the name of those values, sentimentality and a lack of realism" (*MOS,* pp. 439–440)—these too are for the most part images of national scope. If George Wallace is the current spokesman for these ideas and responses, all too many of his followers are from New York, Ohio, and Wyoming.

Cash "disabused" himself from the "myths" of the Old South and went on to give what was supposed to be a realistic account of the rise of the upper class in the South. The settlers, in Cash's book, are simple yeomen who have the frontier as their "predestined inheritance" and who "possessed precisely the qualities necessary to the taming of the land and the building of the cotton kingdom. The process of their rise to power was simplicity itself" (*MOS,* pp. 14–15). As his chief example, Cash writes of a typical "stout young Irishman" who brings his bride into the Carolina upcountry about 1800. He clears the land, plants a little cotton, sells it, buys more land, plants more cotton, sells it, buys an old slave, plants more land, buys more slaves, until by his mid-forties he is a wealthy and prominent citizen of the countryside.

What is supposed to be a historically realistic account follows the outlines of the American success story almost exactly. Economic gain is the reward of long, hard, work and sacrifice. And through all of this acquisition of land and slaves, the man remains at heart a simple yeoman living in harmony with nature. The "big house" which the Irishman eventually builds,

was not, to be truthful, a very grand house really. Built of lumber sawed on the place, it was a little crude and had not cost above a thousand dollars, even when the marble mantel was counted in. . . . But it was huge, it had great columns in front, and it was eventually painted white, and so, in this land of wide fields and pinewoods it seemed very imposing (*MOS,* p. 16).

Even though Cash could see partially through the myth of the "big house," he kept its essential meaning: simplicity and leisure. The old man dies in peace, leaving 2,000 acres, 114 slaves, and four cotton gins. Resolutions of respect are introduced in the Legislature, and one obituary speaks of him as "a noble specimen of the chivalry at its best." In many ways Cash's Irishman, who may remind one of the master of "Tara" in *Gone with the Wind,* is also reminiscent of Thomas Sutpen, even to the point that Cash's Jacksonian frontiersman has admitted no entanglements with history. Although he lives until 1854, he evidently does not get involved with either the politics or the moral issue of slavery. He is presented as apolitical—an archetype, a mythical figure who with "industry, thrift and luck" settled the frontier and established his line of descendants. All that Cash imagines of his political or moral opinions is that as he grew "extremely mellow in age" he liked to pass his time in company, "arguing about predestination and infant damnation, proving conclusively that cotton was king and that the damyankee didn't dare do anything about it" (*MOS,* p. 17).

The irrelevancies of an archaic and decayed Calvinism and the illusions of an economic fiction fit Cash's image of the Southern "ruling class" better than would the moral dilemma in which Faulkner's Sutpen is caught and which Cash himself admits as existing in the pre–Civil War South, which

in its secret heart always carried a powerful and uneasy sense of the essential rightness of the nineteenth century's position on slavery. . . .

This old South, in short, was a society beset by the specters of defeat, of shame, of guilt—a society driven by the need to bolster its morale, to nerve its arm against waxing odds, to justify itself in its own eyes and in those of the world (*MOS,* p. 63).

Cash described here the burden of the South's past. The uncomfortable tensions of his book come from the fact that he was not able to carry the observations of his rational reflection into the mythical world of his Irishman. The indulgent tone of his description makes clear that he believed in his yeoman Irishman, and although he saw the burden of the past, and the burden of history, he could not bring the two worlds together without destroying what was essential in the world of the Irishman—the simplicity and self-sufficient innocence of the democratic American yeomanry. On the one side, the innocence, the gentleness, the "mellowness" of the democratic ruling class; on the other, the guilt, the violence, the crudity of the "schemers" and the Klan. This is the unresolved paradox of Cash's book just as it is the unresolved dilemma in Quentin's mind in *Absalom, Absalom!* In the end, all elements are left isolated by a static irresponsibility and inaction. Neither Quentin nor Sutpen nor the Irishman is able or willing to act. The closing words of *The Mind of the South* might stand for Faulkner's as well as Cash's dilemma in the late 1930s. "In the coming days," wrote Cash, and probably soon, the South "is likely to have to prove its capacity for adjustment far beyond what has been true in the past. And in that time I shall hope, as its loyal son, that its virtues will tower over and conquer its faults and have the making of the Southern world to come. But of the future I shall venture no definite prophecies. It would be a brave man who would venture them in any case. It would be a madman who would venture them in face of the forces sweeping over the world in the fateful year of 1940" (*MOS,* p. 440).

The Form of History

As an artist, Faulkner, unlike even the most imaginatively inclined historian, had the freedom to pursue the complexity and ambiguity of history beyond content, beyond the relatively limited prose of scholarship, to form itself. In the hands of a serious artist such as Faulkner form becomes capable of incorporating abstract content into "a sensuous impression" in which we "confront experience in its immediacy and closeness." In *Absalom, Absalom!* it is the form itself rather than any secondary interpretation or opinion which suggests Faulkner's vision of history. It is also in the form of the novel that we most vividly see Faulkner's disassociation from the main stream of the American literary imagination of the times. So far, this chapter has suggested that during the 1930s, chiefly in the works of Faulkner, the myth of Southern history underwent a significant re-examination. This re-examination led in new directions and was intimately related to a new national examination of the South. We have seen the various other aspects of this re-examination in Dollard's *Caste and Class,* Mitchell's *Gone With the Wind,* and Cash's *Mind of the South.* Further evidence of the divided nature of popular response to the South and its problems is offered by two contemporary journalistic comments on the style of *Absalom, Absalom!*

In a review entitled, "William Faulkner as a Self-Conscious Stylist—His Latest Story Reveals Him as Something Less Than a Novelist," Dorothea Lawrence Mann wrote that while a genuine literary style is "so simple, so natural, so fitted to the subject matter that it is possible to be quite unconscious of it," Faulkner's complicated style and subject matter "reek of decay" and that people who enjoy reading him must have "queer and perverted tastes. . . . We feel in this book a feverish nightmare of unhealthiness. . . . Mr. Faulkner is looking for the decadent, half mad impulses of a defeated and dying people, and these are what he finds. . . . We doubt the story just as we doubt the conclusion that the Jim Bonds and the descendants of the Jim Bonds will ever control the country.[37]

On the other hand, Mary M. Colum, writing for *Forum,* asked this question:

Could we sum up in a few lines what is in these Southern writers that is absent from the bulk of the Northern novels? There is a complexity of interior life; there is the sense of tragedy; there is a sense of the relations of life to the soil, to the earth and the people around . . . [as opposed to the] simple illusions of the northern industrial city novelists, that all life's frustrations can be settled the minute capitalism is liquidated and the "bourgeois ideology" banished from life and that the incompleteness of human destiny can be made complete by some economic arrangements.[38]

Miss Mann's comments in the Boston paper are an illustration of that peculiarly American aversion to the irrational, the unpragmatic, and the unrealistic as well as white America's insensitivity to the burden of racial injustice and its inevitable consequences. Ambiguities and complexities are manifestations of decadence and can only be found among a "defeated and dying" people; no such nightmare of unhealthiness can be found in the "real" world of American progress and simplicity. Like other genteel critics, Miss Mann would have all literature reflect such a world, and in Faulkner she can find only vulgarity and decadence in its negation. Miss Colum's article in the *Forum* suggests an awareness of the same set of responses. She too saw something very different and rather "un-American" in Faulkner and expands it to include Southern novelists in general. Complexity, tragedy, and ambiguity set off the Southerners from their northern counterparts, whose points of view are simplistic to the point of being naive in their narrow

37. Boston *Evening Transcript,* "Book Section," October 31, 1936, p. 6.
38. "Faulkner's Struggle With Technique," *The Forum and Century,* XCVII (1937), 36.

concern with the evils of industrialism and "bourgeois ideology." These northern novelists have no meaningful context in which to examine life's "frustrations" and "incompleteness." She goes on to contrast James T. Farrell's "revolutionary novels," which are "very soothing because they give us the sense that men and women are tamed creatures who can eventually be made satisfied with bread and circuses and with easy sensual gratification," with Faulkner's, which are "very disturbing because they give us the sense that human beings will never be satisfied with anything that society can give them, that they are so tortuous, so mutually destructive, and so self-destructive that there is no possibility of any social change making very much difference in human existence."[39]

What Miss Mann saw as the necessity of genteel reality comes out in Miss Colum's article as the failure of "realism" and the necessity of tragedy. I would suggest that it is a consciousness of history which gives to Faulkner's novels the sense of tragedy and complexity which Miss Colum admired. The characters in the novels of Dreiser, Anderson, and Lewis, writes C. Vann Woodward, "appear on the scene from nowhere, trailing no clouds of history, dissociated from the past . . . and along with their past they checked their forebears, their historical roots and associations. One has the feeling that they considered that heritage a good riddance. . . . A Hemingway hero with a grandfather is inconceivable."[40]

American literary realism then perhaps reflects the American imagination itself. Its directness of approach, its simplicity, and its structural arrangement of words and sentences emphasize the moment, the present, that which is "real." The past is an entangling web of circumstances and relationships which cannot easily be given shape by a literary philosophy of realism based on the depiction of "a slice of life." The literature, like the cultural imagination it expresses, is ahistorical. Lind offers support for this

39. *Ibid.*
40. *The Burden of Southern History,* p. 30.

general interpretation in speaking of Faulkner's ability to convey tragedy. "If, as Emily Dickinson has observed, 'the abdication of belief/makes the behavior small,' so too, it may be argued, does the use of realistic prose style in compliance with an outlook of 'scientific' objectivity. The declining vitality of much realistic writing of the twenties and thirties—of Farrell's fiction, for example, which was also intended to convey the power of relentless forces —is in part a reflection of the inadequacy of realism for tragic themes."[41]

Faulkner, perhaps because of his awareness of history as tragedy, moved beyond realism early in his career. Hints of this are seen as early as *Sartoris* (1929), but his development of a form which would express the complexity of the content becomes more obvious in *The Sound and the Fury* and *Light in August* and finally culminates in *Absalom, Absalom!* By examining certain aspects of the form—namely character, process of narration, and the role of the author in the novel—we shall be better able to understand the "organic interrelationship" which exists between form and meaning in this "exploration of unprecedented depth and scope into the meaning of history."[42] The characters of *Absalom, Absalom!* are projected, as Lind points out, "on a scale larger than life," which puts them on a heroic scale like figures in a Greek tragedy. More specifically, however, it seems both to free them from objective scientific determinism and yet at the same time to deny them the free will associated with the myth of American individualism. There is a determinism, but it is the force of history and not the force of glands and hostile universes. There is free will, but it is in turn determined to some extent by the forces of history. Faulkner's characters then cannot be labeled as "naturalistic" or "Darwinistic" or "materialistic." Their capacity for good and for evil comes not from the present but from the past. Rosa Coldfield and Quentin Compson both feel the presence of the past, and it is

41. Lind, *op. cit.*, p. 291.
42. *Ibid.*, p. 279.

this quality of personality which gives to each a "larger-than-life" dimension which in turn generates a sense of complexity and tragedy. The flaw of Sutpen's character, on the other hand, is that he can never recognize this presence of history in his life.

That a character—if he is going to find the meaning he seeks—must exist simultaneously in the past and in the present, at least imaginatively, is suggested as Shreve and Quentin become more and more involved in the story of Sutpen until they reach a point of involvement so intense that "now it was not two but four of them riding the two horses through the dark over the frozen December ruts of that Christmas Eve: four of them and then just two—Charles-Shreve and Quentin-Henry" (*AA,* p. 334).

Four young men, separated in time by almost a century, come together in imagined space. The whole novel to this point has prepared us for this moment of total identification with the past. Thus Faulkner's characterization, entirely "unrealistic" as an aspect of form, supports and reinforces the content or meaning of the novel, namely the inescapable complexity of historical relationships—the existence of the past in the present.

There is also in the narration an absence of objectivity and narrative omniscience. The resulting ambiguity is never resolved, although the reader sees each narrator—Quentin, Miss Rosa, Mr. Compson, Shreve—reveal himself through the distortions which color his version of the story. These distortions are the building blocks of myth, of what Lind calls "a reality which rests upon unreality." The reader is forced to participate in this narrative quest for the truth, but to direct his judgment he has only the advantage of being able to see the narrators correcting each other. Thus no arbitrary judgments can be made of any of the characters, even Sutpen. The strengths and the weaknesses of each character must be considered. One perceives very early in the novel that "fact" must be, to some extent, discounted because of its failure to relate to meaning.

While the author's active role in the narration is kept to a minimum, he plays his most vital role as stylist. He "describes outward, physical setting, gesture, and speech" but does not enter into "the thoughts, motives and states of feeling of the other narrators and the characters."[43] Yet as stylist he is intricately involved in the development of the story and the quest for meaning. The style of *Absalom, Absalom!* provides a framework in which the narrative of the characters can operate. Like the narrative process and the characterization, the style is complex, sometimes extravagant. Most important, it suggests to the reader the fallacy in oversimplified accounts of any given situation. From the very beginning, this style complements the "larger-than-life" nature of the characters and the distortions and ambiguities of the various narrative efforts. In much of the rhetoric as well as in the sentence structure itself, there is a sense of rigidity and ponderousness which suggests an interest in the events of the present only as they are tied to events of the past. Let us look, for example, at the second sentence of the novel:

There was a wistaria vine blooming for the second time that summer on a wooden trellis before one window, into which sparrows came now and then in random gusts, making a dry vivid dusty sound before going away: and opposite Quentin, Miss Coldfield in the eternal black which she had worn for forty-three years now, whether for sister, father, or nothusband none knew, sitting so bolt upright in the straight hard chair that was so tall for her that her legs hung straight and rigid as if she had iron shinbones and ankles, clear of the floor with that air of impotent and static rage like children's feet, and talking in that grim haggard amazed voice until at last listening would renege and hearing-sense self-confound and the long-dead object of her impotent yet indomitable frustration would appear, as though by outraged recapitulation evoked, quiet inattentive and harmless, out of the biding and dreamy and victorious dust (*AA,* pp. 7–8).

The length of the sentence alone suggests burden and inaction, as do such rhetorical phrases as "impotent and static rage," "grim haggard amazed voice," and "impotent yet indomitable frustration." The past and things long dead are evoked with such images as the "dry vivid dusty sound" and by such rhetorical flourishes as

43. John W. Hunt, *William Faulkner: Art in Theological Tension,* p. 104.

the long-dead object "by outraged recapitulation evoked . . . out of the biding and dreamy and victorious dust." Miss Rosa herself seems harder, if not larger, than life; her legs hanging "straight and rigid as if she had iron shinbones and ankles." Yet she is also likened to a child and then again described as a frustrated, grim, haggard old woman. The phrases "eternal black," "nothusband," and "long-dead object" suggest not only the past and death but various ambiguities in which this old woman and the boy Quentin are inescapably involved. Finally, her impotency, her static outrage, her immobility and bolt uprightness are transferred to Quentin himself. Detachment from the pervasive atmosphere of the burdensome past is for him impossible.

Another even more revealing example of the interrelationship between style, character, and narrative is found much later in the novel, as Shreve and Quentin approach the climax of their quest for the meaning of the Sutpen story. Parts of this chapter have already been quoted separately in our discussion of character and narrative. Now we see the three—style, character, narrative—complementing one another:

Shreve ceased. That is, for all the two of them, Shreve and Quentin, knew he had stopped, since for all the two of them knew he had never begun, since it did not matter (and possibly neither of them conscious of the distinction) which one had been doing the talking. So that now it was not two but four of them riding the two horses through the dark over the frozen December ruts of that Christmas Eve: four of them and then just two—Charles-Shreve and Quentin-Henry, the two of them both believing that Henry was thinking *He* (meaning his father) *has destroyed us all,* not for one moment thinking *He* (meaning Bon) *must have known or at least suspected this all the time; that's why he has acted as he has (AA,* pp. 333–334).

The characters and the narrative which they are creating move freely between the present and the past and back to the present through the flexibility of a style which defies the restrictions of realism with its present-oriented, logic-bound, expository construction. The unevenness of the style and the imaginative links which it reveals between the present and the past make an orderly progression through time impossible. The reader is forced to hesitate, even to repeat, and finally, if he is to understand, to expand both the temporal and spatial limits of his own perceptions to match the imaginations of the narrators and their stories. We are forced to see the entanglement of the past with the future. Lind has caught something of the significance of this style from a technical, poetic standpoint in noting that the "rhetorical" style of *Absalom, Absalom!* is essential to its conception, "excessive as it may at times appear when it fails in that perfect felicity in which rhetoric is never questioned."

The use of polysyllabics and involved—usually periodic—sentences, while natural to the author, is not a surrender to the line of least resistance. Prefixes and suffixes, especially those containing liquids and nasals in combination with vowels, lend sonorous enrichment; sentence units into which are enfolded a series of phrases and clauses which must be gathered sequentially into the mind before the release of meaning afforded in a final verb, are a means of approximating poetic rhythm in prose medium.[44]

The stylistic elements are not only "natural" as Lind suggests; they are vital in Faulkner's conception of history and its meaning. That these essential elements of Faulkner's style, especially as it appears in *Absalom, Absalom!,* did come from a less than totally conscious response to history and to the South in history is suggested by correspondence between Faulkner and Malcolm Cowley. Cowley asked Faulkner how much of the apparent symbolism in such works as *Absalom, Absalom!,* "The Bear," and *Sanctuary* was "intentional and deliberate"; especially that symbolism which suggests judgments and attitudes toward the South. Faulkner replied: "I'm inclined to think that my material, the South, is not very important to me. I just happen to know it," and went on to say that while he "gratefully accepted" all of Cowley's implications (as to the symbolic meaning of the various works) he had not "carried them consciously and simultaneously into the writing . . . In principle I'd like to think I could have. *But I don't believe it*

44. Lind, *op. cit.,* p. 291.

*would have been necessary to carry them or even to have known
their analogous derivation, to have had them in the story.* Art is
simpler than people think because there is so little to write about.
All the moving things are eternal in man's history and have been
written before"[45]

Here, from Faulkner himself, is the essential statement of his
participation in the myth of Southern history. Unlike earlier expo-
nents of Southern uniqueness such as Dixon and the Agrarians,
Faulkner could suggest that his material, the South, was *not* of
central importance. In other words, as is evident in the novels of
the 1930s, Faulkner was not self-consciously rationalizing the
South for its uniqueness or for some other special qualities. But he
did *"know"* it. And it was this knowledge, which was unconscious
or at least not self-conscious, which resulted in the symbolism and,
to some extent, the form. For it was not just the South's burdensome uniqueness which Faulkner discerned but its identification
with "all the moving things" in man's history, which he wrote of as
this same eternal "frantic steeplechase toward nothing . . . no
matter where in time" which shaped and pervaded the form itself.
When Cowley suggested that Faulkner's style was a result of
solitude, Faulkner responded with candid humor:

The style, as you divine, is a result of the solitude, and granted a bad
one. It was further complicated by an inherited regional or geographical (Hawthorne would say, racial) curse. You might say, studbook
style: "by Southern Rhetoric out of Solitude" or "Oratory out of
Solitude."[46]

But while the remark is clothed in humor, the revelation is quite
serious in terms of the point we are trying to make in relating style
to content. This relationship between style and Faulkner's sensitivity to historical complexity is suggested when Faulkner wrote, "My
ambition is to put everything into one sentence—not only the
present but the whole past on which it depends and which keeps

45. Malcolm Cowley, *The Faulkner-Cowley File: Letters and Memories,
1944–1962,* pp. 115–116, emphasis mine.
46. *Ibid.,* p. 78.

overtaking the present, second by second." Cowley says "in writing his prodigious sentences he is trying to convey a sense of simultaneity, not only giving what happened in the shifting moment, but suggesting everything that went before and made the quality of that moment."[47]

The form of *Absalom, Absalom!* might ultimately be understood as a kind of atonement; as, in fact, suffering, as "an uncommon, incessant labor" through which the author attempts—driven by his sensitivity to the position of the South in history and the position of the nation outside of history—to define the present, that is to find an understanding of history which will allow Southerners and Americans to accept the burdens and responsibilities of history. Quentin fails, as is apparent both in *Absalom, Absalom!* and *The Sound and the Fury,* to work this agonizing process of atonement to a resolution; and Sutpen in *Absalom, Absalom!* also fails to accept these responsibilities. Their failure is also the South's failure and the nation's.

As I have already stated, Faulkner's purpose in *Absalom, Absalom!* was neither didactic nor nostalgic. Rather, his concern was the basic symbolic value which the past holds for the present; which Sutpen held for Quentin and which Quentin held for the South of the 1930s. Ten years earlier, Carl Becker had noted that the historian cannot deal with the event of the past itself since the past has disappeared. What he can deal with is the "statement about the event," an affirmation of the event. "In truth," Becker goes on, "the actual past is gone; and the world of history is an intangible world, re-created imaginatively, and present in our minds."[48] This attitude toward history was the approach taken by Faulkner. Because of this, *Absalom, Absalom!*—and Faulkner's other works about the past—is not a work about history, nor a historical novel in the popular sense of the word, but a rendering

47. *Ibid.,* p. 112.
48. *Detachment and the Writing of History: Essays and Letters of Carl L. Becker,* ed. Phil L. Snyder, p. 47.

of history. The facts of the novel are symbols, more than independ-
ent entities, which allow the narrators and reader to reassemble the
past "imaginatively" so that it becomes applicable to the task of
trying to find the meaning of these symbols. Faulkner not only
rejects the barriers of academic scientism (as represented by Dollard) but also those of literary "realism" as this realism restricts
the quest.

Viewed from still another perspective, we see the artistic form of
Faulkner as outside the two camps of literary and historical criticism prevalent in the literary world of 1930 as they symbolically
reflected two extremes of American society in general. On the one
hand, according to Alfred Kazin, were the Marxist critics who
displayed "an unconscious *contempt* for the past, for all that
history which must seem prehistory with the advent of Socialism."
On the other extreme, were the New Critics, such men as Allen
Tate, who "To save criticism from the scientists, . . . disengaged
literature itself from society and men, and held up the inviolate
literary experience as the only measure of human knowledge.[49]
John Crowe Ransom, in answering Calverton's charges in the
Scribner's dialogue on Southern culture, would not even mention
Southern literature. Calverton charged that the Southerners,
among whom he included Faulkner, unlike the proletarian novelists of the North, "adopt the device of escape. Instead of fighting
the evil which confronts them, they either retreat to imaginary
towers of their own construction or to a romantic past which is
equally remote from reality." Calverton regretted that Southern
writers were not politically oriented, that they "escape through
form and manner" and that they had "mounted no crusade against
the evils of the petty-bourgeoisie society which surrounds them."[50]

But if Kazin, as a young liberal writing in 1942, had harsh
words for the Marxists and the New Critics, he too saw little of

49. *On Native Grounds: An Interpretation of Modern American Prose
Literature,* pp. 416, 441.
50. "The Bankruptcy of Southern Culture," *Scribner's Magazine,* XCIX
(1936), 294.

worth in Faulkner, who "was curiously dull, furiously common-place, and often meaningless, suggesting some ambiguous irresponsibility and exasperated sullenness of mind, some distant atrophy or indifference."[51]

His absorption was too complete; it was almost a form of abnegation. . . . his need for pyrotechnics and a swollen Elizabethanism of rhetoric, his delight in difficulty and random inventiveness, became the expression of his need to impose some external intensity, an almost synthetic unity, upon his novels."[52]

Kazin sometimes seemed unable, as did other critics, to see the organic relationship between Faulkner's form and his subject matter. Viewing Faulkner from a cultural point of view, he did see Faulkner's obsession and his style as "the agony of a culture, his culture . . . the agony of his relation to that culture, the tormenting and disproportion between his immersion in the South and his flinging, tumultuous efforts to project it."[53] Yet he wrote with harsh dismissal and contempt, seeing in Faulkner the same nightmare of violence that Miss Mann of the Boston *Transcript* had seen. Because Faulkner's "corn-fed, tobacco-drooling phantoms are not the constituents of a representative American epic,"[54] they were fantasies and exaggerations, creatures of Faulkner's isolated and perhaps disturbed mind. In later years, however, notably in his essay "The Stillness of Light in August," Kazin proved himself a more sensitive and perceptive reader of Faulkner than he had been in 1942.

Some seventeen years after *Absalom, Absalom!*, at the end of the 1950s, another critic, Hyatt Waggoner, concluded of Quentin's and Shreve's quest for meaning in Sutpen's story that

The view in terms of which they operate is that of classical Christian tragedy, at once Greek and Biblical: history contains both God's judgement and men's decision, both necessity and freedom, and it has

51. Kazin, *op. cit.*, p. 456.
52. *Ibid.*, p. 459.
53. *Ibid.*, p. 465.
54. *Ibid.*

sufficient intelligibility for our human purposes. *But its meaning is neither given nor entirely withheld. It must be achieved, created by imagination and faith. Historical meaning is a construct.*[55]

History seen as a construct of imagination and faith is the highest achievement of form in *Absalom, Absalom!* Thus by the end of the 1950s, in the aftermath of Hitler and McCarthy, at least some Americans had evidently discovered Faulkner's essential meaning—that history is tragic complexity and not automatically redemptive progress.

The Mission

In 1948, with the publication of *Intruder in the Dust,* Faulkner moved as close as he ever would toward explicit participation in the final and more directly political aspect of the myth of Southern history; that of the Mission. This short novel, which lacks much of the complexity of form found in the earlier works, reveals perhaps more clearly than any of them the dichotomy within the Southern imagination between escape into the past and use of the past. *Intruder in the Dust* is the story of an attempted lynching, which centers around the efforts of a teen-aged boy, Charles (Chick) Mallison, and his uncle, Gavin Stevens, to save an old Negro, Lucas Beauchamp, from being killed for a murder which he did not commit. Stevens, the meditating, orating lawyer of Jefferson and contemporary of Quentin Compson, is almost fifty at the time the incident takes place about 1938. In one sense the boy represents what has been called the "new hope" of the younger generation of Southerners. His action to save Lucas is possible only in spite of his uncle who, unlike Quentin Compson, has survived the burden of the South's past to rationalize verbosely its inert inability to accept the present. The underlying theme of the story is based upon the relationship which has existed for some four years before the crime between the boy, Chick, and the old Negro. When Chick was twelve years old, Lucas Beauchamp pulled him out of a creek

55. Waggoner, *op. cit.,* pp. 167–168, emphasis mine.

into which he had fallen and took him to his cabin to dry off. When Chick, acting out the role of the white patron, took a few coins from his pocket and offered them to Lucas's wife, Lucas refused the coins and dropped them on the floor.

This Negro who won't "admit that he's a nigger"[56] refuses the white man's patronage. The distinctions of caste have been violated and Chick knows—dreading the knowledge—that the events of this one "irrevocable second" would now be "forever too late, forever beyond recall." Chick's first exposure to the staggering suggestion of the Negro's equality does not convince him, and during the next several months he tries to buy back the immunity he had possessed before the incident at Lucas's cabin. He saves his money and buys a dress to send to Lucas's wife. But Lucas sends back a gallon of fresh homemade sorghum molasses. What makes matters even worse for the baffled boy is that Lucas sends it by a white boy.

Chick still believes that time will bring back the caste status quo which he feels has been violated. He repeats the mistake of his national heritage: that time and space can indeed earn immunity from the commitment of history. Innocence can be regained only if one can escape—figuratively or literally—the complexities which surround him. Chick hopes for the day when Lucas will forget all about him, but when he finally believes that this has happened he learns that the Negro's seeming failure to recognize him on the street is due to the fact that Lucas's wife has just died and he is preoccupied with his own grief. Chick thinks "with a kind of amazement," "He was grieving. You don't have to not be a nigger in order to grieve" (*ID*, p. 25).

Try as he may, he is not able to free himself of an involvement with, and feeling for, the old man, not as a white man patronizing a member of an inferior caste, but as one human somewhat resentfully forced into admitting his involvement with another. Thus there is established very early in the novel this irrevocable relationship between the Negro and the white boy as human beings

---

56. William Faulkner, *Intruder in the Dust*, p. 18.

responsible to each other. The relationship is not entirely satisfac-
tory to either party, but it is one that cannot be escaped. It may be
based on love or charity; it most certainly is based on the burden
of history by way of those "irrevocable seconds" in which relationships and responsibilities in history are established. Chick, like
Quentin, is forced to deal with the burden of his own history and
with the history of his region. When he watches Lucas being
brought to the jail for the murder of a white man, Chick thinks
himself free. But Lucas asks for help, and this begins a long night's
journey through countryside and graveyard in which Chick, in
spite of the rhetorical hindrance of Uncle Gavin, leads the sheriff
to the evidence that will clear Lucas. Waggoner has suggested that
the long monologues of Stevens which accompany the plot are an
indication of Faulkner's sympathy with the Dixiecrat walkout from
the Democratic party in 1948 in protest over President Truman's
advocacy of stronger, more effective civil rights laws, but it should
also be pointed out that it is Gavin Stevens, not Chick, who can be
identified with the Dixiecrats and the Agrarians.[57] He tells Chick
that the South is the only relatively "homogeneous region" of the
country left. In addition, the Negro and Southern white should
confederate. Together they could present "a front not only impregnable but not even to be threatened by a mass of people who
no longer have anything in common save a frantic greed for money
and a basic fear of a failure of national character which they hide
from one another behind a loud lipservice to a flag" (*ID,* p. 156).
If we see Gavin Stevens as the sole spokesman for Faulkner and
for the South, we overlook Chick's role. Insofar as the novel is
concerned, Chick may be seen as the South finally in action; while
his uncle, hampered in action by his membership in the generation
of Quentin Compson, suggests the South in intellectual quandary,
driven back to the same kind of defensiveness that the Agrarians
had displayed in *I'll Take My Stand.* For it is Chick who persuades
his uncle that an element of doubt exists as to Lucas's guilt, and it
is Chick who gets the older man involved in the hectic drive and

---

57. Waggoner, *op. cit.,* p. 219.

chase through the Mississippi countryside to find the necessary evidence. We have only to compare Stevens and Chick speeding through the hot, green countryside toward justice for a black man with Quentin's ponderous internal struggle in the grey New England cold of his Harvard room to see the difference between the two quests. Quentin is defeated before he begins because he himself is a ghost of the tradition of innocence made impossible by his race's own burden of guilt. What action there is, is into the past in a futile search for the meaning of his own and his culture's dilemma. Chick, on the other hand, moves forward through the ruts and loose gravel of time and history, dragging the hindering "truth" of Gavin Stevens's rhetoric with him in an attempt to do justice rather than to preserve the illusions of Southern uniqueness. Gavin Stevens's interest in preventing the lynching is perhaps to prove, as Malcolm Cowley suggested in a review in the *New Republic,* that the federal anti-lynch law which Truman wanted is not a necessity if white Southerners will do their duty as members of a "homogeneous," honor-bound society. But Chick's interest is concerned primarily with the burden of humanity which his association with Lucas has placed upon him. He acts, not only in spite of his uncle's initial hindrance, but also in the face of a whole nation's innocence and "helplessness" as it stares at the burdened South from its vantage point of its own "rich teeming never-ravaged land of glittering undefiled cities and unburned towns and unwasted farms" (*ID,* p. 152). Cowley was wrong to associate Faulkner's position in *Intruder* with the defensive and chauvinistic attitude expressed in *I'll Take My Stand.* The Agrarians made great efforts to avoid coming to grips with the burden of history which Chick encounters—somewhat in the manner of Gavin Stevens at the beginning of *Intruder.* Chick is the first white character in Faulkner's Southern saga to make a positive act, not only of atonement for his region's past, but also toward racial justice for the nation's future. The response to history which is suggested in his action, had it actually materialized among white Americans, might have prevented the tragedies of Oxford, Watts, and Detroit.

✤ IV   Robert Penn Warren and the Promise of History

The Children of Darkness

AGAINST overwhelming odds, the twelve Southerners who wrote *I'll Take My Stand* had defended their concept of Jeffersonian agrarian innocence against the dehumanizing complexity and materialism of the urban-industrial twentieth century. They had chosen to ignore tactfully the problem of race relations in the United States and particularly in the South. William Faulkner, while not wholly divorced from the Nashville group's agrarian romanticism, had nevertheless portrayed the South as part of a great racial tragedy. In turning inward to the dilemma of regional consciousness, Faulkner had criticized some of the same national myths of unlimited acquisitive progress as had the Agrarians. But Faulkner could find no panaceas. At the end of the 1930s, *Absalom, Absalom!* stood, as it still stands, as Faulkner's most profound exploration of the South's problems with its own history and with the history of the nation. It seemed to many that Faulkner's dark and entangled perspective on human nature cut him off from the main stream of American thinking and made of him some kind of exploiter of misery and gloom. And it did certainly make of him a dissenter from prevailing and long-standing American views of

131

man and the sanctity of the individual. Along with the sociologists and psychologists, Faulkner had challenged the concept of the natural goodness of man and of the American individual, and in this sense he was moving with, rather than against, history. Not only were the environmental sciences contributing to a developing new attitude toward human nature, but even theology, adopting some of the attitudes, if not the actual methods, of the social sciences, saw the "religious situation" as a "cultural, historical episode or crisis in which men must face both each other and God in order to make their religious decisions and formulate their faiths."[1] The most outspoken American theologian involved in this effort to turn the "attention of observers of religion from the private and 'solitary' aspects of experience to human history and culture, to man's institutions and customs, to vested interests and funded meanings" was Reinhold Niebuhr.[2] In Niebuhr's basic ideas we see Faulkner's concern with individual guilt within a culture, Robert Penn Warren's concern with individual and collective guilt, and Martin Luther King's concern with individual and collective love and action in the cause of justice—all developments in the uses of Southern history linked together with the nation's painful, hesitant, and sometimes tragic confrontation with history in the decades after 1945.

Reinhold Niebuhr, like Warren, was born in a border state—Warren in Kentucky in 1905, Niebuhr thirteen years earlier in Wright City, Missouri, a small town near St. Louis. Spending his boyhood first in Wright City, then in St. Charles, and then in Lincoln, Illinois, Niebuhr saw, if he did not yet recognize, the evils of racial discrimination and segregation and the division of class and caste. He attended Elmhurst College in Elmhurst, Illinois, Eden Theological Seminary in St. Louis, and Yale University. In 1915 he was ordained as a minister of the Evangelical Synod of the

1. Herbert Wallace Schneider, *Religion in Twentieth Century America,* p. 186.
    2. *Ibid.,* p. 185.

Lutheran church and became pastor of the Bethel Evangelical
Church of Detroit, where he served until 1928. It was here,
according to Niebuhr, that he was first forced by the realities of a
rapidly expanding industrial community to "reconsider the liberal
and highly moralistic creed which I had accepted as tantamount to
the Christian faith."[3] His first book, *Does Civilization Need Religion* (1927), resulted from his experiences in the industrial Detroit
of Henry Ford; and his next book, *Moral Man and Immoral
Society* (1932), "was a somber and powerful rejection of the
Social-Gospel-Dewey amalgam, with its faith in the politics of love
and reason."[4] "Inasfar as this treatise has a polemic interest,"
Niebuhr wrote, "it is directed against the moralists, both religious
and secular, who imagine that the egoism of individuals is being
progressively checked by the development of rationality or the
growth of a religiously inspired goodwill and that nothing but the
continuance of this process is necessary to establish social harmony
between all the human societies and collectives."[5]

What is lacking among all these moralists, whether religious or rational, is an understanding of the brutal character of the behavior of all
human collectives, and the power of self-interest and collective egoism
in all inter-group relations. . . . They do not see that the limitations of
the human imagination, the easy subservience of reason to prejudice
and passion, and the consequent persistence of irrational egoism,
particularly in group behavior, make social conflict an inevitability in
human history, probably to its very end.[6]

Niebuhr would have agreed with the Southern Agrarians that
there was a dehumanizing factor built into the structure of an
industrial society. But while he agreed that in such a society man's
injustice to man was increased, he also believed that this injustice

---

3. *Reinhold Niebuhr: His Religious, Social, and Political Thought,* ed.
Charles W. Kegley and Robert W. Bretall, II, 5.
    4. *Ibid.,* p. 134.
    5. *Moral Man and Immoral Society: A Study in Ethics and Politics,* p.
xii.
    6. *Ibid.,* p. xx.

was merely an aggravation of the injustices "from which men have perennially suffered."[7] There was for Niebuhr nothing uniquely evil about industrial society, nor did he believe that industrial society with all of its injustice and dehumanization could be avoided. It had to be confronted in the political, social, and spiritual realms, which might involve violence and revolution. It most certainly would involve the political process, which is "a twilight zone where ethical and technical issues meet. . . . [where] Immediate consequences must be weighed against the ultimate consequences."[8] This candidly pragmatic approach to the ethics of politics would later be developed by Robert Penn Warren in the character of Willie Stark. Niebuhr, remembering his experiences in Detroit and perhaps his years in Missouri, used race relations to illustrate the problem, noting that, while there were "moral and rational forces at work for the improvement of relations between whites and Negroes," these forces must operate within the larger framework of injustice through political disfranchisement and economic disinheritance. Real equality, which for Niebuhr is a higher value than mere order, could never be achieved without force, preferably nonviolent force.[9] Mere education and faith in the white man's willingness to grant the Negro his equality would not work. "Upon this point one may speak with a dogmatism which all history justifies."[10] Martin Luther King, as we will see in the next chapter, was to be profoundly influenced by Niebuhr's ideas. This was a commitment to the realities of history which the Agrarians had been unable to make, as Warren's essay on race relations illustrates. It was also clear that Faulkner, who shared much of Niebuhr's insight into human nature and the consequent structure and meaning of history, portrayed Quentin Compson and Thomas Sutpen as individuals paralyzed and destroyed by their inability to confront their own responsibilities in history.

7. *Ibid.,* p. 276.
8. *Ibid.,* p. 171.
9. *Ibid.,* pp. 252–254.
10. *Ibid.,* p. 253.

Niebuhr's criticism of liberal optimism continued through the depression into the 1940s. In 1944, as the American invasion of Hitler's Europe progressed, Niebuhr published a small book called *The Children of Light and the Children of Darkness* in which he again noted the danger of the democratic illusion that an "easy resolution of the tension and conflict between self-interest and the general interest" can be achieved. The "Children of Darkness" were those who "know no law beyond their will and interest." Because they understand no law beyond the self, they are evil, but they are also wise because they do understand all too well the power of self-interest. The " 'Children of Light' believe that self-interest should be brought under the discipline of a higher law" and for this reason are virtuous. But the children of light are also foolish "because they do not know the power of self-will," not merely among the children of darkness, but among themselves:

Modern democratic civilization is, in short, sentimental rather than cynical. It has an easy solution for the problem of anarchy and chaos on both the national and international level of community, because of its fatuous and superficial view of man.[11]

The problem was to make the children of light aware of the darkness not only within their enemies but within themselves and within human nature generally. One means to this end was the use of history. For Niebuhr, according to Gordon Harland, history "is never simply something 'back there,' it is the depth dimension of our present. . . . a venture in self-understanding."[12] History is a complex pattern of freedom and necessity. This is history as Faulkner had seen it and as Warren would see it. And Niebuhr, like Faulkner and Warren, understood that those best qualified to interpret this depth-dimension for the sake of national self-understanding might very well be those who had suffered most at the hands of history.

11. *The Children of Light and the Children of Darkness: A Vindication of Democracy and a Critique of its Traditional Defence,* pp. 9–11.
12. *The Thought of Reinhold Niebuhr,* p. 91.

Who is better able to understand the true character of a civilisation than those who suffer most from its limitations? Who is better able to state the social ideal in unqualified terms than those who have experienced the bankruptcy of old social realities in their own lives? Who will have more creative vigor in destroying the old and building the new than those in whose lives hunger, vengeance and holy dreams have compounded a tempestuous passion?[13]

Here, Niebuhr is speaking specifically of the proletariat class, but the assumptions are the same as those underlying the myth of Southern history. While Niebuhr, Faulkner, and Warren moved in the 1930s in parallel lines of intellectual exploration, another event, World War II and its aftermath, was to become the dramatic and visible symbol by which many Americans would finally become aware of the complex and ambiguous world of light and darkness in which their destiny as a nation and as individuals lay. The Depression, the rise of Hitler, the murder of the Jews, and the nuclear attack upon the civilians of two Japanese cities conspired to reveal the shallowness of liberal optimism. It was in 1944, the year of Niebuhr's *The Children of Light and the Children of Darkness* that "genocide" became a part of the language. The legacy of World War II was the violent reassertion of the old Calvinistic concept of human depravity and the total corruption of human nature. Man's potential for evil had not been destroyed or even defeated by this greatest of global wars. It had only been exposed and etched into the minds of all who dared retain their consciences. Americans who had spent three centuries trying to escape the dark insights of their Puritan forefathers, who had built a society and civilization based on the theory of human perfectibility, and who had striven to escape history were suddenly in 1945 drawn back into human history. They were confronted with those Calvinistic visions believed to have been dispatched by H. L. Mencken *et al.,* and forced to observe with Jonathan Edwards, addressing "Sinners in the Hands of an Angry God," that "the corruption of the heart of man is a thing that is immoderate and

13. *Moral Man and Immoral Society,* p. 157.

boundless in its fury and while wicked men live here, it is like fire pent up by God's restraints, whereas if it were let loose it would set on fire the course of nature; and as the heart is now a sink of sin, so, if sin was not restrained, it would immediately turn the soul into a fiery oven, or a furnace of fire and brimstone." In the aftermath of ovens at Buchenwald and firestorms over Hiroshima, Americans in 1945 could not even be sure that God did still restrain the flames.

The story of Nazi atrocities committed against civilians and political prisoners came out through the Nuremberg War Trials and the vivid photographic journalism of American magazines.[14] Stories of Japanese cannibalism and sadism against prisoners of war were common. Returning American soldiers knew too, even if they did not talk about it, that no one side had a monopoly on sadism and the lust for violence and destruction. There *were* Americans like Croft in Norman Mailer's *The Naked and the Dead* and Buzz Marrow in John Hersey's *The War Lover,* and this too was a part of the new heritage. Even in the states, "in every section . . . on all levels of society, the ill-tempered, the mean, the vicious in human beings pushed to the fore."[15] And most terrifying of all, Americans knew that their forces, in two isolated moments, had killed over 100,000 Japanese, most of them civilians, with atomic bombs in "an unparalleled man-made disaster which may or may not have been justified by the ending of a bloody war."[16] The suddenness of the act and the doubts about its justification were to plague the American imagination from that moment, and as a new generation of Americans grew up in the atmosphere of the cold war, even the destruction of the American Indian race in the nineteenth century and the parallels between American racism and Nazi racism—most ironically evident in the discrimination against the Negro servicemen who helped defeat Nazi racism—merged

14. E.g., "Atrocities," *Life,* May 7, 1945, pp. 32–37.
15. Eric F. Goldman, *The Crucial Decade: America, 1945–1955,* p. 42.
16. "Christmas Book," *The Saturday Review of Literature,* XXIX (December 7, 1946), 28.

with the knowledge of Hiroshima into a new burden of guilt and frustration as America tried to justify and to assume its role as leader of the "free world." The spy scandals and subversion investigations of the late forties and early fifties, the loss of China to Communism, the development of the atomic bomb by Russia, and the growing cries of anti-Americanism from abroad merely underlined the fact that this country—as in no other period of its history —was totally involved in a world where the children of darkness could not really be distinguished from the self-willed children of light.

From Guthrie to the World

If, as Hyatt Waggoner's subtitle implies, Faulkner's art carries meaning which expands "from Jefferson to the world," it could also be said that Robert Penn Warren's life experience itself carried his own development as an artist and philosophical historian from the land of his childhood in Kentucky to the world. Both literally and intellectually, Warren's life is a record of movement out from the provincial. He was born in Todd County, Kentucky, on April 24, 1905, three years after the publication of *The Leopard's Spots* and five years before the date given in Faulkner's *Absalom, Absalom!* for Quentin Compson's suicide. As a scholar and as a poet, Warren's quest has been for a critical understanding of the two poles of Southern response that these novels demonstrate. As a Southerner, his quest has been for some middle ground between them—the middle ground between racism and guilt to the point of self-destruction. That he spent his early life in Kentucky and Tennessee, both border states in terms of geography and sympathy, suggests yet another dimension to his point of view. Not only is his view of the South complex, as was Faulkner's, but in addition his view of the relationship between the sections is equally complex, making his understanding of the national imagination even more profound than Faulkner's. Leonard Casper has noted that what he calls Warren's vision of the "dialectic course of man's compulsion to be known" requires in all of its dimensions a "great capacity for discovering a sufficient variety of plausible human references to warrant its existence." While the divided loyalties and unsure position of a resident of a border state might make a man feel estranged from all society, "Warren's adaptiveness has rewarded him instead with a multiplicity of perspectives."[17]

Until he was fifteen, Warren attended school in Guthrie, Kentucky, which would later provide the background for his first novel, *Night Rider*. Already, as a young boy, Warren was a prodigious reader, consuming "the usual nineteenth century novelists, the Boy Scout books, Buckle's *History of Civilization,* Darwin, thrillers, detective stories, a lot of poetry, Macaulay and Gibbon, and a good deal of American history."[18] Even in these early years, then, his perspective was broadening, exposing him not only to such regionally tabooed authors as Charles Darwin but, more important, to liberal quantities of history and poetry, two disciplines which were to figure heavily in his later career. The later effects of this expanding outlook are perhaps suggested in the prefatory note to *Night Rider,* in which he insists that although the events of the novel are based on actual events of the past, the book is not to be construed as a "historical novel." In Warren's statement we sense a possible desire on his part to disassociate his novel from the genre of Southern historical romances which, most recently, had spawned *Gone With the Wind.* In 1939, as the film version of Miss Mitchell's novel was breaking all box office records, it may well have seemed necessary, especially for a young and sensitive Southerner, to make such a qualifying statement explicit in order that his work would not be judged as just another provincial historical romance.

From Guthrie, Warren, sixteen, went in 1921 to Vanderbilt University at Nashville, Tennessee. He went there to study science, but a poor showing in freshman chemistry and "the positive influ-

17. *Robert Penn Warren: The Dark and Bloody Ground,* pp. 11–12.
18. *Twentieth Century Authors: A Biographical Dictionary of Modern Literature,* ed. Stanley J. Kunitz, Supplement I, p. 1477.

ence" of Donald Davidson and John Crowe Ransom altered his plans; and by the second year of college he was "spending a good deal of time writing poetry."[19] This early disenchantment with science as a profession was not, however, to end his concern with science as a cultural phenomenon and as a poetic image through which to portray the problems of the twentieth century. Years later, in *All the King's Men,* he would make one of his most tragic characters a scientist.

In 1925 Warren went to the University of California, where he took an M.A., and, after another year of graduate work at Yale, he went to Oxford as a Rhodes Scholar, where he received the B.Litt. degree in 1930. While he was in England he wrote "Briar Patch" for *I'll Take My Stand.* It was then that Donald Davidson asked what was happening to "Red" over there to lead him to write an essay on the delicate question of race in the South, an essay that to Davidson did not seem quite delicate enough. Already, in 1930, Warren had seen as much of the world as Faulkner would in a lifetime. At the age of twenty-five, he was a published poet and a serious scholar of literature and history. He had come of age as an American in the middle of the 1920s and could share that generation's disillusionment with American life and the failure of the American promise. At the same time, in his traveling he may have sensed something more than the disillusionment of a single generation and a minority at that—something more like the disillusionment of a civilization which, in turn, may have reinforced the tragic view of life and history suggested by his own reading. As a Southerner, he could also look back on the past of his region and find a disillusionment which ran deeper than the expatriates could ever imagine. Here was the potential spark of what both Warren and Woodward would later call the South's identity with a larger world of experience as opposed to the American world of innocence. What Faulkner could suggest with agonizing intensity in *Absalom, Absalom!,* Warren, using the grand framework of Faulk-

19. *Ibid.*

ner's explorations, could explore in *All the King's Men* and *Brother to Dragons* with no less artistic intensity but with the additional aid of a trained, critically and historically oriented mind. As Reynolds Price, a Southern novelist and short-story writer, has written, "the service of Faulkner to subsequent Southern writers has not been that of a rich lode to be prospected by night for plots, characters and rhetoric, but the service of a father to son—to demonstrate a few of the things a man may do, to sketch in the air some of the shapes of possibility."[20]

There is in *Night Rider* an attitude toward the South and some of its myths which opens the doors to a new consciousness of the past in the present and, more specifically, of the South as part of the nation. The novel may be understood as a reaction to that South imagined by the Agrarians in *I'll Take My Stand*. In approaching the novel in this manner, Warren challenges one of the primary tenets of the myth of Southern history; namely, Southern uniqueness.

The story of the Kentucky tobacco wars[21] narrated in *Night Rider* takes place at about the same point in time as Quentin Compson's unsuccessful struggle with the South's past. Warren's concern, however, is neither the burden of race nor the virtues of a peculiar regional past or way of life. The characters are basically Americans rather than "Southerners." One of the board of directors of "The Association of Growers of Dark Fired Tobacco" expresses doubts that the farmers from a particular section can be brought into the Association because "A lot of 'em up there are a mite ornery. Half those folks went with the Yankees in the war." Mr. Christian, another board member, declares, "A hand of tobacco is a hand of tobacco, and I like any Yankee I ever saw a hell of a sight better'n I like a buyer."[22]

The animosities are not between regions but between economic

20. "Speaking of Books: A Question of Influence," New York *Times Book Review,* May 29, 1966, p. 2.
21. *Night Rider,* pp. 14–27.
22. *Ibid.,* p. 17.

classes represented by factions of the tobacco industry. The farmers are stubborn, not because of regional characteristics, but perhaps because of their own rural conservatism, with which all the reform movements of Populism and Progressivism had to contend in all sections of the country during those years of discontent and reform. There are, it is true, several raids and burnings directed against planters because they use Negro help instead of white help. Whether these are manifestations of anti-Negro feeling or thinly disguised retaliation by anti-Association men is not made clear. But these incidents are few and relatively incidental in the over-all story. The suggestion in *Night Rider* is that the danger of moral and economic corruption from the North upon Dixie in the 1930s is little more than part of a myth of national innocence. The tobacco farmers' revolt is not a revolt of virtuous Old South yeomen against the evil capitalists who are building the New South, but a struggle for power between hostile segments of the same economic structure. The picture of Bunk Trevelyan murdering another farmer in a feud over water rights and later trying to blackmail a member of the Association is not the picture of the virtuous Southern agrarian which one finds in *I'll Take My Stand*. Similarly, Mr. Munn, coldly seducing his wife, or coldly putting the first bullet into Trevelyan when he is lynched for betraying the Association, is hardly the philosopher-planter who benevolently reigns over the pastoral, agrarian South imagined by Southerners and Northerners alike. Nor are any of these characters as heroic and imposing in their sin and corruption as the characters of *Absalom, Absalom!* One might read Faulkner's novel and still assume that such people live only in the South, which according to popular thinking tends toward a kind of heroic violence. But Mr. Munn is without regional distinction and could as easily pass for a lawyer and planter from Iowa as from the South. Bunk Trevelyan suggests a dirt farmer in any state, and the revolt of the tobacco farmers is part of the general populist revolt at the turn of the century. W. J. Cash, awed by the uniqueness of the Old South, saw violence itself as a peculiarly Southern quality growing out of

"Southern" individualism. Even Faulkner's characters sometimes suggest this. But in Warren's works, even as early as *Night Rider*, there is no possibility of such a regional limitation. That Warren, as an American author, could write an American novel which takes place in the South but which is *not* a "Southern historical" novel is the essential meaning of his insistence that he has "not written in any strict sense, a historical novel." Instead, it was a ground-clearing novel in which a great many of the stereotyped characters and images found in the novels of Faulkner and Dixon were put aside in preparation for a new synthesis of Southern life as part of the national life.

This development toward an "American" South continued in *At Heaven's Gate* (1943), which is a story set in the South of the 1920s. The novel's characters reflect all of the cultural and moral confusion and drift associated with the 1920s nationally. Bogan Murdock, "the finance capitalist *par excellence*," whose grandfather had grown rich through land speculation, whose father had killed a political opponent, and whose own financial corruption is finally exposed, uses the death of his daughter, Sue, to distract public attention from a scandal involving his financial manipulations. He poses with the rest of his family in mourning and invokes the memory of another Southerner and patriot, Andrew Jackson, whose portrait hangs on the wall: " 'Courage, it is the heritage of all of us—of all citizens of this State. Courage,' he says, and turns and indicates with a glance the portrait, as large as life, above the fireplace."[23] The seeming irony of a man like Murdock speaking of the old Jacksonian courage is lessened by the closing paragraph in the book which describes the painting:

It is the portrait of a man who, more than a century ago, endured cold and hunger, who killed men with his own hand, who survived steaming malarial swamps and long marches, who was ruthless, vindictive, cunning, and headstrong, who was president of his country, who died in the admiration, or hatred, of millions of men. There is the painted face: the sunken flesh over the grim jawbone, the deep, smoldering

23. Robert Penn Warren, *At Heaven's Gate*, p. 391.

eyes, the jutting beak of a nose, and the coarse crest of grayish hair, like an old cockatoo (*AHG,* p. 391).

At work here was Warren's own developing consciousness of the past in the present. All of what Bogan Murdock represents, all of what America of the 1920s represents, is encompassed in the dark, grim face of this ruthless, vindictive, and cunning man, who—like Thomas Sutpen—epitomizes his own century. The similarities between Sutpen and Horatio Alger are implicit. The link between Murdock and another cultural hero, Andrew Jackson, is explicit. Nature and man have always been conquered and, if necessary, destroyed in the quest for whatever designs or ideals draw individuals toward their destiny. The tragedies and horrors of the present are rooted in the past, thus making the past part of the present. As we realize this, our conception of the past changes to make our present more comprehensible and our future more hopeful. It is the full development of this point of view which makes *All the King's Men* and *Brother to Dragons* two of the most significant artistic and intellectual works of this century.

More than either of Warren's first two novels, *All the King's Men* (1946) is an *American* novel which happens to take place in the South. It is narrated by Jack Burden, a Southerner by birth and an American of the Lost Generation by commitment—or rather lack of commitment—who is suddenly forced to live in a world in which romantic disenchantment and indifference lead only to destruction. At the very beginning, the reader is confronted by imagery which aptly combines a regional phenomenon—climate —with a national symbol—the machine—to present a gripping and terrifying picture of the American landscape in the twentieth century: an endless trip down an endless, well-engineered road of smooth concrete and tar cutting through the countryside, heading toward what might be water and coolness but which is only an illusion created by the heat reflecting up from the hot surface of the pavement. The dazzling heat, the whining tires, and the endless black line can hypnotize and destroy whoever lets himself be lured by the painless monotony of the new highway and the age of concrete and steel and rubber. This is an age which derives some kind of morbid satisfaction by keeping score of its own self-destruction with little "white metal squares" along the highways to mark the scenes of fatal accidents. The young men—the Cavalier candidates of earlier fiction—now take race-car drivers as their idols. And in this land where "the smell of gasoline and red-eye is sweeter than myrrh," the Southern belle is transformed into a crooked-spined little provincial flapper who perspires, wears no underclothes, and is not above spreading her legs to bathe the very seat of her maidenly virtue in the hot, humid air blowing in through the hood ventilator of the roaring machine (*AKM*, p. 4). In such an environment, the stereotypes of Southern womanhood, Southern chivalry, and Southern hospitality are without meaning.

In the characters of Jack Burden and Willie Stark we see more fully the national aspects of the novel. Burden explains his "Idealism":

I had got hold of the principle out of a book when I was in college, and I had hung on to it for grim death. I owed my success in life to that principle. It had put me where I was. What you don't know don't hurt you, for it ain't real. They called that Idealism . . . If you are an Idealist it does not matter what you do or what goes on around you because it isn't real anyway (*AKM*, p. 33).

With this philosophy, Burden is able to remain detached for the complex and ambiguous events shaping the destruction of his friends Willie Stark and Adam Stanton. When Judge Irwin and Willie confront each other and exchange contemptuous insults, Burden stands removed, refusing to participate: "From my spot by the wall, I looked at both of them. *To hell with them,* I thought, *to hell with both of them.* When they talked like that, it was to hell with both of them" (*AKM*, p. 49).

Like the "lost" generation of Americans of which he is a member, Burden had made a separate peace, refusing to become involved or committed in the struggle between idea and action, between good and evil. The Jack Burden of most of the novel's plot—as distinguished from Jack Burden the narrator, who is a sadder and wiser man—is a participant and an observer, but morally he is a "piece of furniture" to be moved around at will by those who command his loyalty.

This noninvolvement is suggested most dramatically in the chapter where, as college students, Jack Burden and Anne are left alone in his house on a dark, stormy night. They go to his bedroom, where he undresses her and almost makes love to her. But in undressing Anne, he does not touch her and cannot bring himself to make the initial and symbolic contact of flesh with flesh. His image of Anne is the essence of innocence. He cannot commit himself by touching her, for this would spoil the innocence of their relationship. Making love to Anne would commit both of them to the "violent" sky and shadows and beating rain of the world outside the window, and to each other. He cannot sacrifice his conceptions of innocence to the world of knowledge and evil. He must keep the two separated.

Willie Stark, on the other hand, is a practical Calvinist, a man of action, a pragmatist drawn in part, according to Warren, after the "scholarly and benign figure of William James" (*AKM,* p. vi). As a Calvinist he believes in original sin. "You don't have to frame somebody," he tells Jack Burden when Burden balks at digging up "dirt" on Judge Irwin to force him to withdraw his opposition to Willie Stark's governorship. "You don't ever have to frame anybody, because the truth is always sufficient. . . . I went to a Presbyterian Sunday school . . . and that much of it stuck (*AKM,* p. 358) . . . Man is conceived in sin and born in corruption and he passeth from the stink of the didie to the stench of the shroud. There is always something" (*AKM,* p. 54). As a pragmatist, Willie believes that the law is like "a single-bed blanket on a double bed and three folks in the bed and a cold night. . . . The law is always too short and too tight for growing humankind" (*AKM,* p. 145).

Law and institutions, he believes, must give way to need. "Your need," he cries to a crowd of citizens, "is my justice." It is not always possible to wait around for the law to be changed before the need is met. The means are to be judged by the end. Good comes out of evil. "Dirt's a funny thing," he tells the Judge on that night in the Judge's library.

There ain't a thing but dirt on this green God's globe. . . . It's dirt makes the grass grow. A diamond ain't a thing in the world but a piece of dirt that got awful hot. And God-a-Mighty picked up a handful of dirt and blew on it and made you and me and George Washington and mankind blessed in faculty and apprehension. It all depends on what you do with the dirt (*AKM*, p. 50).

This philosophy is the dynamics of Willie Stark. Neither Quentin Compson in *Absalom, Absalom!* nor Jack Burden can understand this. Quentin is unable to act and finally is destroyed by the burden of man's evil. Jack Burden unwittingly destroys his friends by allowing himself to be held immobile by the burden of innocence, disguised as "Idealism."

It is in the story of the early Willie Stark that we see the development and historical implications of his philosophy. As an honest county treasurer, he objects when the contract for a new school building is given to the highest instead of a lower bidder. Willie's suggestions of political graft and corruption go unheeded, and he is defeated. The school is built, but during a fire drill three years later a fire escape filled with children collapses because of the faulty bricks which had been used in its construction. Three children are killed, and several more are permanently crippled. Willie becomes a local hero but does not run for office until one of the warring factions of the state Democratic machine sets him up as a gubernatorial candidate to split the vote of the other faction's candidate. In the still-lingering afterglow of his local vindication on the schoolhouse issue, Willie does not suspect that he is being used. He is deceived by the apparent or at least potential good of rational human nature. With calm reason and the God of the Universe on his side he sets out to lead the people from the darkness toward a new justice and a better life. But his Jeffersonian idealism is badly shaken when first Jack Burden and then

Sadie Burke fill him in on the facts of political life. Burden tells
him to forget the facts and figures and high ideals. If he wants
votes, he must entertain the people and "stir 'em up and make 'em
feel alive again. Just for half an hour. That's what they come for.
Tell 'em anything. But for Sweet Jesus' sake don't try to improve
their minds" (*AKM*, p. 77).

After Sadie Burke tells him that he is being deliberately used to
split "the hick vote," Willie is forced to admit the general corruption of human nature, which his earlier experiences with particular
individuals had already demonstrated. Now, Willie, "the sap,"
becomes Willie, the boss. He destroys the Democratic party machine and becomes governor and government. In destroying or
intimidating the institutions of government, he takes the first step
toward ultimate failure, for he has eliminated the possibility that
whatever good he might do might be preserved, after his death, in
a permanent institutional structure. Obviously, the character of
Willie Stark is much too complex to be defined only in terms of the
"Southern demagogue" stereotype. Willie Stark, as an American, is
caught between the Jeffersonian view of man and the Calvinistic
view of man. The quest for justice through reason must be evalu-
ated in terms of man's general evil and irrationality. Willie's belief
that good must come out of evil comes from his discovery that
justice must be achieved in history with the materials and terms
that history offers. These materials include the "hicks" and the
grafters—the children of darkness—as well as the dreamers and
thinkers—the children of light. Willie's tragic flaw, however, is that
he understands the content of history without really understanding
the form. He understands that history must contain evil as well as
good, commitment through action as well as commitment to ideal.
But as an American committed to the tenets of individualism, he
does not understand the necessity for institutional form in history.
When life in the corrupted and complex areas of civilization
becomes impossible, Thomas Sutpen strikes out on his own as an
individual. Similarly, when Willie Stark learns that there is evil in
the political institutions of his state, he strikes out as an individual;

in this case, destroying the political machinery in order to implement his ideals outside the inefficient and corrupted institutional organization of democratic politics; in other words, without regard for history. As Niebuhr noted, those who would be children of light often do fail to recognize the existence of darkness within their own motivations and actions. Such individuals believe that they can use corruption to work good without in turn being corrupted. Such self-reliance is not enough to guarantee the survival of the dream of a great society against the outraged innocence of an Adam Stanton. Adam as a scientist is committed to an ideal, "tidy," rather romantic world of mathematical, logical relationships. Willie Stark is committed to the less tidy world of action. After Adam and Willie destroy each other, it is Jack Burden who is left to ponder the meaning behind the tragedy—to resolve, if he can, the conflict between innocence and knowledge, between idea and action. Ultimately, for Warren, this amounted to a quest for a resolution between the myths of American history and the unpleasant realities of Southern history.

From "Sutpen's Hundred" to the *Maison Carrée*

Warren's control of his Southern themes, settings, and characters so that they merge into a greater thematic framework of national implication builds upon Faulkner's achievement, in which the regional dimension of character, setting, and theme more nearly dominate the form. To understand this development in Warren's thought more clearly, we may turn to *Brother to Dragons,* published seven years after *All the King's Men.* Here we will examine in particular Warren's use of the imagery of neoclassical architecture which we have already examined in works by Dixon and Faulkner.

For Dixon, the plantation house with its Grecian columns and white portico represented the order and simplicity of a social order based on white supremacy. For Faulkner, the house and the style represented irresponsible innocence, greed, racial irresponsibility, and, in general, the decay of the Old South, mythical or otherwise.

In *Brother to Dragons*, we find the national hero Thomas Jefferson —a Southerner as well as a founding father—explaining his conception of man's innocence and how an ancient Roman temple in France had come to symbolize for him the hopes of rational men. Jefferson is the man of the Enlightenment, with no illusions about the potential evil of men, yet sure of man's redeemability through reason. He is contemptuous of "the Gothic night," the medieval Christian world which had erected the "abominable relics of carved stone" as monuments to darkness and ignorance. But then, in the same country of Chartres and Notre Dame he comes upon the "Square House," the "Maison Quarree" [*sic*] at Nîmes:

I stood in the *place* and saw it. There is no way
For words to put that authoritative reserve and glorious frugality.
. . . .
                                              . . . It spoke
Of a fair time yet to come, but soon
If we might take man's hand, strike shackle, lead him forth
From his own monstrous nightmare—then his natural innocence
Would dance like sunlight over the delighted landscape.[24]

For Warren's Jefferson, the Roman temple symbolizes the goodness and rationality of human nature just as the medieval cathedrals symbolize the malevolence and perversity of which man is capable. The *Maison Carrée* symbolizes the rational civilization which man is capable of building; nature redeemed from the corruptions of religious ignorance and superstition. In its "authoritative reserve and glorious frugality"—diction reminiscent as much of the New England Puritan as of the Virginia Cavalier—the temple suggests a future when man would live in a state of natural innocence, free from the dark medieval world, free from the "monstrous nightmare" which had oppressed him for centuries. It would be an ordered universe, a Newtonian universe, which Jefferson imagines as "bright pendentives, coigns, and cornices of the sky."

The *Maison Carrée,* for all of its grandeur, is only the symbol of

24. Robert Penn Warren, *Brother to Dragons,* pp. 39–41.

man's potential, of his ability to redeem nature and man in nature. For all of the temple's simplicity and honesty, it stands on a continent covered and corrupted by the "abominable relics" of medieval civilization. But the American West—for Jefferson all of that great area of Louisiana west of "the mountains"—offers an ideal site for man's monuments to order and rationality, to simplicity and innocence:

Swale and savannah and the tulip-tree
Immortally blossoming to May,
. . . .
It was great Canaan's grander counterfeit.
Bold Louisiana,
It was the landfall of my soul (*BTD*, p. 11).

The great American West seems to Jefferson the promised land for his fellow children of light and for all the hopes which fill his soul at Nîmes. He pictures himself as an American Moses, bringing his people into "his" West, into the new land of Canaan, fertile, "immortally blossoming to May"; where all of nature, the sun, the moon, the tame bison and seal await "in delight" the coming of man, and where the "illimitable glitter of distance dazzles" in anticipation of the great fulfillment of redeemed nature and humanity which man will render in this new land where he is unencumbered by the fetters of evil European institutions such as the church and the crown.

In Jefferson's conception of the West, shared by countless eighteenth- and nineteenth-century Americans, Warren found the origins of the Myth of the American Garden which historians—notably Frederick Jackson Turner and Henry Nash Smith—have examined in great detail. This is not to say that no one before Jefferson had dreamed of the great inner continent in such terms. But in Warren's poem Jefferson provides a focal point, for it was he who, as President, ordered the exploration of the West by Meriwether Lewis and William Clark. In addition, it is in Jefferson's vision that the mythology of the American West and the mythology of the European Enlightenment of the eighteenth century join into a positive, optimistic synthesis combining nature with civilization. The order and wisdom of the classical world as understood by the eighteenth-century mind were to be combined with the virtues of American republicanism and agrarianism. This is the vision of the "real" America for which the Nashville Agrarians, one hundred thirty years after the journeys of the Lewis and Clark expedition, were to take their stand arguing that, historically, only the South had actually had such a way of life, and that in twentieth-century America only the South had been able to preserve such a way of life. What is understood in *Brother to Dragons,* however, is that Jefferson is not just a Southerner but also an American and that whatever good or evil is rendered by his dreams of the *Maison Carrée* and of the Louisiana Territory must belong to the nation.

It is around the image of the *Maison Carrée* that Warren constructed the irony of the Jeffersonian dream. After Jefferson describes the temple at Nîmes as a "shape that shines," where "a man who hoped to be a man, and be free,/Might enter in," R. P. W., described in the cast of characters only as "the writer of this poem," sarcastically questions Jefferson's vision:

R. P. W.: So you—so you find evidence for innocence
In such a heap of organized rubble
(I call it cold and too obviously mathematical)
Thrown up by a parcel of those square-jawed looters
From the peninsula, stuck in a foreign land? (*BTD,* p. 40).

Warren had moved from the terrible internal conflict which the house at "Sutpen's Hundred" represents in Faulkner's novel, to its European prototype, the *Maison Carrée* and the spirit of the Enlightenment. But just as we move from "Sutpen's Hundred" to the *Maison Carrée,* so we are forced to move back again from the noble ideals of innocence of the "Square House" at Nîmes to a meat house in Kentucky where human butchery stains the virgin soil with guilt.

The story told in *Brother to Dragons* was taken from an actual incident which took place in Kentucky in 1811. Some years earlier

Dr. Charles Lewis, whose wife, Lucy, was the sister of Thomas Jefferson, moved from Virginia to Kentucky with his wife, slaves, and two grown sons, Lilburn and Isham. Lucy soon died, and Dr. Lewis returned to Virginia, leaving Lilburn and his wife and children and Isham to live on the place which he had established on a bluff overlooking the Ohio River. "On the night of December 15, 1811—the night when the New Madrid earthquake first struck the Mississippi Valley—Lilburn, with the assistance of Isham and in the presence of his Negroes, butchered a slave named George, whose offense had been to break a pitcher prized by the dead mother, Lucy Lewis" (*BTD,* pp. ix–x). The two brothers were arrested and indicted, but before they could be brought to trial Lilburn had died in a suicide pact with Isham which miscarried, and Isham had fled. Isham was caught and sentenced to be hanged but escaped again and supposedly died at the Battle of New Orleans.

In the Foreword, Warren wrote:

In regard to the role of Jefferson, several eminent students of his life and work have assured me that they can find no reference by him to the tragic end of his family in Kentucky, and one has even gone so far as to offer the opinion that Jefferson could not bring himself to discuss the appalling episode. If this is true, it is convenient for my poem, but the role of Jefferson in the poem does not stand or fall by this historical fact—which later research may prove not to be a fact at all. If the moral shock to Jefferson caused by the discovery of what his own blood was capable of should turn out to be somewhat short of what is here represented, subsequent events in the history of America, of which Jefferson is the spiritual father, might still do the job (*BTD,* p. xi).

Here Warren defends the license which he believes poetry must take with factual record in order to find its imaginative meaning rather than its "scientific" construction. The thematic focus of Warren's poetic account is the sadistic murder of the Negro slave, George, which takes place on a large chopping block in the plantation meat house. Earlier, Jefferson had spoken of the tulip tree in the West, "Immortally blossoming to May." But it is tulip wood of which the chopping block is made, and it is here that human life is violently destroyed. Not only had Jefferson's image of the West been defiled, but even more shocking was the fact that Lilburn, who had butchered a young boy for his insolence and for the petty vandalism of the other slaves, was of Thomas Jefferson's own blood. For Jefferson, who in life had once believed in the innocence of natural man and in the possibility of a redemption of innocence, the murder destroys his faith in man's future. Thus, when in the poem Jefferson as "spiritual father" does speak of the family tragedy, it is to reveal the futility of his dream of the West. "I said I must cling more sternly to the rational hope," he says, but "The axe had been laid, in secret, at the root of hope" (*BTD,* p. 135). The tulip tree was to have blossomed in "immortal" innocence. Now the bloody chopping block made from the wood of that tree is to "bloom in Time" rather than in eternity because of the crime committed upon it. The horror of the meat house, which is a burden upon the Southern conscience, is also a burden upon the national conscience, for it symbolizes the racial injustice, class exploitation, and social irresponsibility upon which the whole nineteenth century—the molding century in American history—is built. After the murder of George, neither Southerner nor American can deny his own guilt and involvement in an imperfect history which suggests man's animalism more than his progress toward perfection. But rather than give himself over to this guilt, as does Quentin, Warren's Jefferson, as a Southerner *and* as an American, is able to expand its meaning. If the South is guilty, then surely too the nation:

> I'll be sarcastic and remember
> A few more items from the ample documentation,
> And Pittsburgh and Pinkerton and the Polak bleeding
> In some blind angle while the snow falls slow,
> And Haymarket, and Detroit, and Henry's goons (*BTD,* pp. 136–137).

The central tragedy of Southern history reveals the tragic irony of American history. The ironic illusions of the pre–Civil War

South that a great civilization could be built on the bedrock of institutional slavery—the same institution which makes possible George's fate—suggest an analogy with the national illusion that a great civilization could be built in the name of Progress—the same "Progress" which allows starving workers to be shot down in the street and political scapegoats to be executed in the name of a justice which "pimps for brokers."

If such a meaning exists in *Brother to Dragons,* it also provides a context in which Willie Stark in *All the King's Men* appears as much more than a mere fictionalization of Huey Long or of a "Southern" demagogue. The education of Willie Stark in the earlier work is analogous to the education of Thomas Jefferson in *Brother to Dragons.* The young Willie believes in the basic goodness of man just as he believes in a just universe, although he also knows that evil does exist within that universe. As Jefferson finds evidence of this potential goodness in the *Maison Carrée,* Willie finds it through his vindication in the schoolhouse affair. Willie, like Jefferson, like every young, concerned American, is at first a man of ideas and ideals. Eventually, however, he is made wiser by a baptism of fire in which the potential evil in man touches him directly for the first time. Both Jefferson and Willie learn what their common blood—mankind—is capable of doing.

Jefferson is discouraged and disillusioned when he discovers that the meat-axe has been lifted in the "elation of love and justice," for there is no doubt that Lilburn did love his mother and that his intention, mad though it was, was to render justice against the Negroes who he thought were profaning her memory, and, perhaps, the image of white womanhood. Willie Stark, on the other hand, is only momentarily discouraged when he learns that he has been duped in the primary. The practical man of action moves beyond the Jeffersonian idealist. Willie screams, "Gimme that meat-axe" (*AKM,* p. 277), but the "meat-axe" of his wrath is raised by a man who paradoxically gives the people new roads, new economic hopes, and the promise of such humane benefits as free medical service in return for power. The West of Jefferson's dream represents hope and innocence. But, to carry the axe analogy one step farther, the land, to fit man's needs, must first be cleared with the axe, and in the very act of clearing it—whether in love or greed or hope—the innocence of the land, and *man's* hopes for redemptive innocence in nature, are both destroyed. As the wilderness becomes the frontier and the frontier becomes the settlement and the settlement becomes a civilization, inhabited by the children of darkness as well as by the children of light, man's hope of living in any kind of natural simplicity and harmony with a perfectly harmonious universe recedes farther and farther beyond possibility; for it is history—man's actions—which threatens to clear the land of men's ideals. The dilemma for the American imagination—an imagination shaped by Jeffersonian idealism—is that it seeks both innocence and progress. This makes it necessary to deny the reality of history, for history destroys the myth of innocence, as well as the possibility of unending progress. Willie, caught in this Jeffersonian dilemma, attempts to balance the three concepts—innocence, progress, and history. He is destroyed by Adam Stanton who, as an Innocent, cannot tolerate Willie's philosophy which combines Calvinistic pessimism with Jamesian pragmatism into a dynamic yet violent and sometimes irresponsible philosophy for action, which exploits weakness and evil for the sake of good. Adam Stanton is the post-Hiroshima American driven to violent repression by a complex, shaded world of ambiguities and tragedy in which the pieces of progress and scientism no longer fit. Rather than tolerate even the *idea* of his sister's seduction, Adam Stanton, in effect like Quentin, destroys himself, but even more terrible, he destroys the man who had brought the healing skill of his hands to the people. Rather than tolerate the existence of evil, he destroys both good and evil. For as a self-defined moral man, he cannot function in an "immoral" society. Instead he takes up the meat-axe in despair and destroys all in vengeance for a lost innocence. It is not a "white backlash" which we have witnessed in the second half of this decade but rather a backlash of innocence in which such Americans as George Wallace, caught in the same dilemma between innocence and knowledge, between ideal and action, as Quentin and Willie Stark and Warren's Jefferson, once more seek to bring about that clearing of the land which will deliver America from the corruptions and ambiguities of history and also, in Wallace's case, bring vindication for the South.

Warren's insights into American innocence—like Niebuhr's—do not end in despair or destruction but finally in the wisdom of responsibility, the one quality which most of Faulkner's struggling characters never really achieve because they are always held immobile by the burden of their region's past. In the final humility of Jack Burden, aptly named protagonist of *All the King's Men,* there is both wisdom and hope for progress in history. When he discovers that even Anne Stanton is involved in the corruption of the world as Willie Stark's mistress, Jack Burden's mask of neutrality breaks apart, and he is forced by his heritage as an American into a sterile burlesque of the old Jeffersonian panacea—escape to the West.

For West is where we all plan to go some day. It is where you go when the land gives out and the old-field pines encroach. It is where you go when you get the letter saying: *Flee, all is discovered.* It is where you go when you look down at the blade in your hand and see the blood on it (*AKM,* p. 286).

The West is where one seeks redemption in nature when he has failed in the corrupted world of institutions. When innocence has been either threatened or destroyed, one goes West to protect or regain its simplicity. The West, where innocence blossoms forever in May, is Jack Burden's destination. But for Burden the image of the West is no longer that of blossoming life and the future, but of death and the past. He finds temporary redemption in the clichés of a shallow naturalism. Love becomes only a "mysterious itch in the blood," and "life is but the dark heave of blood and the twitch of the nerve" (*AKM,* pp. 327–328, 329). This is the innocence offered by a capitulation to science, the same science which had distorted Adam Stanton's perspective. From this point of view, "The words *Anne Stanton* were simply a name for a peculiarly complicated piece of mechanism which should mean nothing whatsoever to Jack Burden, who himself was simply another rather complicated piece of mechanism" (*AKM,* p. 329). Thus he can return from the West, believing that "nothing was your fault or anybody's fault, for things are always as they are. And you can go back in good spirits, for you will have learned two very great truths. First, that you cannot lose what you have never had. Second, that you are never guilty of a crime which you did not commit. *So there is innocence and a new start in the West, after all*" (*AKM,* p. 330).

But the new start which Burden believes he has gained is to no avail. The fate of his friends, Willie and Adam, has already been sealed by their being what they are—the man of action *versus* the man of idea; knowledge *versus* innocence.

In addition, Jack Burden's research project into the history of Judge Irwin does produce the "dirt" that Willie Stark needs to intimidate Irwin. But when Jack Burden confronts Irwin with the evidence, asking him if it is true, giving him a chance to deny it, Irwin kills himself. Only then, only after Jack Burden's final blundering act of moral neutrality in a world supposedly governed by the "big twitch," does he learn from his hysterical mother that the Judge had been her lover—that he, Jack Burden, has driven his own father to suicide. The man he had always thought of as his father had walked out on his adulterous wife and had never come back. He had become a religious fanatic, a hermit who had crawled "into a hole in the slums" to lie there "like a wounded animal and let his intellect bleed away into pious drivel and his strength bleed away into weakness." "And," Jack Burden thinks, "*he* had been good,"

but his goodness had told me nothing except that I could not live by it. My new father, however, had not been good. He had cuckolded a friend, betrayed a wife, taken a bribe, driven a man, though unwittingly to death. But he had done good. He had been a just judge. And he had carried his head high (*AKM,* p. 375).

Years before, Jack Burden had encountered in his research for a Ph.D. dissertation another man, Cass Mastern, who had cuckolded a friend, betrayed a wife, and finally driven that friend to self-destruction. Later, in retribution, he had tried to undo at least part of the evil which his own sin had caused by trying to save the "high yellow" slave whom his mistress, his friend's widow, had sold down the river, because the slave had discovered the secret of the adultery. He had freed his own slaves, though he knew that he was sending them to even greater miseries, and when he had failed to find the slave girl who had been separated from her husband, he joined the Confederate Army, carrying a rifle which he never used, waiting for a bullet to find him that he might sacrifice his life to atone for his sins. Later, as Burden narrates the story of Willie Stark, which, as he says, is also his own story, he writes that Cass Mastern had "learned that the world is like an enormous spider web and if you touch it, however lightly, at any point, the vibration ripples to the remotest perimeter." At the time, however, Burden could not understand the implications of Mastern's story, "Or perhaps he laid aside the journal of Cass Mastern not because he could not understand, but because he was afraid to understand for what might be understood there was a reproach to him" (*AKM,* pp. 200–201).

What Cass Mastern, a Southerner, had learned was that men are responsible for their acts and that their sins not only destroy their own innocence but the lives of others. What Jack Burden finally learns, years later, is that if we do not recognize change, if we insist upon preserving our innocence in the face of time, this too brings tragedy for ourselves and for those with whom we come in contact. Thus, as he drives West, he reflects back upon his affair with Anne and concludes that even if they had been caught there in his room and forced into marriage by their parents, at least Anne would never have become Willie Stark's mistress. Nor, it must follow, would Adam Stanton ever have killed Willie Stark.

So, I observed, my nobility (or whatever it was) had had in my world almost as dire a consequence as Cass Mastern's sin had had in his. Which may tell something about the two worlds (*AKM,* p. 315).

The problem for twentieth-century man is not as simple as the mere rejection of evil. He must also refrain from insisting upon his innocence, for an evil and complex world needs for its salvation the strong commitments and humility symbolized by the love between two individuals. "That first trifling contact of flesh with flesh" which Jack Burden cannot bring himself to make, either that night or for many years afterward, must be made. Finally, however, after the deaths of Judge Irwin, Willie Stark, and Adam, Burden is able to tell Anne "how if you could not accept the past and its burden there was no future, for without one there cannot be the other, and how if you could accept the past you might hope for the future, for only out of the past can you make the future" (*AKM,* p. 461). Some time after this they are married.

The burden of his past includes the sins of his father and his own guilt—whatever the extent—for the deaths and betrayals of his friends. Dixon had suggested in *The Sins of the Father* that to atone for them, the sons must eliminate the source of sin, the Negro. Warren's novel suggests that atonement must come by accepting the source of this sin, human nature. But more than merely accepting, men must attempt to bring good out of what is potentially evil. We must live, not in the "moral neutrality" of innocence, but in the "agony of the will."

Neither Dixon nor the Agrarians had dealt with this dark side in humanity or with this responsibility in history. They had attempted to preserve a concept of innocence which had already been violated by the movement of history. Faulkner suggested the fallacy of innocence. His characters and the form of *Absalom, Absalom!* make manifest the overwhelming burden of indecision and guilt which destroys Quentin and Thomas Sutpen. There is, as we have mentioned before, a frenzy, a lack of control and comprehension, in Quentin's last panting cries when Shreve asks him why he hates the South: "I don't hate it! I don't hate it!" (*AA,* p. 378).

On the other hand, *All the King's Men* ends in prose made memorable by the sense of resolution and wisdom gained through tragedy:

We shall come back, no doubt, to walk down the Row and watch young people on the tennis courts by the clump of mimosas and walk down the beach by the bay, where the diving floats lift gently in the sun, and on out to the pine grove, where the needles thick on the ground will deaden the footfall so that we shall move among the trees as soundlessly as smoke. But that will be a long time from now, and soon now we shall go out of the house and go into the convulsion of the world, out of history into history and the awful responsibility of *Time* (*AKM,* p. 464).

Jack Burden accepts the burden of history—the burden of the past as he calls it—and responsibility for the future in a society which believes in the free will of the individual as the basis of order and justice. This "terrible responsibility of time," symbolized specifically by America's new role in world affairs and its own internal crisis of race relations, became the new mission of Southern history as both Warren and Woodward envisioned it in the years after 1950.

White Impasse

When Senator Joseph R. McCarthy told a Wheeling, West Virginia, audience on February 9, 1950, that he held in his hand a list of 205 members of the Communist party who were, at that time, working in the American State Department, that very department had already been cleared of such charges by Republican Congressman Bartel Jonkman of Michigan on behalf of the House Foreign Affairs Committee. "Before the Eightieth Congress adjourns," Jonkman said, ". . . I want the members to know that there is one department in which the known or reasonably suspected subversives, Communists, fellow travelers, sympathizers, and persons whose services are not for the best interests of the United States have been swept out. This is the Department of State." McCarthy's early charges, and later charges made on the Senate floor, were denied by both President Truman and Secretary of State Dean Acheson. McCarthy was asked to name names and would not. Such responsible and conservative newspapers as the New York *Times* labeled the attacks of McCarthy against the State Department as "campaigns of indiscriminate character assassination." But it was neither the time nor the place to ignore such charges, even if they were irresponsible and slanderous. And with the decision to "conduct a full and complete study and investigation as to whether persons who are disloyal to the United States are or have been employed by the Department of State," the "McCarthy era" was born.

Any study of this pathetic moment in American history makes clear the fact that "McCarthyism" did not rise and fall with the rise and fall of Senator McCarthy. The association of the "ism" with the man, without consideration of a broader national imagination, is misleading. Too few of his critics in the 1950s saw this, and still fewer saw the implications of the panic and fear which led so many Americans to follow McCarthy while he lived and to continue his efforts to purge the country of unseen evil after his death. The implications were that such attitudes, with their narrowing of permissible belief and action in the political and social arenas, might continue to spread indefinitely unless Americans could come to grips with the complexities of the twentieth century. Unfortunately, the empty victories of two world wars and the responsibilities which these victories had cast, ironically, upon a nation seeking only those simplicities which would make the world safe for their brand of democracy, had seemingly dulled the American imagination to the point where, though military "isolation" was admitted by all to be no longer practical, intellectual isolation was still coveted as a way of life. If political and military isolation were no longer possible, because of a new concept of power paternalism —seen by some as an updated revision of the white man's burden —there could be at least intellectual isolation to protect the American god and the American economic system, as well as the always sacred "American way of life," from what seemed to be the dark conspiracies of foreigners bent on the destruction of the old individualism and "free enterprise."

It was in this climate of opinion that in November of 1952 Arkansas-born C. Vann Woodward (whose *Origins of the New South* was awarded the Bancroft prize that same year) read to the Southern Historical Association meeting at Knoxville, Tennessee, a paper entitled "The Irony of Southern History." The title had been suggested by Reinhold Niebuhr's just-published *The Irony of American History*. Niebuhr's book was a specific application of ideas set down in both *Moral Man and Immoral Society* and *The Children of Light and the Children of Darkness*. American illusions of innocence and virtue, according to Niebuhr, had led to "dreams of bringing the whole of human history under the control of the human will." Such dreams, however, "are ironically refuted by the fact that no group of idealists can easily move the pattern of history toward the desired goal of peace and justice. The recalcitrant forces in the historical drama have a power and persistence beyond our reckoning."[25] In the 1950s, the irony of illusions of innocence and virtue in the face of history was heightened for Niebuhr by the fact that the historical experience which refutes these illusions is "occasioned by conflict with a foe who has transmuted ideals and hopes, which we most deeply cherish, into cruel realities which we most fervently abhor."[26] "The ironic elements in American history can be overcome, in short, only if American idealism comes to terms with the limits of all human striving, the fragmentariness of all human wisdom, the precariousness of all historic configurations of power, and the mixture of good and evil in all human virtue."[27]

But only an observer who is neither too hostile nor too sympathetic can perceive the ironies of history. This balance, according

25. *The Irony of American History,* pp. 2–3.
26. *Ibid.,* p. 11.
27. *Ibid.,* p. 133.

to Niebuhr, is difficult for an observer to achieve and almost impossible for a participant in an ironic situation to achieve. It was at this point that Woodward saw the possibility of a special role for the South as observer-participant in the affairs of the nation.

"In a time when nationalism sweeps everything else before it, as it does at present," Woodward wrote, "the regional historian is likely to be oppressed by a sense of his unimportance." More specifically, while the other sections of the country are sometimes allowed to speak for the whole, the South "is thought to be hedged about with peculiarities that set it apart as unique." In fact, according to Woodward, the South *is* unique:

I do not think, however, that this eccentricity need be regarded as entirely a handicap. In fact, I think that it could possibly be turned to advantage by the Southern historian, both in understanding American history and in interpreting it to non-Americans. For from a broader point of view it is not the South but America that is unique among the peoples of the world. This peculiarity arises out of the American legend of success and victory, a legend that is not shared by any other people of the civilized world.[28]

While it is true that "there have been many Southern converts to the gospel of progress and success," and that there was even a period following Reconstruction "when it seemed possible that these converts might carry a reluctant region with them," the "conversion was never anywhere near complete. . . . For the South had undergone an experience that it could share with no other part of America—though it is shared by nearly all the peoples of Europe and Asia—the experience of military defeat, occupation, and reconstruction."[29]

It was this uniqueness which, in Woodward's words, "may be turned to advantage by the Southern historian." Dixon and the Agrarians had seen Southern uniqueness as the answer to the national problems of race and industrial capitalism. In viewing the

28. "The Irony of Southern History," in *The Burden of Southern History,* pp. 167–168.
29. *Ibid.,* p. 170.

national crisis of the 1950s—world leadership in a divided and impoverished nonwhite world by a white, affluent, and proud, yet suspicious, inner-directed nation—Woodward reasserted the mission of Southern history. It was based, not on theories of racial or economic superiority, but upon historical irony. It seemed ironic to Woodward that the South, which once had dreamed of a powerful Confederate empire based on the institution of slavery, should be defeated in war, occupied by enemy armies, and finally reconstructed according to the enemy's morality. It was also ironic that the South, although part of affluent, historically innocent America, should have experienced history in all of its catastrophic force. It seemed ironic that in a land of plenty and victory, there existed people who had known hunger and defeat.

By taking advantage of the perspective offered by this irony, Woodward suggested that the South might better understand both itself and the nation and might make possible better communications between America and the world. For "the ironic interpretation of history is rare and difficult. In the nature of things the participants in an ironic situation are rarely conscious of the irony, else they would not become its victims. Awareness must ordinarily be contributed by an observer, a nonparticipant,"[30] yet someone who can be sympathetic as well as detached. To recognize the ironies of history, one must have already experienced history. This was the vantage point open to the Southerner.

As a case in point, Woodward compared the transition in public opinion between the 1930s and the late 1940s with a similar transition in Southern history during the 1830s. "In both cases," while no exact parallels could be drawn, there were "some unhappy similarities" between the periods. Like the South of the 1830s, "We have showed a tendency to allow our whole cause, our traditional values, and our way of life to be identified with one economic institution. . . . We have shown a strong disposition to suppress criticism and repel outside ideas. We have been tempted

30. *Ibid.,* p. 173.

to define loyalty as conformity of thought, and to run grave risk of moral and intellectual stultification."[31]

Because of the South's experience, Woodward contended, each of these tendencies should be "the subject of gravest concern." Southern historians, if they could purge "their minds of rancor" and "narrow parochialism" should also be in a singularly strategic position—in this age of the Marshall Plan and foreign aid and what has since been called "welfare imperialism"—"to teach their fellow countrymen something of the pitfalls of radical reconstruction: of the disfranchisement of old ruling classes and the indoctrination of liberated peoples. . . . They should at least have a special awareness of the ironic incongruities between moral purpose and pragmatic result, of the way in which laudable aims of idealists can be perverted to sordid purposes, and of the readiness with which high-minded ideals can be forgotten."

He could have been referring to the dilemma of Willie Stark as well as suggesting that America's great weakness in its age of nuclear power and staggering responsibilities was that it did not understand the nature of its own history. The nation needed historians "who can penetrate the legend without destroying the ideal, who can dispel the illusion of pretended virtue without denying the genuine virtues."[32] Such historians would know that there are no geographical or party monopolies on virtue and morality and rectitude. They would show the "futility" of intellectual isolation and the transitory nature of *all* economic systems. Their historical scholarship would also constitute a warning "that an overwhelming conviction in the righteousness of a cause is no guarantee of its ultimate triumph, and that the policy that takes into account the possibility of defeat is more realistic than one that assumes the inevitability of victory."

Finally he concluded that while America might find such historians anywhere, North or South, surely "some of them might reason-

31. *Ibid.*, p. 184.
32. *Ibid.*, pp. 188–190.

ably be expected to rise from that region where it is a matter of common knowledge that history has happened to our people in our part of the world."[33] The South's mission then was to make America aware of history and to make it aware of the rest of the world's right to its own values and beliefs; to hold back against the tide of international reconstruction; and finally, and perhaps more important, to urge the nation toward internal freedom and openness.

Woodward's call in the early 1950s for a broader perspective on the part of America toward the world and its problems now, at the end of the 1960s, seems prophetic. His warnings of dangerous tendencies in foreign policy seemed to anticipate the dispute between the administration and a minority of congressmen and intellectuals which developed in the late 1960s over the Viet Nam war. A complicating factor was that both President Lyndon B. Johnson and his chief critic, Senator J. W. Fulbright, were Southerners. Parallels between the latter's thoughts and Woodward's counsel are nevertheless suggested by an interview in which a columnist wrote that Senator Fulbright "intends to go on trying to persuade the country to break the behavior pattern of rich, successful and mighty nations and to abandon the historical 'tendency of such nations to get puffed up about all the terrific things they think they ought to be doing with their power.' "[34]

But even as Woodward was voicing his hopes concerning a new mission for the South, the greatest irony of all was taking shape. The decades in which Woodward had hoped the South would play a new role of leadership in bringing the nation to understand the ironies of their own history was, instead, to be marked by new sectional animosities concerning the oldest burden of all: race.

The nature of this development is to some extent documented by Alfred O. Hero Jr. in *The Southerner and World Affairs.* In

33. *Ibid.,* pp. 190–191.
34. Mary McGrory, Minneapolis *Tribune,* May 20, 1966, p. 4.

prefacing his study of Southern opinion, Hero recalled that as an adolescent growing up in New Orleans during the late 1930s and early 1940s, he had come to think of the South as generally more favorable to a more active role in world affairs than other regions of the country such as the Middle West and the Rocky Mountain region. Southerners, for instance, seemed to Hero to be much more willing at an earlier date to involve American power in the European struggle against Axis aggressions than were other Americans. By the late 1950s, however, he noted "certain disturbing trends in replies by Southerners as compared with those of other Americans" in regard to foreign affairs. Southern opinion seemed to be moving toward isolationism and protectionism and growing more and more hostile to foreign aid and United States co-operation with the United Nations. Like Dixon, Faulkner, Warren, and Woodward, Hero had found evidence of a Southern uniqueness which manifested itself, not only in a concern for the traditions of the past, but also in a disbelief in "Progress" and in the perfectibility of human nature. After the Civil War, Hero wrote, the Northerners "innocently could dream of human perfectibility," but Southern whites were laden with guilt. The Protestant ethic, with its promise of environmental control through hard work, did not seem to work as well in the South, and there have been "greater tendencies in the South toward fatalism, inertia, feelings of inability to improve or 'reform' one's environment and the social and economic forces determining one's future, and disbelief (or cautious hesitation) that change would be for the better have been reflected in replies to survey questions."[35]

This greater tendency of Southerners to disbelieve in progress . . . has been closely associated with more widespread inclinations in the South than in the North to reject optimistic assumptions of many Northern "progressives" or rationalist liberals about the nature of mankind. "Acceptance by perhaps most Southerners of the Calvinist emphasis on original sin and their intimate contact with racial inequality, poverty, and violence have reinforced the impacts of Southern

35. *The Southerner and World Affairs*, pp. 342–344.

tradition and experiences of an agrarian people, producing the rather general view that evil and guilt are everywhere, in every human being to some extent and in considerable numbers of people to a rather large extent. Society and the life of the individual in it have been viewed as made up of continuing struggles between the forces of good, reason, honor, and integrity against deeply rooted irrationality, depravity, cruelty, and threat of ruin.[36]

Hero's evidence suggests that the South had experienced history and its attitudes were markedly affected by the exposure. Yet, in the late 1950s and after, in the aftermath of the 1954 Supreme Court decision on segregation and the decisions and incidents which followed, Hero found another interpretation of this Southern pessimism and a new effect of the South's exposure to the currents of historical change. As outside censure reached new intensity, a noticeable difference appeared between the opinions of those Southerners who thought Negroes were treated fairly in this country and those Southerners who did not. The former group was more pessimistic about the possibility of avoiding a thermonuclear war, more concerned that all domestic Communists be rooted out than that innocent citizens be protected from harassment, and less inclined to give foreign aid or to participate in the United Nations. It seemed as if Southerners were rejecting what Woodward had called the ironic perspective provided by their own history and had instead been taken in by what Niebuhr had called the irony of American history, preferring to reassert innocence in the face of complex and traumatic change, yet willing to use all possible force —political, social, and even physical—to maintain the illusions of innocence. Such white Southerners as Warren, who attempted to assert the meaning of Southern history as a tempering baptism by fire through which individuals learned to assume responsibility for their actions and for the actions of their societies by struggling to assert what Niebuhr had called the qualities of "Light," the well-being of the many, over the qualities of "Darkness," the selfish interests of the few—these Southerners found little response in a

36. *Ibid.,* pp. 345–346.

South whose spokesmen were such men as Governor Herman Talmadge of Georgia and, later, George Wallace of Alabama. By the mid-fifties, it was obvious that one branch of the myth of Southern history ran in a rather direct line from Dixon through the Agrarians to George Wallace. Still, as recently as 1966, two well-meaning, though still somewhat defiant, Southerners in introducing an anthology of contemporary Southern fiction could claim that there is a uniquely Southern "homogeneity," "wholeness," and "community of the spirit" which, even now "amidst the South's agony," could "be the basis for a new and dynamic society that might offer fresh hope to the world."[37] But such academic echoes of *I'll Take My Stand* rang hollow by the time of the presidential campaign of 1968 when the two most prominent Southerners were Wallace and Strom Thurmond. The myth as explored and interpreted by such Southerners as Faulkner, Warren, and Woodward was perhaps not dead, but within the white community at least it had reached an impasse. Increasingly, after 1960, the burden and the mission of Southern history seemed, to some at least, to rest with those Southerners who were black.

37. *Southern Writing in the 60's: Fiction,* ed. John William Corrington and Miller Williams, p. xxii.

✤ V Black Man's Burden

The Leopard's Spots

THE school segregation decision which the Supreme Court handed down on May 17, 1954, had not come about overnight. In fact, the seeds of the simple statement which was to bring social revolution to the nation lay as far back as the one dissent to *Plessy v. Ferguson* (1896) in which the Court had upheld Jim Crow segregation if tangible facilities were equal for the two races. Justice John Marshall Harlan had written that the Court had placed a "brand of servitude and degradation" on the Negro and that no "thin disguise of 'equal' accommodations could atone for the wrong this day done." Harlan implied that there were intangible as well as tangible factors in equality and that these intangible factors were as important if not more important than mere tangible ones. And it was in recognition of these factors that the Court in 1938, 1948, and again in 1950 decided against segregation in legal education. In *Sweatt v. Painter* (1950), Chief Justice Fred M. Vinson wrote that regardless of tangible factors, there are other factors "which are incapable of objective measurement but which

171

make for greatness in a law school." These factors included "the reputation of the faculty, experience of the administration, position and influence of the alumni, standing in the community, traditions and prestige."

Thus, it could not have come as a great surprise to anyone familiar with the direction in which the Court was moving that the basic question asked in *Brown et al. v. Board of Education of Topeka et al.* was: "Does segregation of children in public schools solely on the basis of race, even though the physical facilities and other 'tangible' factors may be equal, deprive the children of the minority group of equal educational opportunities?" In answering the question, Chief Justice Earl Warren wrote that the Court could not "turn the clock back" to the America of *Plessy v. Ferguson.* "We must consider public education in the light of its full development and its present place in American life throughout the Nation." Education today, he continued, "is the principal instrument in awakening the child to cultural values, in preparing him for later professional training, and in helping him to adjust normally to his environment." In this light the Court agreed unanimously that segregation solely on the basis of race does deprive children of equal educational opportunities. "To separate them [on such a basis] generates a feeling of inferiority as to their status in the community that may affect their hearts and minds in a way unlikely ever to be undone. . . . Whatever may have been the extent of psychological knowledge at the time of *Plessy v. Ferguson* this finding is amply supported by modern authority." The "modern authority" was quoted in the form of a bibliographical footnote which was itself significant, not only because of the high repute of the authorities cited, but also because of the nature of the evidence itself.[1] This was not judicial or legal precedent. This was empirical evidence from the fields of psychology and sociology. This was a culmination of the scientific environmentalistic study of race about

1. Brown *et al.* v. Board of Education of Topeka *et al.,* 347 U.S. 483 (1954).

which Dixon and the Agrarians had expressed so much apprehension.

The immediate Southern response to the *Brown* decision was predictable. According to Alfred Hero, it was overwhelmingly negative in so far as newspaper editorial comment surveyed was concerned. But the comments and excerpts reprinted in the New York *Times* suggested a slightly more balanced picture, a picture which seemed to reflect the two responses of Southerners toward the South and its past suggested earlier in this study. Governor Talmadge of Georgia predicted bloodshed if schools were integrated, accused the Court of "blatantly" ignoring "all law and precedent," usurping "from the Congress and the people the power to amend the Constitution." Its decision "confirms the worst fears of the motives of the men who sit on its bench and raises a grave question as to the future of the nation. . . . Georgians will fight for their right under the United States and Georgia Constitutions to manage their own affairs." The Supreme Court "had lowered itself to the level of common politics."[2]

The Jackson (Mississippi) *Daily News* shared Talmadge's tone of outrage and defiance:

Human blood may stain southern soil in many places because of this decision, but the dark red stains of that blood will be on the marble steps of the United States Supreme Court Building. White and Negro children in the same schools will lead to miscegenation. It means racial strife of the bitterest sort. Mississippi cannot and will not try to abide by such a decision.[3]

Once again, the old fear of miscegenation was raised as a threat to white America. Georgians and Mississippians would meet the challenge and would take their stand to preserve American innocence even if the Supreme Court had chosen to dirty its hands in the "common politics" of historical change. The innocence of Southern soil might be stained by blood, but the guilt would lie with the judges of the Court who had betrayed the classical sim-

2. New York *Times*, May 18, 1954, pp. 1, 20.
3. Quoted, *ibid.*, May 19, 1954, p. 20.

plicity and the historical illusions symbolized by the "marble" edifice of their building.

But there were other tones of Southern response. In Virginia, the State Superintendent of Public Instruction declared that there "will be no defiance of the Supreme Court decision. . . . We are trying to teach school children the law of the land and we will abide by it."[4] The Nashville *Tennessean* touched most directly on the meaning of Southern history: "The South is and has been for years a land of change. Its people—of both races—have learned to live with change. They can learn to live with this one. Given a reasonable amount of time and understanding, they will."[5]

The South's past had taught that history is change. If the North could understand that history is also time—that there are no sudden leaps in history—the adjustment for justice could and would be made. A Southern mission similar to that suggested by Woodward was implied by several newspapers which viewed the decision and its implementation as a great victory for the free world over Communism, for it would demonstrate that the American pledge "of the worth and dignity of the humblest individual means exactly what it says."[6] If the South could respond to this historical crisis with wisdom and humanity, it would lead the nation in taking the message of a democratic society to the emerging masses of Africa and Asia. The task, however, was to prove overwhelming.

A year later, in the Preface to his short monograph, *The Strange Career of Jim Crow,* Woodward wrote that one of the problems in achieving a rational and humane understanding of the race controversy is overcoming, or putting into their true historical perspective, all of the distortions and perversions which all sides and factions of the controversy have harbored over the years since the beginnings of the Jim Crow laws in the late 1890s. "The twilight

4. *Ibid.,* May 18, 1954, p. 20.
5. Quoted, *ibid.,* May 19, 1954, p. 20.
6. Quoted, *ibid.*

zone that lies between living memory and written history is one of the favorite breeding places of mythology. This particular twilight zone has been especially prolific in the breeding of legend. The process has been aided by the old prejudices, the deeply stirred emotions, and the sectional animosities that always distort history in any zone, however well illuminated by memory or research."[7]

It was this twilight zone which obscured the mission of the South as outlined in "The Irony of Southern History." By the 1950s agrarianism and racism as concepts of Southern identity and vindicated reconciliation had failed. And yet both concepts, especially that of race, existing as it did in the twilight zone between "living memory" and "written history," paralyzed the South, making it impossible to find a new synthesis, a new basis of identification in the present. Once again, as in the 1860s and -70s, the screws of national righteousness began to turn in Southern flesh, and once again the South resisted. The mind of the South itself remained in a twilight zone between action and reaction. There are those people, wrote Warren two years after the Supreme Court's segregation decision of 1954, "whose eyes brighten at the thought of the new unity in the South, the new solidarity of resistance. . . . they dream of preserving the traditional American values of individualism and localism against the anonymity, irresponsibility and materialism of the power state, against the philosophy of the ad-man, the morality of the Kinsey report, and the gospel of the bitch-goddess."[8]

But as Woodward noted, this South—the South envisioned by Dixon as well as by the Nashville Agrarians—contained "no promise of continuity and endurance for the Southern tradition,"[9] since this resistance, based as it was on race, would simply hasten the entrance of the "anonymity, irresponsibility and materialism of the power state" acting as moral spokesman for the nation. And

---

7. *The Strange Career of Jim Crow*, p. viii.
8. *Segregation: The Inner Conflict in the South*, p. 96.
9. *The Burden of Southern History*, p. 9.

Warren himself looked elsewhere for a resolution and found it, at least in part, in the remarks of a taxicab driver: There is hate, admits the taxicab driver,

but it ain't our hate, it's the hate hung on us by the old folks dead and gone. Not I mean to criticize the old folks, they done the best they knew, but that hate, we don't know how to shuck it. We got that Goddamn hate stuck in our craw and can't puke it up. If white folks quit shoving the nigger down and calling him a nigger he could maybe get to be a asset to the South and the country. But how stop shoving?[10]

Are we then the prisoners of our history? Must we always live under the burden of the past, unable to "get out of history into history" as Jack Burden had finally succeeded in doing? There is hope, according to Warren, but first there must be the perspective in which desegregation would appear, not as some kind of Armageddon, but only as "one small episode in the long effort for justice."[11] There must be gradualism, he insists, for if the change in the South is to mean anything, it must be based on education. "It's a silly question, anyway, to ask if somebody is a gradualist. Gradualism is all you'll get. History, like nature, knows no jumps. Except the jump backward, maybe."[12]

"If the South is really able to face up to itself and its situation," Warren concludes, "it may achieve identity, moral identity. Then in a country where moral identity is hard to come by, the South, because it has had to deal concretely with a moral problem, may offer some leadership. And we need any we can get. If we are to break out of the national rhythm, the rhythm between complacency and panic."[13]

Once again Southern history and the Southerner's consciousness of this history might raise the South out from under its burden of race and national humiliation into a position of national and perhaps even world leadership. The white South, as well as the

10. *Segregation*, p. 109.
11. *Ibid.*, p. 113.
12. *Ibid.*, p. 114.
13. *Ibid.*, p. 115.

black South, could at last attain first-class citizenship in the nation. But whether or not the myth of Southern history in this era would furnish a cultural point of view for American society to any greater extent than in the past remained to be seen. Little Rock, Atlanta, Oxford, Selma, and Grenada had not yet happened in 1956. George C. Wallace had not yet become Governor of Alabama. Five years later, looking back at the South's past, Warren seemed less sure of the merits of the heritage, for it had resulted in the "Great Alibi" that the Southerner was an innocent victim of a cosmic conspiracy and thus justified in his "frozen" attitude toward the contemporary situation. In anguish, Warren asked: "Does [the Southerner] ever realize that the events of Tuscaloosa, Little Rock, and New Orleans are nothing more than an obscene parody of the meaning of his history? . . . Can the man howling in the mob imagine General R. E. Lee, CSA, shaking hands with Orval Faubus, Governor of Arkansas?" And in conclusion, Warren could only hope, in a kind of existential resignation, that in the contemplation of the Civil War, we might see how individual men, despite failings, blindness, and vice, "may affirm for us the possibility of the [tragic] dignity of life" so that some of the "grandeur" of that affirmation, "even in the midst of the confused issues, shadowy chances, and brutal ambivalences of our life and historical moment, may rub off on us. And that may be what we yearn for after all."[14]

In 1956, Warren had hoped for "moral leadership" from the South. By 1961, he struggled with resignation to tragedy. Between 1956 and 1961, the pattern of the Civil Rights revolution had been set: black petition and nonviolent resistance would be met by white indifference and violent rejection. The year 1956 saw calculated opposition to the *Brown* decision from legislatures and from Southern senators and congressmen. On February 3, Autherine Lucy, under heavy police guard, became the first Negro student at

14. *The Legacy of the Civil War: Meditations on the Centennial,* pp. 57, 108–109.

the University of Alabama. The next day, 1,000 students marched and demonstrated against her admission. A cross was burned on the campus. At the end of the month, Miss Lucy was expelled. At the same time, Louisiana State University officials made what the New York *Times* called "decisive moves" to stop interracial football games and to stop Negro admissions to the University. And less than two years after Miss Lucy's admission to the University of Alabama, Governor Orval E. Faubus placed state militiamen and state police around Central High School in Little Rock to obstruct the school's scheduled integration. On September 9, six-year-old Negro pupils and their mothers were stoned and spat upon in Nashville. A Negro clergyman was beaten in Birmingham, and in North Little Rock Negro youths were taunted by white youths, at least one with a Confederate flag on the back of his black leather jacket, and told "you can't come in the school, nigger." Early the next day in Nashville, a newly integrated grammar school was virtually destroyed by a bomb. Southern response to federal troops in Little Rock seemed to echo Warren's concern that "gradualism" decay into backward leaps. A cartoon in the Greensboro *Daily News* entitled "Casualty of Little Rock" showed a man, representing "Southern Moderation" and "Years of Race Relations Work" beaten and trampled in the aftermath of the force and violence which both sides had used at Central High School. The Arkansas *Gazette* sided with President Eisenhower against the actions of Faubus, but the Jackson (Mississippi) *Clarion Ledger,* again representing the extreme reaction wrote:

The South's darkest day since Reconstruction I dawned Wednesday in Little Rock, as Federal bayonets in the hands of Federal troops inaugurated Reconstruction II.
    President Eisenhower, seated at the core of centralized Federal Government in Washington, has looked on Arkansas as a satellite almost like Hungary, where efforts at local freedom were ruthlessly suppressed.[15]

Once again, the "Great Alibi" of conspiracy and self-righteousness was to lead the South to take its stand in the bastion of

15. Quoted in New York *Times*, September 29, 1957, IV, p. 5.

Americanism. If Washington was corrupt and dictatorial, the South at least could defend the freedom and individualism upon which an older America had been founded. On September 23rd in Little Rock, "a mob of belligerent, shrieking and hysterical demonstrators" had forced the withdrawal of nine Negro students from the school. President Eisenhower threatened to use force if the obstructors did not "cease and desist." Faubus denied Eisenhower's authority to call in federal troops, and on September 24, U.S. paratroopers, under the command of General Edwin A. Walker, were posted at the school to enforce compliance with the law. In early January of the next year, a short story in the New York *Times* reporting the bombing of a Negro school in Chattanooga, Tennessee, appeared next to the story of a young circuit judge in Alabama, George C. Wallace, who had refused to release the records of his court to investigators from the Civil Rights Commission. There were more bombings and more defiance, such as the bill signed in May by Mississippi Governor J. P. Coleman, authorizing him to close any state school at his discretion in order to keep the federal government from enforcing integration. More and more states were passing such anti-integration legislation, and by August of 1958 the New York *Times* concluded that progress toward the integration of Southern public schools "seems to have come to a dead stop."

In November of 1960, 2,000 white youths rioted in protest against integration in New Orleans; Molotov cocktails, rock-throwing, and cross-burning marred another attempt to integrate the schools. And in 1961, the year Warren's *Legacy* was published, Freedom Riders were beaten, threatened, and harassed at such places as Birmingham and Anniston, Alabama. A little less than a year later, three men were killed and 50 injured, as 2,500 military policemen and infantrymen converged on Oxford, Mississippi (where William Faulkner had been buried three months earlier), to keep order, or some semblance of order, while James H. Meredith became the first Negro to enroll at the University of Mississippi. A month later, George Corley Wallace was elected governor of Alabama.

In mid-July 1968 George Wallace's third-party presidential candidacy loomed hard and cold along the edges of the political scene. Earlier in the month he had picked up more than enough signatures in Minnesota—the home state of both major Democratic contenders—to get his name on that state's ballot in November, and Wallace spokesmen predicted that his name would appear on all state ballots but one. The national polls showed his support up to an unprecedented high of 16 percent, and his critics could take little comfort in the fact that most of his support came from those with little or no formal education. No major violence had yet erupted in any American city that summer, but neither of the national conventions had been held (the Democrats had unwittingly picked Chicago for their site) and the hottest weather was yet ahead. If incidents such as the shouting and fist-fighting which had prevented Wallace from addressing a Fourth-of-July-weekend crowd in Minneapolis were to continue and expand in level of violence, support for Wallace would obviously rise even higher as the white middle class—the "forgotten men"—reacted to the complexity of a national tragedy which threatened their hard-earned, if naive, security. More and more, in letters to the editor and in political speeches, one found reference to the "forgotten middle class," and the "betrayal of the tax-paying, law-abiding citizen," and for these people Wallace offered a simplistic return to normalcy through force which fed self-righteous indignation and soothed away any twinge of guilt which the Kerner *Report* and Resurrection City might have raised during the evening news program.

Other Southerners before him had battled for Southern vindication, and Wallace was caught up in the same basic struggle to reconcile the South with the nation on the South's own terms. His mission was to establish the South's uniqueness and then to use that uniqueness to save America from the anarchists, communists, and bearded professors who threatened it. Even in the most camelotian days of the New Frontier, the goals of Joe McCarthy, if hushed momentarily, were not forgotten; and when the black revolution and the crisis of the cities began to threaten the sanctity of white America in the 1960s, Wallace stepped forward to champion the lost cause of innocence redeemed, if necessary, through violence. Black power meant the same thing to many frightened Americans as black franchisement had meant to Dixon. Science, the cities, and liberals were all part of the conspiracy which Wallace, as something of a neo-populist, rose to expose and destroy. Wallace clutched the meat-axe which Lilburn in *Brother to Dragons* had raised to vindicate innocence by a violent spilling of blood in outraged frustration at forces and acts which he could neither understand nor rationally control. Unlike Warren's Willie Stark, who had become entangled in a doomed attempt to use power and evil to create demonstrable justice and opportunity, Wallace in his national campaign promised only destruction, which when completed, would somehow reveal American innocence still intact.

Wallace had grown up as one of four children of an Alabama farmer. In high school he was a quarterback on the school football team and twice, in 1936 and 1937, had won the state Golden Gloves bantamweight boxing championship. He worked his way through law school by such part-time jobs as taxi-driving and professional boxing, and graduated in 1942. In World War II he served as a B-29 flight engineer in the Pacific theater, during which he flew numerous missions over Japan. After the war he served briefly as assistant attorney general of Alabama, then as a state legislator for two terms, and finally as a judge of the Third Judicial Circuit, a position which he held from 1953 to 1959. It was during this period that he became known as the "Fighting Judge" for his refusal to release voter-registration records to the United States Civil Rights Commission. After he had been cleared of contempt of court charges, he declared, "These characters from the Civil Rights Commission and Justice Departments are backed to the wall—they were defied and backed down. This 1959 attempt to have a second Sherman's March to the Sea has been stopped in the

Cradle of the Confederacy."[16] After an unsuccessful attempt to become governor in 1958, he won in 1962, promising to "refuse to abide by any illegal federal court order [to integrate schools] even to the point of standing in the schoolhouse door." And on June 11, 1963, he blocked the entrance of two Negro students, James A. Hood and Vivian J. Malone, to the University of Alabama. Standing before the brick and concrete, six-column, classical facade of Foster Auditorium, Wallace told the world:

I stand before you today in place of thousands of other Alabamians. . . . It is the right of every citizen however humble he may be, through his chosen official of representative government to stand courageously against whatever he believes to be the exercise of power beyond the constitutional rights conferred upon our Federal Government. . . .
Again I state—This is the exercise of the heritage of freedom and liberty under the law.[17]

It is symbolically convenient that Wallace took his school-house-door stand under the classical facade of Foster Auditorium, for it helps us to see that the "heritage" of which he spoke is also the heritage of Thomas Dixon and the Southern Agrarians, and even of W. J. Cash. The architectural imagery remains constant and is a clue to the fact that whatever one may think of Wallace's ideas, both he and his ideas are a part of a historically traceable imagination. The South's burden of oppression would be thrown off and its integrity and patriotism vindicated through a mission to defend individuals against centralization.

A racist, according to Wallace, "is someone who dislikes people because of color," and he flatly denies that he is a racist. Nevertheless, his attitudes concerning the Negro in the South often gave evidence of being those passed down from the era of Jim Crow. For Wallace, segregation was necessary because distinctions between the races made the Negro race unqualified for full participation in that society. For instance, according to Wallace, Negroes in

16. *Current Biography Yearbook*, 1963, p. 455.
17. New York *Times*, June 12, 1963, p. 20.

Alabama vote, presumably unlike Southern white Democrats, as a block rather than as individuals, and such voting is not "conducive to good government."[18] He also claimed that in effect God himself segregated the races. Thus segregation was in the best interests of both races. Yet these racial attitudes were only implicit, for Wallace did not speak about the Negro threat to democracy but about the federal threat to democracy through such schemes as interference with local schools and school transportation of students, fair-housing and equal-opportunity laws, urban-renewal programs, and the "soft" attitudes toward campus disorders and urban riots. Yet the fact that all of these issues have the question of race relations at their core was not coincidental. Where the Agrarians failed and where even Dixon really succeeded only in the South, Wallace sought triumph on a national scale by making the burden of Southern history as he understood it the essence of a mission to save all America and in the process redeem the South. His cry for law and order set the trend for the campaigns yet to come in such cities as New York, Minneapolis, and Los Angeles.

There had never been any doubt in Wallace's mind that the South did have a leading role to play in this return to innocence. Philosophically a Jeffersonian populist in his distrust of big government and urban civilization, Wallace found ample evidence, federal laws notwithstanding, that American society has been corrupted by urban or communal substitutes for the agrarian simplicity lauded by Jefferson. Individuals are "manipulated . . . as cogs in a gigantic socialistic pattern . . . reduced to the status of a mere thinking animal, to be bedded, clothed and housed by

18. Quoted from testimony of George C. Wallace before Senate Committee on Commerce, *Hearings, A Bill to Eliminate Discrimination in Public Accommodations Affecting Interstate Commerce,* Part I, 88th Congress, 1st Session, July 15–16, 1963, p. 498, in John W. Schmidt, "Rhetoric, Theology and George Wallace," p. 17. I gratefully acknowledge my use of Professor Schmidt's manuscript, which contains numerous quotations from many of Wallace's unpublished speeches, which Professor Schmidt obtained directly from Wallace.

sociological zookeepers . . . to satisfy the social whims of some social engineers."[19] The cities are full of violence and danger, and no citizen can walk the streets of a Northern city in safety. The news media mislead the masses, and Wallace proposes that the solution to this problem is to "have a big final rally, invite the press, then sic the crowd on them. One purge and get rid of the whole problem."[20] Since, according to Wallace, one can travel in the South "without fear of bodily harm," one must presume that this purge would take place someplace else, perhaps at Wallace headquarters in Chicago. The burden of Southern alienation and humiliation provided the essential motivation, while the meat-axe approach of the outraged Jeffersonian innocents provided the means of execution. High-rise apartment complexes, "concrete jungles fit for habitation only by subjects of the state who are in the process of reduction to animalistic existence," were also seen by Wallace as part of the corruption process.[21] The plantation-house imagery which we have followed through previous pages stood, not only for peace and tranquillity, but also for freedom and individual strength. This was what Jefferson saw in the *Maison Carrée*. No urban cubicles for the residents of the simple Greek temples. Thus could a large brick structure such as Foster Auditorium be reduced to the "schoolhouse door" in order to provide the appropriate symbolic setting for the defense of nineteenth-century individualism against the ambiguities of an urban civilization in a pluralistic age. It was such a dark picture for Wallace that he saw it as a "revolution of government against the people," much as Dixon had seen Reconstruction and Donald Davidson the probings of the neo-"abolitionists" such as Dollard.

19. Quoted from testimony of George C. Wallace before House Committee on the Judiciary, *Hearings, On Proposed Amendments to the Constitution Relating to Prayers and Bible Reading in the Public Schools,* Part I, 88th Congress, 2nd Session, April 30, 1964, p. 845, *ibid.,* pp. 5–6.
20. Quoted from *Esquire,* April 22, 1966, p. 114, *ibid.,* p. 29.
21. Quoted from speech given June 6, 1965, *ibid.,* p. 32.

Yet Wallace believed that the South had prevailed against all of these conspiracies and misguided reformations and through the years had progressed and pulled itself and its black burden up in spite of a "vengeful government." And in taking its stand, the South had become, according to Wallace, an example for people all over the United States who also believe in the conspiracy. "Today," proclaimed Wallace, "it is the Alabamian who has told the world that tyranny, by whatever name, shall be challenged in the pit of struggle and shall meet its match in the spirit of free men."[22] The South has a great destiny because of its great history. "Southerners played a most magnificent part in erecting this great divinely inspired system of freedom—and as God is our witness Southerners will save it. Let us, as Alabamians, grasp the hand of destiny and walk out of the shadows of fear—and fill our divine destination. Let us not simply defend—but let us assume the leadership across this nation. God has placed us here in this crisis —let us not fail in this our most historical moment."[23]

For four centuries white Americans have believed in their manifest destiny to lead a righteous struggle for freedom, thereby fulfilling their divine destiny. Wallace called America back to that mission, proclaiming (implicitly if not explicitly now that he was using prime time on national television) that the South, because it had remained true to the covenant of American innocence, would assume the leadership of this great march back to the simple world of Thomas Jefferson. The same fears, frustrations, and frenzied hopes which had lifted Thomas Dixon onto the best-seller lists of his day now drove Wallace into a well-planned, efficiently run campaign for the presidency, in which he bluntly promised to destroy or silence all evil—all those who did not share this vision —after he won in November. The hopes of Warren and Wood-

22. Quoted from speech at the Inauguration of Governor Lurleen B. Wallace, January 16, 1967, Montgomery, Alabama, *ibid.*, p. 34.
23. Quoted from Inaugural Address of Governor George C. Wallace, January 14, 1963, Montgomery, Alabama, *ibid.*, p. 35.

ward were lost—if they had ever been noted—in the backlash of outraged innocence. The burden and the hope, according to some, now rested with the black man.

God's Appeal to the Age

It is well beyond the scope of this book to trace in any kind of detail the black freedom movement in the United States. Its past is too long and too complex, its present too dynamic. And if there was a time in this movement when it involved *only* the South, that time was long ago and short-lived. The problem and the response have been, at least since the time of the Constitutional Convention in 1787, national in scope, and today, in thinking of the race problem, one is as likely to think of Detroit or New York City or Los Angeles as of Little Rock or Selma. Nevertheless, in examining the uses of Southern history and the response of Southerners to history, it is appropriate to come finally to a brief consideration of the relationship between the black freedom movement and the myth of Southern history. For, as one would suspect, there are points where they intertwine and overlap. As we have seen the existence of a concept called the burden of Southern white history, so is it also possible to define a burden of American black history. The mission of Southern history with which we have dealt finds its sometimes strikingly similar counterpart in a concept of a black mission to America and to the South. And finally, there are indications that some black Southerners as well as some white Southerners have found in the South and its way of life a counter-force to the technological and commercial degradation which seems to them to be running rampant across the nation. It is not possible, of course, to speak only of a Southern black burden or of a mission of just Southern Negroes to the nation. Yet it is a fact that the civil rights movement of the early 1960s focused in the South where the burden of Black America at first appeared most obvious, and it is also a fact that many, though not all, of the Negro leaders of this movement have come out of the South and have spoken against the backdrop of their regional memories and experiences.

The black man's burden in America has been white racism, that racism as old as America itself which found its roots and justification in the early genocidal wars against the American Indians and which was easily transferred to other races, particularly the black race. "This long-standing racist ideology," wrote Martin Luther King in *Why We Can't Wait* (1964), "has corrupted and diminished our democratic ideals." Under this racist ideology, black people have been "harried by day and haunted by night . . . and are plagued with inner fears . . . forever fighting a degenerating sense of 'nobodiness.' "[24] On the one hand, the burden has bred bitterness. Ida Scott, in James Baldwin's *Another Country,* expresses this hatred:

They keep you here [in the ghetto] because you're black, the filthy, white cock suckers, while they go around jerking themselves off with all that jazz about the land of the free and the home of the brave. And they want you to jerk yourself off with that same music, too, only keep your distance. Some days, honey, I wish I could turn myself into one big fist and grind this miserable country to powder.[25]

The obscenity of the metaphor reflects the obscenity of the perversion of the ideal by white hypocrisy. In *Black Boy,* Richard Wright recalled that whenever he thought of the "essential bleakness of black life in America," he knew that "Negroes had never been allowed to catch the full spirit of Western civilization, that they lived somehow in it but not of it."[26] Yet, on the other hand, this living in but not of a society was the experience Warren and Woodward had pointed to as affording the ironic perspective so necessary to come to grips with American history. John Oliver Killens, Alabama-born Negro novelist and essayist, wrote in *Black*

---

24. *Why We Can't Wait,* p. 84.
25. *Another Country,* p. 295.
26. *Black Boy: A Record of Childhood and Youth,* p. 45.

Man's Burden: "the problem facing most of the races of mankind is: 'What are we going to do about these white folk? How are we going to get them off our backs; how can we undo their centuries of deliberate dehumanization? How are we going to teach them the meaning of some of the phrases they themselves claim to have invented but never practiced so far as we are concerned—democracy, human dignity, and the brotherhood of man?' This is the enormous Black Man's Burden today."[27]

Killen's words are an ironic twist of the old concept of the White Man's Burden which has dominated Western attitudes toward the colored races down to our own day. The white man's imagined burden was to minister to an inferior race with minimal gestures toward his well-being, a ministry designed to soothe the white conscience and keep the caste system intact. On the other hand, the Black Man's Burden, as Killens views it, is to bring a backward race—the white race—into the integrated equality of a new world where all men will be brothers. Like most of the white Southerners talking about the South's mission and uniqueness, Killens overstates the potential of the mission which he envisions as well as the uniqueness which he attributes to the colored races of the world. To some extent this overstatement is due to the fact that Killens's sense of burden, like Martin Luther King's, is political, born of political injustice and demanding political solution. Historical irony and the detachment, compassion, and vision which it makes possible begin with the recognition and confession of one's own sins and shortcomings. This is a luxury which groups politically on the make usually cannot afford, at least in very large doses, for it seems to interfere with political efficiency. The Southern white imagination is in a similar situation because the quest for national inclusion and reconciliation does not allow it to take advantage of the ironies of its own history. Killens, like the Southern Agrarians, is sometimes too sure of the uniqueness and virtue of his own

27. *Black Man's Burden*, pp. 149–150.

cause to be politically realistic. On the other hand, Martin Luther King understood, besides the burden of being black, the burden of belonging to human history. In the 1960s it was King who took up the thread of the myth of Southern history which ran from Niebuhr through Woodward and Warren, while the other thread, as we have seen, ran all too swiftly from Dixon to the rhetoric of Wallace.

When Martin Luther King was assassinated in Memphis on April 4, 1968, he was at 39 already one of the great Americans. Brought up in the relative security of a middle-class Negro home in Atlanta, Georgia, with those advantages which love and education afford, he could easily have avoided getting involved in the racial crisis. Yet even for a middle-class Negro the caste system of the South was always present and sometimes almost unbearable. As a boy, King "could never adjust to the separate waiting rooms, separate eating places . . . partly because the separate was always unequal, and partly because the very idea of separation did something to my sense of dignity and self-respect."[28] Thus aware of the great burden of his race, King continued his education at Morehouse College, Crozer Theological Seminary, and Boston University. By 1953, now married to Coretta Scott and near completion of the Ph.D. degree in Systematic Theology, he turned down churches in Massachusetts and New York to take the pastorate at the Dexter Avenue Baptist Church in Montgomery, Alabama. In taking this job, King and his bride faced the first and probably most profound decision of their married life. There were so many personal advantages in staying in the North and so many disadvantages, if not dangers, in returning to the South. But after much discussion and prayer, they agreed that "in spite of the disadvantages and inevitable sacrifices, our greatest service could be ren-

28. *Stride Toward Freedom: The Montgomery Story,* p. 6.

dered in our native South. We came to the conclusion that we had something of a moral obligation to return—at least for a few years."[29]

Having chosen to enter the turmoil of history at its most sensitive point—in the very "Cradle of the Confederacy"—King committed himself to a struggle in which very soon he was to be acknowledged as leader. From the Montgomery bus boycott and the marches on such cities as Selma and Birmingham to the great Washington march of 1963 and the "Dream" which was proclaimed at that gathering, King led the black people and the poor people and the people of peace in protest against a rigid injustice which they could not understand in all of its complexity, but which they were determined to "overcome" through the power and force of nonviolent resistance and love. And to a greater extent than at any other point in the long struggle for racial justice, King had the strength of national and world opinion behind him.

In explaining King's philosophical position, major credit is usually given to the influence of Mahatma Gandhi, in whose teachings on love and nonviolence King "discovered the method for social reform" which he had sought. Yet King himself, in *Stride Toward Freedom,* also put great emphasis on the influence of Reinhold Niebuhr's "prophetic and realistic style and profound thought." Having been convinced by his reading of Gandhi that true pacificism is not nonresistance to evil but nonviolent resistance to evil, King could not agree with what he felt was Niebuhr's misunderstanding of pacifism as "a sort of passive nonresistance to evil expressing naive trust in the power of love." What Niebuhr did contribute, however, according to King, was a refutation of liberal Protestantism's "false optimism," through his "extraordinary insight into human nature" and his insistence in "the reality of sin on every level of man's existence. . . . While I still believed in man's potential for good, Niebuhr made me realize his potential for evil as well. Moreover, Niebuhr helped me to recognize the complexity

29. *Ibid.,* p. 7.

of man's social involvement and the glaring reality of collective evil."[30]

King's own experience as a black American and particularly as a black Southerner, underlined Niebuhr's ideas, and the theologian's concept of moral and immoral society became a central concept in King's rationalization of nonviolent resistance. In his "Letter from Birmingham Jail" written in April of 1963, he reminded a group of Alabama clergymen who had called his march in Birmingham "unwise and untimely" that no gains could be made without "legal and nonviolent pressure," since groups, unlike individuals, seldom give up their privileges voluntarily because, "as Reinhold Niebuhr has reminded us, groups tend to be more immoral than individuals."[31] Here, too, was the perspective to see with Woodward the "tragic aspects and the ironic implications" of American history that "have been obscured by the national legend of success and victory and by the perpetuation of infant illusions of innocence and virtue."[32] Finally, here was the motivation to act, and it was suggested that it was the oppressed, not the oppressors, as Warren and Faulkner had hoped possible, who must act in the cause of racial justice, not only for themselves but also for their oppressors.

For King, Communism was like the doom hanging over the Sutpen mansion, for Communism is "a judgment against our failure to make democracy real and follow through on the revolution that we initiated."[33] Communism and other forms of tyranny and injustice can only be defeated, King believed, not by self-righteous reaction and violence, but by nonviolent, love-centered revolution. Those who take this path toward justice do "not seek to defeat or humiliate the opponent, but to win his friendship and understanding. . . . The end is redemption and reconciliation. . . . the attack is directed against forces of evil rather than against persons who happen to be doing the evil." There is a "willingness to accept

30. *Ibid.*, pp. 79–81.
31. *Why We Can't Wait*, p. 82.
32. *The Burden of Southern History*, p. 189.
33. *The Trumpet of Conscience*, p. 33.

suffering without retaliation," for, according to Gandhi, "Suffering is infinitely more powerful than the law of the jungle for converting the opponent and opening his ears which are otherwise shut to the voice of reason!" Furthermore, "At the center of nonviolence stands the principle of love . . . in the struggle for human dignity, the oppressed people of the world must not succumb to the temptation of becoming bitter or indulging in hate campaigns." And finally, there is "the conviction that the universe is on the side of justice."[34]

The myth of Southern history, which we have traced through 65 years of this century, suggests that out of suffering comes wisdom and that out of wisdom comes the ability to redeem American life. The nonviolent, love-centered quest for justice of Martin Luther King stood in the eyes of many as one of the most profound contributions to this national redemption made by any Southerner in the nation's history. If the white Southerner has felt alienated from the mainstream of American life, then how much greater has been the black Southerner's alienation? And while it was just the material opulence and cultural innocence from which the Southerner felt excluded, the black man knew that in addition *he* was cut off from the essential rights and guarantees—tangible and intangible—granted to every first-class citizen. For white Southerners, the clash between what their own experience with history had put on them as burden and what their birthright as innocent ahistorical Americans excused them from produced violence—an obsession with violence, a fear of violence, a reliance on violence—and it is of great significance that in so many of the works by Southerners discussed in this study—those of Dixon, Warren, Cash, and Faulkner, for example—we have seen this violence in one form or another as part of the Southern imagination. But for King, the burden of Negro history taught that violence breeds only more violence. It was not innocence which he sought for his people but justice, and by this quest would the black man redeem America.

34. *Stride Toward Freedom,* p. 88.

In speaking of the race problem in the South, King noted that while not all whites were hostile to Negro equality, many who might support the cause were silent. This was a dilemma for the South, and King, once again reflecting his debt to Niebuhr, wrote, "Our generation will have to repent not only for the acts and words of the children of darkness but also for the fears and apathy of the children of light."[35] The mission must begin in the South, for by "grasping his great opportunity in the South [the Negro] can make a lasting contribution to the moral strength of the nation and set a sublime example of courage for generations yet unborn."[36] King believed that "Today the Negro is fighting for a finer America, and he will inevitably win the majority of the nation to his side because our hard-won heritage of freedom is ultimately more powerful than our traditions of cruelty and injustice."[37] More specifically, for example, "American politics needs nothing so much as an injection of the idealism, self-sacrifice and sense of public service which is the hallmark of our movement."[38]

According to King, it was Negro youth who lifted "the blanket of fear" left by the social paralysis of McCarthyism, and it certainly can be suggested that the political awakening which may have culminated in Senator Eugene McCarthy's candidacy had its roots in the civil rights movements beginning in the late 1950s. Beyond the nation's destiny, the Negro mission expands to the world. King believed, along with Arnold Toynbee, that Western civilization might gain a new spiritual dynamic from the Negro. "The spiritual power that the Negro can radiate to the world comes from love, understanding, good will and nonviolence," King wrote. "It may even be possible for the Negro, through adherence to nonviolence so to challenge the nations of the world that they will seriously seek an alternative to war and destruction." Here too King was applying the myth of Southern history to the particular

35. *Ibid.*, p. 179.
36. *Ibid.*, pp. 190–191.
37. *Why We Can't Wait,* p. 132.
38. *Ibid.*, p. 167.

crisis of his times, just as white Southerners before him had done. "The Negro may be God's appeal to this age—an age drifting rapidly to its doom. The eternal appeal takes the form of a warning: 'All who take the sword will perish by the sword.' "[39] C. Vann Woodward warned of the danger in romanticizing the Negro as a new savior of a decadent civilization.[40] Yet on the other hand, one could not deny the part which such men as King had played in the 1950s and 1960s in forcing at least some Americans to re-examine their assumptions about the past and the future.

"Nonviolence," King wrote in 1965, "the answer to the Negroes' need, may become the answer to the most desperate need of all humanity."[41] When, in 1967, King took a stand against American involvement in Viet Nam, it was, he made clear, his sense of love, his quest for nonviolent paths to peace, and his sensitivity to the ironies of the United States position in the Far East which guided him. Although the Vietnamese people had proclaimed their independence in 1945, quoting the American Declaration of Independence in their own declaration, King noted, "Our government felt then that the Vietnamese people weren't ready for independence, and we again fell victim to the deadly Western arrogance that has poisoned the international atmosphere for so long."[42]

Let us try to see the irony of our position from the point of view of those who have been "designated" our enemies, wrote King: "Here is the true meaning and value of compassion and non-violence, when they help us to see the enemy's point of view, to hear his questions, to know his assessment of ourselves. For from his view we may indeed see the basic weaknesses of our own condition, and if we are mature, we may learn and grow and profit from the wisdom of the brothers who are called the opposition."[43] And always, perception must lead to action, for this is the ultimate

39. *Stride Toward Freedom*, p. 201.
40. "What Happened to the Civil Rights Movement," *Harper's Magazine*, CCXXXIV (1967), 35–36.
41. *Why We Can't Wait*, p. 169.
42. *The Trumpet of Conscience*, p. 26.
43. *Ibid.*, p. 29.

mission. "If we do not act, we shall surely be dragged down the long, dark, and shameful corridors of time reserved for those who possess power without compassion, might without morality, and strength without sight."[44]

King understood, like Warren, that Americans must see behind the illusionary facade of the *Maison Carrée* if they were to avoid the "dark corridors" and self-condemning butchery of the meat house.

Other Negroes—John Oliver Killens, Ralph Ellison, Charles V. Hamilton, Stokely Carmichael, Whitney Young, among others—have also spoken of this mission which the black man must take to redeem America and the West. And Robert Penn Warren—who had tried to find the key to redemption within the white community —writes finally that as "the 'existentialist' American," the Negro may in fact play a central role in the redemption of America because of his courage and clarity in pointing out "that the white man is to be indicted by his own self-professed, and self-created, standards." If the Negro does this—as he is in fact doing—then, according to Warren, "we may redeem ourselves—by confronting honestly our own standards. For in the end, everybody has to redeem himself."[45] This was Warren's position in 1965—a position evolved out of thirty-five years of intellectual and artistic confrontation with the burden of race and innocence in America.

Whitney Young, Kentucky-born executive director of the Urban League, told Warren:

The Negro says, "I think I can bring something to a new society, even though I can't bring, certainly, a superior technological know-how, certainly I can't bring money, I can't bring in many cases the same level of education—but out of suffering one develops something that goes beyond just jazz. One develops compassion, one develops humaneness—certainly the Negro has developed a tolerance, a patience, that maybe the larger society can use. Maybe General Motors can use some of our compassion."[46]

44. *Ibid.*, p. 34.
45. *Who Speaks for the Negro?*, p. 442.
46. *Ibid.*, pp. 159–160.

John Oliver Killens believes that the achievements of freedom and human dignity for most of mankind will, in the histories yet to be written, far outweigh the technological and scientific accomplishments of this age. And King, only months before his death, wrote that "Nothing in our glittering technology can raise man to new heights, because material growth has been made an end in itself, and, in the absence of moral purpose, man himself becomes smaller as the works of man become bigger. . . . instead of strengthening democracy at home, [the technological revolution] has helped to eviscerate it. Gargantuan industry and government, woven into an intricate computerized mechanism, leave the person outside."[47]

Whitney, Killens, and King, like some of the white Southerners we have examined in this study, and like many in the mainstream of Romantic dissent in America, including Emerson and Thoreau, had linked the "sickness" of Western society in general and American society in particular to the dehumanization which accompanies technology and industrialization. Following in the steps of the Southern Agrarians, some Negro writers and spokesmen believed that the South might in the long run prove the better environment for the type of society they envisioned. Charles Evers spoke on the Mississippi white man some time after the murder of his brother, Medgar, and the release of his accused killer: "He [the white Southerner] admires any man who stands up for what he believes. . . . we know where this man stands. In Chicago and New York . . . They rub you down and they grin in your face and they stab you in the back. . . . Once we can prove to the Mississippi whites that what we are fighting for is right and just, then Mississippi will be the best place in the world to live."[48] George Wallace, too, has often said that segregation in the South is much less a threat to one's humanity because it is overt, out in the open, so that everyone knows where he stands, with none of the hypocrisy or false sympathy which marks race relations in the North.

---

47. *The Trumpet of Conscience,* pp. 43–44.
48. *Who Speaks for the Negro,* p. 107.

Besides the absence of bitterness and the spirit of nonviolent persistence reflected in such comments as those of Evers, we are also able to see that same distrust of the impersonal urban North that we have witnessed in other Southerners, such as Dixon and Faulkner. Ralph Ellison pointed out in the same series of interviews "that there is an area in Southern experience wherein Negroes and whites achieve a sort of human communication, and even social intercourse, which is not always possible in the North. I mean, that there is an implacably human side to race relationships."[49] Bayard Rustin notes that when Southerners finally are convinced, "they are often infinitely more consistent than a number of people in the North, who have never been through the traumatic experience of change. They often come out with more insight, and that is my hope for the South."[50] The burden of Southern history could, after all, provide the key to racial peace. King, in *Stride Toward Freedom,* wrote of the South as his beloved home and noted that at the time he had decided to take the position at the Dexter Avenue Church, he and his wife had felt that "something remarkable was unfolding in the South," and that "the region had marvelous possibilities." Once it "came to itself and removed the blight of racial segregation, it would experience a moral, political, and economic boom hardly paralleled by any other section of the country."[51] King too had partaken of the myth of Southern history, although his feeling and hope for the South could also have come in part from his reading of *Moral Man and Immoral Society.* Several years later, when Warren asked him about the idea that there were grounds for a more human recognition between the races in the South than in a big "anonymous city" of the North, King replied that there was probably some truth in this at an individual level, but that it was "mainly a paternalistic thing, a law of servantry."[52] Remembering Niebuhr, King knew that men might be moral, but seldom if ever could societies follow. In

49. *Ibid.,* p. 344.
50. *Ibid.,* p. 243.
51. *Stride Toward Freedom,* pp. 7–8.
52. *Who Speaks for the Negro,* p. 217.

later books such as *Where Do We Go From Here: Chaos or Community?* and *The Trumpet of Conscience,* he seemed less concerned with the South than with the nation and with Western civilization.

Reading these opinions and hopes of black Southerners, one was reminded of Gavin Stevens, Chick's reluctant uncle in *Intruder in the Dust,* who had said:

We [Southern whites and blacks] should confederate: swap him the rest of the . . . privileges which are his right, for the reversion of his capacity to wait and endure and survive. Then we would prevail; together we would dominate the United States; we would present a front not only impregnable but not even to be threatened by a mass of people who no longer have anything in common save a frantic greed for money and a basic fear of a failure of national character.[53]

It was *almost* all here, in Gavin Stevens's words, as in some of the statements from the Negroes: Southern burden, Southern uniqueness, and Southern mission. Faulkner's character, however, does not speak of the other concept—Union—but of "domination" and of an "impregnable front" to defy the damyankees. It was left for the black Southerner, King, and those who might choose to follow the fallen leader, to speak of forgiveness and reconciliation between the races, the classes, and the nations.

53. William Faulkner, *Intruder in the Dust,* p. 156.

✤ Bibliography

Allen, Frederick Lewis. *Only Yesterday: An Informal History of the Nineteen-Twenties.* New York: Harper and Brothers, 1931; Bantam Books edition, 1957.

Allen, John D. "Southerntown." *The Saturday Review of Literature,* XVI (June 26, 1937), 17.

Baldwin, James. *Another Country.* New York: Dial Press, 1962; Dell Book edition, 1963.

Beard, Charles A., and Mary R. Beard. *The Rise of American Civilization.* One-volume edition. New York: Macmillan, 1930.

Beck, Warren. *Man In Motion: Faulkner's Trilogy.* Madison: University of Wisconsin Press, 1961.

Becker, Carl L. *Detachment and the Writing of History: Essays and Letters of Carl L. Becker,* ed. Phil L. Snyder. Ithaca, N.Y.: Cornell University Press, 1958.

Berman, Daniel M. *It Is So Ordered: The Supreme Court Rules on School Segregation.* New York: W. W. Norton & Co., 1966.

Binnon, Randolph B. "Solving the Negro Problem through Education." *Current History,* XXX (May 1929), 231–236.

Bloomfield, Maxwell. "Dixon's *The Leopard's Spots:* A Study in Popular Racism." *American Quarterly,* XVI (Fall 1964), 387–401.

Brickell, Herschel. *"Absalom, Absalom!" Review of Reviews,* LXXXXIV (December 1936), 15.

———. *"Gone With the Wind." Review of Reviews,* LXXXXIV (August 1936), 8.

Brooks, Cleanth. *William Faulkner: The Yoknapatawpha Country.* New Haven, Conn.: Yale University Press, 1964.

Brown, William Garrott. *The Lower South in American History.* New York: Macmillan, 1903.

Bruce, Philip A. *The Rise of the New South.* Philadelphia: G. Barrie and Sons, 1905.

Buck, Paul H. *The Road to Reunion, 1865–1900.* Boston: Little, Brown and Co., 1937.

Butcher, Margaret Just. *The Negro in American Culture.* Based on materials left by Alain Locke. New York: Alfred A. Knopf, 1956.

Caldwell, Erskine. *Tobacco Road.* New York: Grosset and Dunlap, 1932.

Calverton, V. F. "The Bankruptcy of Southern Culture." *Scribner's Magazine,* XCIX (1936), 294–298.

Carmer, Carl. *Stars Fell on Alabama.* New York: Blue Ribbon Books, Inc., 1934.

Carmichael, Stokely, and Charles V. Hamilton. *Black Power: The Politics of Liberation in America.* New York: Vintage Books, 1967.

Carter, Hodding. *Southern Legacy.* Baton Rouge: Louisiana State University Press, 1950.

Cash, Wilbur J. *The Mind of the South.* Vintage Books edition. New York: Alfred A. Knopf, Inc., 1941; Random House, 1960.

Casper, Leonard. *Robert Penn Warren: The Dark and Bloody Ground.* Seattle: University of Washington Press, 1960.

Chase, Stuart. *Men and Machines.* New York: Macmillan, 1929.

Colum, Mary M. "Faulkner's Struggle With Technique." *The Forum and Century,* XCVII (January 1937), 35–36.

Commager, Henry Steele. "The Civil War in Georgia's Red Clay Hills —Vividly Told from the Viewpoint of the Women Left Behind," New York *Herald Tribune Books,* July 5, 1936, XII, 1–2.

Cook, Raymond A. "The Man Behind the Birth of a Nation," *The North Carolina Historical Review,* XXXIX (Autumn 1962), 519–540.

————. "Thomas Dixon: His Books and His Career." Unpublished Ph.D. dissertation, University of Georgia, 1953.

Corrington, John William, and Miller Williams, eds. *Southern Writing in the 60's: Fiction.* Baton Rouge: Louisiana State University Press, 1966.

Couch, W. T., ed. *Culture in the South.* Chapel Hill: The University of North Carolina Press, 1934.

Cowley, Malcolm. *The Faulkner-Cowley File: Letters and Memories, 1944–1962.* New York: The Viking Press, 1966.

———. "Poe in Mississippi." *The New Republic,* LXXXIX (November 4, 1936), 22.

———. *The Portable Faulkner.* New York: The Viking Press, 1946.

Dabbs, James McBride. *Who Speaks for the South?* New York: Funk & Wagnalls Co., 1964.

Dabney, Virginius. *Liberalism in the South.* Chapel Hill: The University of North Carolina Press, 1932.

———. *Below the Potomac: A Book about the New South.* New York: D. Appleton-Century Co., 1942.

Daniel, Frank. "Cinderella City—Atlanta Sees 'Gone With the Wind.' " *The Saturday Review of Literature,* XXI (December 23, 1939), 10–12.

Davidson, Donald. "First Fruits of Dayton: The Intellectual Evolution in Dixie." *The Forum,* LXXIX (1928), 896–907.

———. "Gulliver With Hay Fever." *American Review,* IX (Summer 1937), 152–172.

De Voto, Bernard. "Witchcraft in Mississippi." *The Saturday Review of Literature,* XV (October 31, 1936), 3–4.

Dixon, Thomas. *The Clansman: An Historical Romance of the Ku Klux Klan.* New York: Grosset and Dunlap, 1905.

———. *Comrades: A Story of Social Adventure in California.* New York: Grosset and Dunlap, 1909.

———. *The Fall of a Nation: A Sequel to the Birth of a Nation.* New York: D. Appleton and Co., 1916.

———. *The Foolish Virgin: A Romance of Today.* New York: D. Appleton and Co., 1915.

———. *The Leopard's Spots: A Romance of the White Man's Burden —1865–1900.* New York: Doubleday, Page and Co., 1902.

———. *The One Woman: A Story of Modern Utopia.* New York: Grosset and Dunlap, 1903.

———. *The Root of Evil.* New York: Grosset and Dunlap, 1911.

———. *The Sins of the Father: A Romance of the South.* New York: D. Appleton and Co., 1912.

———. *The Traitor: A Story of the Fall of the Invisible Empire.* New York: Grosset and Dunlap, 1907.

Dollard, John. *Caste and Class in a Southern Town.* New Haven, Conn.: Yale University Press, 1937.

Dunning, William Archibald. *Essays on the Civil War and Reconstruction and Related Topics.* New York: Macmillan, 1910.

Ellison, Ralph. *Invisible Man.* New York: Random House, 1952.

Faulkner, Harold U. *From Versailles to the New Deal: A Chronicle of the Harding-Coolidge-Hoover Era.* The Chronicles of America Series. New Haven, Conn.: Yale University Press, 1950.

Faulkner, William. *Absalom, Absalom!* Modern Library edition. New York: Random House, 1951.

———. *Essays, Speeches and Public Letters,* ed. James B. Meriwether. New York: Random House, 1965.

———. *Go Down, Moses.* Modern Library edition. New York: Random House, 1955.

———. *Intruder in the Dust.* Modern Library edition. Random House, 1948.

———. *Light in August.* Modern Library edition. Random House, 1956.

———. *The Mansion.* New York: Random House, 1959.

———. *Sanctuary.* Modern Library edition. New York: Random House, 1932.

———. *Sartoris.* New York: Harcourt, Brace & Co., 1929.

———. *The Sound and the Fury and As I Lay Dying.* Modern Library edition. New York: Random House, 1946.

———. *The Unvanquished.* New York: Random House, 1938.

Franklin, John Hope. *From Slavery to Freedom: A History of American Negroes.* Second edition. New York: Alfred A. Knopf, 1961.

Freidel, Frank. *F. D. R. and the South.* Baton Rouge: Louisiana State University Press, 1965.

Gabriel, Ralph Henry. *The Course of American Democratic Thought.* Second edition. New York: The Ronald Press Co., 1956.

Gaines, Francis Pendleton. *The Southern Plantation: A Study in the Development and the Accuracy of a Tradition.* New York: Columbia University Press, 1924.

Glasgow, Ellen. *Barren Ground.* Garden City, New York: Doubleday, Page and Co., 1925.

———. *The Battle Ground.* New York: Doubleday, Page and Co., 1902.

———. *The Deliverance: A Romance of the Virginia Tobacco Fields.* New York: Doubleday, Page and Co., 1904.

———. *The Voice of the People.* New York: Doubleday, Page and Co., 1900.

Goldman, Eric F. *The Crucial Decade: America, 1945–1955.* New York: Alfred A. Knopf, 1956.

"Gone With the Wind: After Three Years of Hullabaloo, It Emerges a Great Motion Picture." *Newsweek,* XIV (December 25, 1939), 26–29.

Grady, Henry W. *The New South and Other Addresses.* New York: Charles E. Merrill Co., 1904.

Graves, John Temple. *The Fighting South.* New York: G. P. Putnam's Sons, 1943.

Harland, Gordon. *The Thought of Reinhold Niebuhr.* New York: Oxford University Press, 1960.

Hazlitt, Henry. "So Did King Canute." *The Nation,* CXXXII (January 14, 1931), 48–49.

Hero, Alfred O. Jr. *The Southerner and World Affairs.* Baton Rouge: Louisiana State University Press, 1965.

Hesseltine, William B. *A History of the South.* New York: Prentice Hall Co., 1936.

————, and David L. Smiley. *The South in American History.* Second edition. Englewood Cliffs, N.J.: Prentice-Hall, Inc., 1960.

Hoffman, Frederick J. *The Twenties: American Writing in the Postwar Decade.* New York: Viking Press, 1955.

————. *William Faulkner.* New Haven, Conn.: College and University Press, 1961.

————, and Olga W. Vickery, eds. *William Faulkner: Three Decades of Criticism.* Harbinger Book edition. New York: Harcourt, Brace and World, Inc., 1960.

Hofstadter, Richard. *The Age of Reform: From Bryan to F.D.R.* New York: Alfred A. Knopf, 1955.

Hunt, John W. *William Faulkner: Art in Theological Tension.* Syracuse, N.Y.: Syracuse University Press, 1965.

James, F. Cyril. "I'll Take My Stand." In "Book Department," *The Annals of the American Academy of Political and Social Science,* CLIII (January 1931), 268–269.

Karanikas, Alexander. *Tillers of A Myth: Agrarians as Social and Literary Critics.* Madison: University of Wisconsin Press, 1966.

Kardines, Abraham. "The Anatomy of Jim Crow." *The New Republic,* XCII (September 1, 1937), 109.

Kazin, Alfred. *On Native Grounds: An Interpretation of Modern American Prose Literature.* New York: Harcourt, Brace & World, 1942.

Kegley, Charles W., and Robert W. Bretall, eds. *Reinhold Niebuhr: His Religious, Social, and Political Thought.* The Library of Living Theology Series. New York: Macmillan, 1956.

Kendrick, Benjamin B., and Alex M. Arnett. *The South Looks At Its Past.* Chapel Hill: The University of North Carolina Press, 1935.

Killens, John Oliver. *And Then We Heard the Thunder.* New York: Alfred A. Knopf, 1964.

————. *Black Man's Burden.* New York: Trident Press, 1965.

King, Martin Luther Jr. *Stride Toward Freedom: The Montgomery Story.* New York: Harper and Brothers, 1958; Perennial Library edition, 1964.

————. *The Trumpet of Conscience.* New York: Harper and Row, 1968.

————. *Where Do We Go From Here: Chaos or Community?* New York: Harper and Row, 1957; Bantam Book edition, 1968.

————. *Why We Can't Wait.* New York: Harper and Row, 1964.

Knickerbocker, William S. "Back to the Land." *The Saturday Review of Literature,* VII (December 20, 1930), 467.

Krock, Arthur. "Industrialism and the Agrarian Tradition in the South: Two Forces Are at War for Control of the Future Below the Mason and Dixon Line." New York *Times Book Review,* January 4, 1931, 3.

Kunitz, Stanley J., ed. *Twentieth Century Authors: A Biographical Dictionary of Modern Literature—Supplement I.* New York: H. W. Wilson, 1955.

Link, Arthur S., and Rembert W. Patrick, eds. *Writing Southern History: Essays in Historiography in Honor of Fletcher M. Green.* Baton Rouge: Louisiana State University Press, 1965.

Longley, John Lewis Jr., ed. *Robert Penn Warren: A Collection of Critical Essays.* New York: New York University Press, 1965.

————. *The Tragic Mask: A Study of Faulkner's Heroes.* Chapel Hill: The University of North Carolina Press, 1963.

Lynd, H. M. "Social Cleavage in the South." *The Nation,* CVL (July 17, 1937), 77.

McGrory, Mary. "Fulbright: L. B. J.'s Formidable Foe." Minneapolis *Tribune,* May 20, 1966, 4.

McKinney, John C., and Edgar T. Thompson. *The South in Continuity and Change.* Durham, N.C.: Duke University Press, 1965.

Mann, Dorothea Lawrence. "William Faulkner as a Self-Conscious Stylist—His Latest Story Reveals Him As Something Less Than a Novelist." Boston *Evening Transcript,* October 31, 1936, VI, 6.

Marx, Leo. *The Machine in the Garden: Technology and the Pastoral Ideal in America.* New York: Oxford University Press, 1964.

Meriwether, James B. *The Literary Career of William Faulkner: A Bibliographical Study.* Princeton, N.J.: Princeton University Library, 1961.

Millgate, Michael. *The Achievement of William Faulkner.* New York: Random House, 1966.

Mitchell, Margaret. *Gone With the Wind*. New York: Macmillan, 1938.

Moore, Virginia. "What is the Southland." New York *Herald Tribune*, "Books," November 30, 1930, 21.

Mumford, Lewis. *Technics and Civilization*. Harbinger Book edition. New York: Harcourt, Brace and World, Inc., 1963.

Niebuhr, Reinhold. *The Children of Light and the Children of Darkness: A Vindication of Democracy and a Critique of Its Traditional Defence*. New York: Charles Scribner's Sons, 1946.

—————. *The Irony of American History*. New York: Charles Scribner's Sons, 1952.

—————. *Moral Man and Immoral Society: A Study in Ethics and Politics*. New York: Charles Scribner's Sons, 1932.

Nilon, Charles H. *Faulkner and the Negro*. New York: Citadel Press, 1965.

Noble, David W. *The Eternal Adam and The New World Garden: The Central Myth in the American Novel Since 1830*. New York: Braziller, 1968.

—————. *Historians Against History: The Frontier Thesis and the National Covenant in American Historical Writing Since 1830*. Minneapolis: University of Minnesota Press, 1965.

O'Connor, William Van. *The Tangled Fire of William Faulkner*. Minneapolis: University of Minnesota Press, 1954.

Odegard, Peter H. "A Review of Caste and Class in a Southern Town." *American Political Science Review*, XXXI (October 1937), 982–983.

Odum, Howard W. *An American Epoch: Southern Portraiture in the National Picture*. New York: Holt and Co., 1930.

—————. *Southern Regions of the United States*. Chapel Hill: The University of North Carolina Press, 1936.

Osofsky, Gilbert. "Symbols of the Jazz Age: The New Negro and Harlem Discovered." *American Quarterly*, XVII (Summer 1965), 229–238.

Patterson, Isabel. "An Unquiet Ghost Out of the Old South—William Faulkner Evokes the Civil War Period Again, in This Tale of Evil and Doom." New York *Herald Tribune*, "Books," October 25, 1936, 3.

Price, Reynolds. "Speaking of Books: A Question of Influence." New York *Times Book Review*, LXXI (May 29, 1966), 2.

Proceedings of the National Conference of Social Work—55th Annual Session—Memphis, Tennessee, 1928. Chicago, 1928.

Ransom, John Crowe. "The South is A Bulwark." *Scribner's Magazine,* XCIX (1936), 299–303.

Rock, Virginia J. "The Making and Meaning of *I'll Take My Stand:* A Study in Utopian-Conservatism, 1925–1939." Unpublished Ph.D. dissertation, University of Minnesota, 1961.

Schmidt, John W. "Rhetoric, Theology and George Wallace." Unpublished manuscript in the author's possession.

Schneider, Herbert Wallace. *Religion in Twentieth Century America.* The Library of Congress Series in American Civilization, ed. Ralph Henry Gabriel. Cambridge, Mass.: Harvard University Press, 1952.

Seligmann, Herbert J. "Twenty Years of Negro Progress." *Current History,* LXXX (January 6, 1929), 614–621.

Sellers, Charles Grier Jr., ed. *The Southerner as American.* Chapel Hill: The University of North Carolina Press, 1960.

Slatoff, Walter J. *Quest for Failure: A Study of William Faulkner.* Ithaca, N.Y.: Cornell University Press, 1960.

Smith, Henry. "Notes on Recent Novels." *The Southern Review,* II (Winter 1937), 577–593.

Smith, Henry Nash. *Virgin Land: The American West as Symbol and Myth.* Cambridge, Mass.: Harvard University Press, 1950.

Smith, Lillian E. *Killers of the Dream.* New York: W. W. Norton, 1949.

———. *Strange Fruit.* New York: Reynal and Hitchcock, 1944.

Stewart, John L. *The Burden of Time: The Fugitives and Agrarians, The Nashville Group of the 1920's and 1930's, and the Writing of John Crowe Ransom, Allen Tate, and Robert Penn Warren.* Princeton N.J.: Princeton University Press, 1965.

Strandberg, Victor H. *A Colder Fire: The Poetry of Robert Penn Warren.* Lexington: University of Kentucky Press, 1965.

Strauss, Harold. "Mr. Faulkner Is Ambushed in Words." The New York *Times Book Review,* November 1, 1936, 7.

Swiggart, Peter. *The Art of Faulkner's Novels.* Austin: University of Texas Press, 1962.

Tate, Allen, ed. *A Southern Vanguard.* New York: Prentice-Hall, 1947.

Taylor, William Robert. *Cavalier and Yankee: The Old South and American National Character.* New York: Braziller, 1961.

Tindall, George Brown. *The Emergence of the New South: 1913–1945. A History of the South,* ed. Wendell Holmes Stephenson and E. Merton Coulter, Vol. X. Baton Rouge: Louisiana State University Press, 1967.

Troy, William. "The Poetry of Doom." *The Nation,* CXXXIII (October 31, 1936), 524–525.

Turner, Frederick Jackson. *The Frontier in American History.* New York: Henry Holt and Co., 1937.

Twelve Southerners. *I'll Take My Stand: The South and the Agrarian Tradition.* Harper and Brothers, 1930. Reprint. New York: Peter Smith, 1951.

Vandiver, Frank E. *The Idea of the South: Pursuit of A Central Theme.* Chicago: University of Chicago Press (for William Marsh Rice University), 1964.

Vickery, Olga W. *The Novels of William Faulkner: A Critical Interpretation.* Baton Rouge: Louisiana State University Press, 1959.

Waggoner, Hyatt. *William Faulkner: From Jefferson to the World.* Lexington: University of Kentucky Press, 1959.

Warren, Robert Penn. *All the King's Men.* Modern Library Edition. New York: Random House, 1953.

————. *At Heaven's Gate.* New York: Harcourt, Brace and Co., 1943.

————. *Band of Angels.* New York: Random House, 1955.

————. *Brother to Dragons: A Tale in Verse and Voices.* New York: Random House, 1953.

————, ed. *Faulkner: A Collection of Critical Essays.* Englewood Cliffs, N.J.: Prentice-Hall, Inc., 1966.

————. *The Legacy of the Civil War: Meditations on the Centennial.* New York: Random House, 1961.

————. *Night Rider.* New York: Random House, 1939.

————. *Segregation: The Inner Conflict in the South.* Modern Library Paperbacks edition. New York: Random House, 1957.

————. *Who Speaks for the Negro?* New York: Random House, 1965.

White, Walter. "Solving America's Race Problem." *The Nation,* CXXVIII (January 9, 1929), 42–43.

Wilson, Woodrow. *George Washington.* New York: Harper and Brothers, 1897.

————. *Reunion and Nationalization. A History of the American People,* Vol. V. New York: Harper and Brothers, 1903.

Wolfe, Thomas. *The Web and the Rock.* Harper's Modern Classic edition. New York: Harper and Brothers, 1958.

Woodward, C. Vann. *The Burden of Southern History*. Baton Rouge: Louisiana State University Press, 1960; New York: Vintage Books, 1961.

————. *Origins of the New South: 1877–1913*. Baton Rouge: Louisiana State University Press, 1951.

————. "The South in Search of a Philosophy." Phi Beta Kappa Address, University of Florida, Gainesville, Fla., 1938.

————. *The Strange Career of Jim Crow*. New York: Oxford University Press, 1955.

————. *Tom Watson: Agrarian Rebel*. New York: Rinehart and Co., 1938. Reprint. New York: Oxford University Press, 1955.

————. "What Happened to the Civil Rights Movement." *Harper's Magazine,* CCXXXIV (January 1967), 29–37.

Wright, Richard. *Black Boy: A Record of Childhood and Youth*. New York: Harper and Brothers, 1945; Perennial Classic edition, 1966.

❦ Index

Anderson, Sherwood, 117

Baldwin, James: *Another Country*, 187
Beard, Charles, 51
Becker, Carl: history as creative construct, 124
Brown, William Garrott: and the South's past, 15; and the Negro, 16; Southern violence, 16; concept of burden, 17
Brown et al. v. Board of Education (1954), 172–173; Southern response to, 173–174

Caldwell, Erskine, 3
Calverton, V. F.: on the South, 93; on Southern literature, 125
Carmer, Carl: description of South, 63–64
Cash, W. J.: *The Mind of the South*, 84, 110–114; on *Gone With the Wind*, 92
Clemens, Samuel, 48
Commager, Henry Steele: on *Gone With the Wind*, 92
Couch, W. T.: *Culture in the South* and the revisionist movement, 107–108
Cowley, Malcolm: correspondence with Faulkner, 122–124; links Faulkner with Dixiecrats, 130

Dabney, Virginius, 107
Davidson, Donald: on industrialism, 46; on democracy, 58; reaction to Warren's "Briar Patch," 71–72
Dixon, Thomas: as racist, 23; early life, 23–24; promotes *The Birth of a Nation*, 24; *The Leopard's Spots*, 24–30, 34–39, 44, 78; and myth of Southern history, 25; and concept of union, 27; and concept of burden, 27–32 *passim; The Sins of the Father*, 30–32, 91; and national crisis, 32–34; and concept of mission, 32, 38–43; *The Root of Evil*, 32–34, 50; uses of plantation imagery, 34–37, 86; and industrialism, 36–37, 40–41, 62–64 *passim;* and science, 37; *The One Woman: A Story of Modern Utopia*, 39–40; *The Foolish Virgin*, 40–41; *The Fall of a Nation*, 41–42; defense of agrarian values, 44–45; and the Negro, 46–47; and Southern Agrarians, 62–64 *passim; The Traitor*, 86. *See also* Frontier; Wallace, George C.
Dollard, John: *Caste and Class in a Southern Town*, 84, 93–94; reviews of, 94–95
Dos Passos, John, 49
Dreiser, Theodore, 48, 117